John H. Walton (Ph.D., Hebre
lege) teaches Old Testament a
Moody Bible Institute. He
contributor to scholarly jour
Biblical Archaeologist and *Vetus Testamentum*, and
the author of several books.

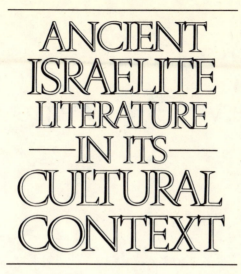

ANCIENT ISRAELITE LITERATURE IN ITS CULTURAL CONTEXT

Library of Biblical Interpretation

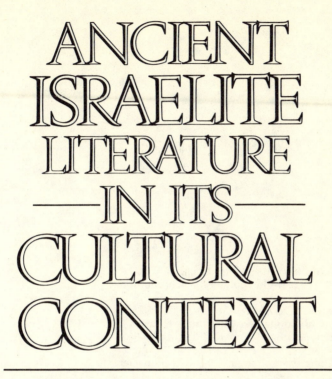

ANCIENT ISRAELITE LITERATURE —IN ITS— CULTURAL CONTEXT

A Survey of Parallels Between
Biblical and Ancient Near Eastern Texts

JOHN H. WALTON

Regency
Reference Library
Zondervan Publishing House
Grand Rapids, Michigan

ANCIENT ISRAELITE LITERATURE IN ITS CULTURAL CONTEXT
Copyright © 1989 by the Zondervan Corporation

REGENCY REFERENCE LIBRARY
is an imprint of Zondervan Publishing House
1415 Lake Drive, S.E., Grand Rapids, MI 49506

Library of Congress Cataloging-in-Publication Data
Walton, John H., 1952-
    Ancient Israelite literature in its cultural context : a survey of
parallels between biblical and ancient Near Eastern literature /
John H. Walton.
      p.   cm.
    Includes bibliographies and index.
    ISBN 0-310-36590-2
    1. Middle Eastern literature–Relation to the Old Testament.
2. Bible. O.T.–Criticism, interpretation, etc. 3. Bible. O.T.-
-Comparative studies. 4. Bible. O.T.–Extra-canonical parallels.
I. Title.
BS1171.2.W35   1989
221.6–dc20   89-33403
                                                  CIP

Unless otherwise noted, all Scripture references are taken from the *Holy Bible: New International Version* (North American Edition), copyright © 1973, 1978, 1984 by the International Bible Society. Used by permission of Zondervan Bible Publishers.

Printed in the United States of America

89 90 91 92 93 94 95 96 / DH / 10 9 8 7 6 5 4 3 2 1

In Memory of Cyril F. Carr
1949–1982

CONTENTS

LIST OF ABBREVIATIONS

AASOR	*Annual of the American Schools of Oriental Research*
AEL	*Ancient Egyptian Literature*, 3 vols., Miriam Lichtheim (University of California, 1976)
AfO	*Archiv für Orientforschung*
AHw	*Akkadisches Handwörterbuch*, Wolfram von Soden
AJA	*American Journal of Archaeology*
AJSL	*American Journal of Semitic Languages and Literature*
AnBib	*Analecta Biblica*
ANET	*Ancient Near Eastern Texts*, 3d ed., ed. James Pritchard (Princeton, 1969)
AOAT	*Alter Orient und Altes Testament*
ARM	*Archives royales de Mari*
AS	*Assyriological Studies*
AUSS	*Andrews University Seminar Studies*
BA	*Biblical Archaeologist*
BASOR	*Bulletin of the American Schools of Oriental Research*
BG	*The Babylonian Genesis*, A. Heidel (Chicago: University of Chicago Press, 1951)
BibSac	*Bibliotheca Sacra*
BM	British Museum
BO	*Bibliotheca Orientalis*
BWL	*Babylonian Wisdom Literature*, W. G. Lambert (Oxford, 1960)
CAD	*Chicago Assyrian Dictionary*
CAH³	*Cambridge Ancient History*, 3d ed.
CBQ	*Catholic Biblical Quarterly*
CBS	*Catalogue of the Babylonian Section* (University Museum, Philadelphia)
CT	Cuneiform Texts of the British Museum
CTA	*Corpus des Tablettes en Cunéiformes alphabétiques*, Andrée Herdner (Geuthner, 1963)
EQ	*Evangelical Quarterly*
G	Gadd, C. J., publication of Nuzi texts in RA 23 (1926): 49–61
GTJ	*Grace Theological Journal*
HSS	*Harvard Semitic Series*
HTR	*Harvard Theological Review*
HUCA	*Hebrew Union College Annual*
IDB	*Interpreter's Dictionary of the Bible*, ed. G. A. Buttrick et al. (Nashville, 1962)
IEJ	*Israel Exploration Journal*
JANES	*Journal of the Ancient Near East Society*
JAOS	*Journal of the American Oriental Society*
JBL	*Journal of Biblical Literature*
JCS	*Journal of Cuneiform Studies*
JEA	*Journal of Egyptian Archaeology*
JEN	Joint Expedition with the Iraq Museum at Nuzi
JEOL	*Jaarbericht van het Vooraziatisch—Egyptisch Genootschap ex Orient Lux*
JESHO	*Journal of Economic and Social History of the Orient*
JETS	*Journal of the Evangelical Theological Society*

JNES	*Journal of Near Eastern Studies*
JQR	*Jewish Quarterly Review*
JSOT	*Journal for the Study of the Old Testament*
JTS	*Journal of Theological Studies*
KAR	*Keilschrifttexte aus Assur religiösen Inhalts*, E. Ebeling (Leipzig, 1919, 1923)
KTU	M. Dietrich, O. Loretz, J. Sanmartín, *Die kielaphabetischen Texte aus Ugarit* (Neukirchener, 1976)
MB	Middle Babylonian Period
MAOG	*Mitteilungen der altorientalischen Gesellschaft*
MDOG	*Mitteilungen der deutschen Orient-Gesellschaft*
MSL	*Materielien zum sumerischen Lexikon*
NASB	*New American Standard Bible*
NB	Neo-Babylonian Period
Ni	Nippur Text
NIV	*New International Version*
OB	Old Babylonian Period
OECT	Oxford Editions of Cuneiform Texts
Or	*Orientalia*
OTS	*Oudtestamentische Studiën*
PBS	Publications of the Babylonian Section, University of Pennsylvania
PS	Pfeiffer and Speiser, AASOR 16 (1936) Publication of Nuzi Texts
RA	*Révue d'Assyriologie et d'archaeologie orientale*
RAI	*Compte rendu de la . . . Rencontre Assyriologique Internationale*
RB	*Révue Biblique*
RLA	*Reallexikon der Assyriologie*
Si	Sippar Text
SKL	Sumerian King List
TB	*Tyndale Bulletin*
UET	Ur Excavation Texts
UF	*Ugarit-Forschungen*
VAT	*Vorderasiatische Abteilung Tontafeln* (Texts in the Berlin Museum)
VT	*Vetus Testamentum*
ZA	*Zeitschrift für Assyriologie*
ZAS	*Zeitschrift für ägyptische Sprache und Altertumskunde*
ZAW	*Zeitschrift für die alttestamentliche Wissenschaft*

ACKNOWLEDGMENTS

Many people have had input on this project, and I cannot begin to thank all of them. There are those, however, who have put extra time and effort into it, and they ought to be recognized. For reading parts (and sometimes extensive parts) of the manuscript and for numerous helpful suggestions, I thank the following professors: Alan R. Millard, Kenneth A. Kitchen, Samuel Greengus, and James Hoffmeier. Furthermore, to the editors who faced a mammoth task and to my family for support and endurance, I offer thanks.

INTRODUCTION

Abraham is presented in the Bible as having come from Mesopotamia. The descendants of Abraham spent centuries in Egypt and then came to dwell in the midst of a Canaanite civilization. The language spoken by the Israelites is historically related to the languages of the Semitic world around them. Copies of ancient Near Eastern literature have been discovered in the excavations of Israelite cities. It is profitable to compare the Israelites to the peoples living around them. The historical and linguistic connections are undeniable, and the Israelites' awareness of the cultures and literature of the ancient Near East is demonstrable from the biblical record as well as from the archaeological data.

The basic premise of this book is that Israel, while being the recipient of divine revelation that gave her a unique theological distinctiveness, reflected in many ways the culture of the ancient Near East. Such a reflection implies that Israelite thinking cannot be understood in isolation from its ancient Near Eastern cultural context. The similarities that exist can be very instructive and should not be ignored. The ancient Near Eastern literature should and can instruct us about the common worldview of biblical times. Israel at times conformed to that worldview and at times departed from it; in either case, we can appreciate and understand Israel better once we know what informed the assumptions of the surrounding cultures. Israelite theology becomes more meaningful if we are aware of the world in which it took shape and of the tensions that were tugging at its perimeters.

In 1902 Franz Delitzsch delivered his now famous "Babel and Bible" lectures in which he attempted to elevate the religion of the Babylonians at the expense of the Israelites and the Old Testament literature. Defending the ancient Babylonians against the claims made by Old Testament scholars, Delitzsch attempted to demonstrate that the Israelite religion, far from being superior to the supposed crude paganism of the Babylonians, had actually evolved from the Babylonian culture. He presented certain significant Old Testament texts as being merely edited versions of Babylonian myths.

Needless to say, devout Jews and Christians of every label saw this as an affront to their faith, an attack on their heritage, and no less than an insult to their God. The negative reaction was swift and of immense scope and gave comparative studies a bad reputation that persists in some circles even today. Since then, scholars have had their hands full trying to reverse the damage Delitzsch caused.

A significant step in a more moderate and positive direction was made in the publication in 1958 of Assyriologist J. J. Finkelstein's article entitled "Bible and Babel" in the magazine *Commentary*. Finkelstein recounted the lectures of Delitzsch and the response to them and then proceeded to present a very balanced survey of the positive results of comparing the Bible with the literature of Mesopotamia.

This century has produced a wealth of literature from Mesopotamia, as well as from Syro-Palestine, Egypt, and Anatolia, that provides an opportunity for comparative studies. More and more scholarly research has been conducted on comparisons of various sorts. Much of this research is not readily available even to scholars working in related fields, and students (not to mention interested nonspecialists) have very few resources to introduce them to this area of study. As a result, there is still much popular misunderstanding regarding the results and present status of comparative studies. Many still respond to studies comparing the Bible and the ancient Near East as if the claims of Delitzsch were the only possible result. Francis Andersen has assessed the present entrenchment of the various views regarding comparative studies and offers this advice:

> Two extremes should be avoided. Nothing is gained by contending so energetically for the uniqueness of Israel's life, especially its religion, as the product of special revelation, that the people of God are cut off from the rest of the world. Some scholars have not been prepared to recognize much affinity between the Old Testament and "pagan" writings and insist on interpreting the Bible solely in terms of itself. At the other extreme, the culture of the ancient Near East is sometimes viewed as if it were uniform from the Persian Gulf to the upper reaches of the Nile. "Comparative" studies of myths and rituals have highlighted similarities between the gods and institutions of the people of the region; and the impression is sometimes given that the Israelites invented nothing on their own but borrowed everything, just as they borrowed the alphabet, from one or other of their neighbors.[1]

PURPOSE

This book will survey the parallels that exist within the various genres of literature between the Old Testament and the primary cultures of the ancient Near East. A number of caveats must be mentioned regarding my interpretation of the material.

1. The comparisons have been largely genre oriented. Though I have

---

[1] Francis Andersen, *Job* (Downers Grove, 1976), 24. See similar identification of excesses in D. Damrosch, *The Narrative Covenant* (San Francisco, 1987), 28.

not worked within a technical definition of "genre," the comparisons that are the focus of this volume concern literatures that serve similar functions. One must certainly acknowledge, for instance, that the patriarchal narratives are not of the same genre as the Nuzi texts or epics. Yet the comparisons that I have worked with are from those pieces of literature which, in my estimation, inform us of the same aspects of their respective civilizations.[2] Concentrating my efforts on this literary class of comparison, I have not pursued the many potential cultural comparisons (e.g., sacrifice, priesthood) or linguistic comparisons that could each be the focus of entire studies in their own right. These are simply beyond the scope of the book.

2. The survey is not intended to break new ground. I have attempted to organize the materials and to review what scholarship has done in each of the areas studied. This may tend at times to cause the book to take on the appearance of an anthology, but I wanted the reader to be able to see for himself what scholarship has proposed or concluded. I have tried to make clear what presuppositions have at times affected the judgment of scholarship and to discuss the implications of various viewpoints. I have also included my analysis of each area once the survey has been completed.

3. This study is not intended to be a comprehensive treatment of the literature of the ancient Near East. I have concentrated on the types of literature that have been viewed as most important regarding the light they shed on the literature of the Old Testament or the value they have for comparative study. This means that whole genres have been passed over (e.g., temple hymns, letters, etc.) because there is little to compare them with in the Old Testament. Even in the genres that I have included in the study, not all examples of that genre have been introduced. I have made every attempt to include those of greatest comparative value.

4. The study is directed to the nonspecialist. I am certain that Assyriologists and Egyptologists will find that this study leaves much to be desired. I can only hope that they will find it to be of some use as an aid to their students. While there certainly is a technical aspect to the information presented here, I have not dealt with material in the original languages. Likewise, I have not done firsthand form criticism. It was not my intention to repeat the research, so I have made abundant and critical use of my predecessors' work. This was a practical necessity and in the interest of those whom this book hopes to serve.

PITFALLS

Many pitfalls confront the student who attempts to do comparisons of this sort. Most dangerous is the tendency to create uniform views where none exist. To speak of "Mesopotamian thinking" or "Egyptian theology" or "Israelite worldview" is unquestionably presumptuous. It is like speaking of

---

[2]This reflects my view that literary genres are, at best, abstractions and are seldom static. See R. Sonsino, *Motive Clauses in Hebrew Law* (Chico, Calif., 1980), 7. Note also the statements by D. Damrosch, *Narrative Covenant*, who concludes, "Our sense of the texts must be derived purely from the thematic and formal shape of the text and from any indications there may be as to the purposes for which it was produced and the ways in which it was used" (pp. 38–39).

"European culture" today. The distinctions between the Assyrians and the Sumerians would be no less than present-day differences between the Swiss and the Italians. Furthermore, the Babylonians of Hammurabi's time may have viewed many things differently than the Babylonians of Nebuchadnez-zar's time. The generalizations that result from large-scale comparisons must be understood to be just that—generalizations. It is hoped that the necessity of doing a certain amount of generalizing will not mislead the reader. No society is totally homogeneous in its viewpoints, though there is more agreement on some things than on others, and major points of general overall agreement do exist.

A second potential pitfall is the related danger of overpolarization. While there is something to be gained by understanding the ways in which Israel was unique, there is no merit in overemphasizing its uniqueness or ignoring or denying the existence of similarities with other cultures. Comparative studies profit just as much from similarities as they do from differences.

Finally, any introduction needs to be selective. I have made every attempt not to allow selectivity to reflect my bias. In cases where information argues against a point I have made, I have tried to bring that data to the attention of the reader by offering a qualifying statement.

PERSPECTIVE

Everyone has presuppositions, both blind and acknowledged ones. Scholars who can bring all of their work under the umbrella of objectivity are rare. Perhaps a more manageable task is to separate objective data from subjective opinions, and that is what I have tried to do throughout this work. I believe in the authority of the Old Testament as the Word of God and would categorize myself as an evangelical. In this book, however, my intention is *not* to produce an apologetic for that position. I have avoided a polemical approach. It is my hope that I have achieved such objectivity in presenting the data that scholarship at large will find this book a useful tool. Generally, in each chapter I have also included a discussion regarding evangelical concerns and perspectives. I have tried to confine those thoughts to certain sections so that those to whom these are of no interest may easily pass by them. I do not believe that the evangelical cause is threatened by comparative studies, so I have not felt that I had to avoid certain issues or ignore some of the data. All scholarship benefits from the objective presentation of data, and that has been my primary concern. I do not doubt that some of my evangelical colleagues might have wished me to take a more aggressive position, but such a task was not my burden.

PROCEDURE

Each chapter begins with a presentation of the extant ancient Near Eastern materials. In some cases the listing is exhaustive, while in other cases only a sampling can be given. With each piece of literature, I provide information concerning the manuscript's description, location, designation, date, and publication (including text, transliteration, and translation). The publication data is not intended to be comprehensive, but I attempted to list the most up-to-date, complete, or significant treatments. When I was aware of sources that gave full bibliographic data, I brought them to the attention of the reader also.

While this section will perhaps not be of interest to the general reader, I felt that it would be useful for graduate students who may spend hours trying to track these things down, as I did. The materials section also includes a brief synopsis of the content of each work covered.

Following the materials section is the discussion of the literature. The discussion is organized differently depending on the nature of the literature. In some cases the discussion is divided into sections concerning style and content, but other approaches are used when appropriate. The main concern in the discussion section is to present the various similarities and differences between the biblical and ancient Near Eastern material.

A final section in each chapter treats cases of alleged borrowing— where the literature is thought to be sufficiently similar that borrowing is suspected or has been suspected by some. In this section I examine the similarities in detail and then try to assess what conclusions may legitimately be drawn concerning the relationship between the works.

PROSPECTS

I hope that, besides being a reference tool, this book will serve a curricular function. I envision three areas that could be served. First, some universities offer a course introducing ancient literature. This book could be used along with James Pritchard's *Ancient Near Eastern Texts* to provide the student some guidance in this area. Second, many schools offer a course in biblical or Near Eastern archaeology. If it is deemed important to discuss the ways in which archaeology has influenced biblical studies, a large percentage of time will be spent on the texts that archaeology has provided us. This book could then serve as supplemental reading for such a course. Finally, professors of the religion of Israel, Old Testament theology, or even religions of the ancient Near East may find this a helpful supplement.

Chapter 1

COSMOLOGY

Cosmology is the term I have chosen to encompass the comparative study of the foundational elements in the perceived origin and operation of the universe. I will introduce the primary literature concerning creation of the cosmos, creation of man, and the flood.

Mesopotamian literature has no extant literature that systematically recounts the details of creation. There are, however, numerous references to aspects of creation in a wide range of literature. It would be a similar case if in biblical material we had to construct a creation account from the Psalms. As a result there are many gaps. There are also inconsistencies. As mentioned in the introduction, we do not expect homogeneity of Mesopotamian thinking, even in a given time period. Certainly over the millennia differences are expected. We are not trying to suggest a form of systematic theology for Mesopotamian thought. Rather, based on observations from the literature, as diverse as it is, we are attempting to comprehend how their worldview fitted together.

In Egyptian literature, the case is similar to that of Mesopotamia, except that here the element of rival theologies is more evident. Creation accounts from Memphis, Hermopolis, and Heliopolis compete with one another. Again our object is not to reach some conclusive "view of creation," for no such thing existed. We hope to come to some conclusions, however, on some of the common factors that provide a foundation for understanding the origin of the cosmos and humanity.

MATERIALS

I. Mesopotamian

A. Eridu Genesis

Approximate Date of Composition
    Sources date from late in the Old Babylonian period (ca. 1600), and it is difficult to extrapolate beyond this.

Manuscript Data
    Sumerian OB tablet (CBS 10673) from Nippur (ca. 1600) of which only the lower third is preserved.
    Sumerian OB fragment from Ur.
    Bilingual Sumerian/Akkadian copy from Ashurbanipal's library.

Publication Data
    Text:
        CBS 10673—PBS V:1.
        Ur Fragment—UET VI:61.
        Bilingual—F. W. Geers, AS 11; W. G. Lambert, CT XLVI, pl. 23:5.
    Translation:
        T. Jacobsen, "The Eridu Genesis," JBL 100 (1981): 513–29. Translation, discussion, and frequent transliteration notes.
        ANET, 42–44 ("The Deluge").
        M. Civil, "The Sumerian Flood Story" in W. G. Lambert and Alan Millard, *Atraḫasis: The Babylonian Story of the Flood* (Oxford, 1969), 138–45, 167–72. Also includes transliteration.
        A. Heidel, *The Babylonian Genesis* (Chicago, 1951), 102–6.

Content
    The preserved section begins with humanity becoming civilized. Later, because of their excessive noise, a flood is sent. Ziusudra, the king, is given the forewarning and builds a boat. Gaps make it impossible to know who else is spared.

B. Atraḫasis

Approximate Date of Composition
    Earliest surviving copies are from the seventeenth century B.C. The composite nature of the work makes conclusive statements beyond this impossible. W. G. Lambert and A. R. Millard suggest that the text could not have taken its present form earlier than the eighteenth or nineteenth centuries B.C.

Manuscript Data
    The most complete edition dates from 1635 B.C. and is on three tablets copied by Ku-Aya. There is a total of about two dozen fragments dating from the seventeenth to the sixth centuries B.C., and the complete listing may be found in W. G. Lambert and Alan Millard, *Atraḫasis: The Babylonian Story of the Flood* (Oxford, 1969), 40–41.

Publication Data
    All the publication data as well as the texts, transliterations, and translations can be found in W. G. Lambert and Alan Millard, *Atraḫasis: The Babylonian Story of the Flood* (Oxford, 1969). A somewhat outdated translation may also be found in ANET, 104–6, 512–14.

Content

The lower deities become tired of their work and rebel. The gods' solution is to create man to do the work. Populations proliferate and become too noisy; the multitudes are reduced respectively by plague, then twice by famine and drought. Finally a flood is sent. Atraḥasis is told of the coming destruction and builds a boat in which animals and birds are saved. It is assumed that other people were saved besides Atraḥasis, but breaks in the text obscure the details.

C. Enuma Elish

Approximate Date of Composition

Manuscripts are all from the first millennium B.C. Estimates of the date of composition usually center on the Kassite period. Lambert suggests a strong connection to the developments under Nebuchadnezzar I (ca. 1100).

Manuscript Data

The epic is written on seven tablets and was first discovered in Ashurbanipal's library at Nineveh by Rassam about 1850. Fragments from an Assyrian version were found at Assur in the early twentieth century. Tablets I and VI were found in a Neo-Babylonian version at Kish, 1924–25, and another Neo-Babylonian version of tablet VII was found at Uruk a few years later. Sultantepe and Babylon also yielded tablets.

Publication Data

Text:
W. G. Lambert and S. B. Parker, *Enuma Elish: The Babylonian Epic of Creation* (Oxford, 1966).
 Composite text without critical notes; see also O. R. Gurney, AfO 17 (1956): 353–56.
E. Ebeling, *Keilschrifttexte aus Assur religiösen Inhalts* (Leipzig, 1919, 1923).
L. W. King, *The Seven Tablets of Creation* (London, 1902).
CT XIII (1901)
S. Langdon, OECT VI (Kish) tablets.
Translation:
ANET, 60–72, 501–3.
A. Heidel, *The Babylonian Genesis* (Chicago, 1951).
Discussion:
T. Jacobsen, *Treasures of Darkness* (New Haven, 1976), 167–91.

Content

This composition tells of Marduk's ascension to the head of the Babylonian pantheon. It is recorded on seven tablets as follows:

Tablet One: Cosmogony/Theogony including a long description of Marduk, born of Ea and Damkina. Describes the discontent between the boisterous younger gods and the older gods, Apsu and Tiamat (representing sweet water and salt water respectively), who are seeking peace and quiet. When Apsu decides to respond destructively, Tiamat joins the rebel cause.

Tablet Two: The older gods unsuccessfully seek a champion to represent them against Tiamat until Marduk steps forward to accept the challenge. In exchange for his leadership, he asks to be made the head of the pantheon.

Tablet Three: Marduk's proposal is presented before Laḥmu and Laḥamu (the oldest children of Apsu and Tiamat) and is accepted.

Tablet Four: Decrees are given to Marduk, and his weapons for battle are prepared. The battle is enjoined, and Marduk is victorious. Using Tiamat's corpse, Marduk lays out the cosmos.

Tablet Five: Stars and constellations, moon, and probably the sun are arranged in the firmament. Marduk reorganizes the divine realm and is proclaimed king of the gods.

Tablet Six: Man is created so that the gods will not have to work. Kingu, the partner of Tiamat, is slain, and his blood is used by Ea to form man. Babylon is constructed as the first city. The last part of the tablet begins the proclamation of Marduk's fifty names by the *Igigi* gods.

Tablet Seven: The proclamation of the fifty names is completed. The work ends with an exhortation to be vigilant in praising Marduk.

D. The Gilgamesh Epic

The Gilgamesh Epic seems to have had more influence on international literature than any other piece known to us from antiquity. Though it is not cosmological literature, I have included it here because the foremost correlation between it and biblical literature occurs in its recounting of the flood story.

Approximate Date of Composition

The Gilgamesh Epic is an edited work comprised of several ancient works. According to the reconstruction of the evolution of the work by Jeffrey Tigay, Gilgamesh tales may well have begun circulating in writing as early as the twenty-fifth century B.C. The earliest copies known are Sumerian; they date to the Old Babylonian period, 2000–1600, though it is reported that the Ebla tablets attest some Gilgamesh material. If so, then this would move the date back to within a couple of centuries of the historical Gilgamesh (ca. 2600). The current Akkadian Epic draws from four (or more) separate Sumerian Gilgamesh tales: Gilgamesh and the Land of the Living; Gilgamesh, Enkidu, and the Netherworld; Gilgamesh and the Bull of Heaven; The Death of Gilgamesh; and original material from several editors. The initial editing is thought to have taken place in the Old Babylonian period. The Middle Babylonian period, 1600–1000, witnessed international circulation with some editing. Tigay further understands three sections as being still later additions: the prologue, the flood story, and tablet XII. The flood story is borrowed from the Atraḥasis Epic. Thus some material in the Gilgamesh Epic dates back into the third millennium, but its final form as we know it was achieved in the first part of the first millennium B.C.

Manuscript Data

Dozens of fragments are used to piece together the epic. Modern scholarship got its first glimpse of the material in the considerable fragments found in Ashurbanipal's library. Other fragments have been found both in Mesopotamia (Nippur, Nimrud, Ur, Uruk, and Ischali) and in such faraway places as the Hittite capital, Boghazkoi, and in Israel at Megiddo. Tigay has a very helpful listing on pages 304–6.

Publication Data

To date, the most comprehensive publication of the text, transliteration, and translation is R. Campbell Thompson, *The Gilgamesh Epic* (Oxford, 1930).
Translation:
ANET, 72–99; 503–7.
A. Heidel, *The Gilgamesh Epic and Old Testament Parallels* (Chicago, 1946).

Discussion:
D. Damrosch, *The Narrative Covenant* (San Francisco, 1987), 88–143.
J. Tigay, *The Evolution of the Gilgamesh Epic* (Philadelphia, 1982).
T. Jacobsen, *Treasures of Darkness* (New Haven, 1976), 195–219.

Content
The first-millennium Gilgamesh Epic is composed of twelve tablets documenting Gilgamesh's search for immortality. The epic progresses as follows:

Tablet One: Description of Gilgamesh. Creation of Enkidu as a distraction for Gilgamesh. The seduction and civilizing of Enkidu.

Tablet Two: Gilgamesh and Enkidu fight to a draw and become friends.

Tablet Three: Gilgamesh and Enkidu decide to embark on a journey to the cedar forest to fight the Ḥuwawa.

Tablet Four: Arrival at the cedar forest.

Tablet Five: Ḥuwawa defeated.

Tablet Six: Gilgamesh turns down a proposal of marriage from the goddess Ishtar. She, in a rage, demands that Anu send the Bull of Heaven to revenge the rejection. Enkidu and Gilgamesh kill the Bull.

Tablet Seven: Because of the death of the Bull and the Ḥuwawa, it is decided that Enkidu must be punished, so he falls ill and dies.

Tablet Eight: Gilgamesh's eulogy for Enkidu.

Tablet Nine: Gilgamesh ponders his mortality and begins a search for eternal life.

Tablet Ten: Gilgamesh receives advice from the barmaid Siduri: death comes to all, so enjoy the pleasures of life. He finally meets Urshanabi, who can take him to see Utnapishtim, a mortal who has gained immortality.

Tablet Eleven: Gilgamesh hears how Utnapishtim gained immortality. Here the flood story is retold. Utnapishtim = Atraḥasis = Ziusudra, is the individual who was spared. This way is not open to Gilgamesh, so it is suggested that if he can refuse to sleep, he may be able to escape death. At this he is unsuccessful. As a final chance, Gilgamesh is told of a rejuvenating plant growing at the bottom of the sea. He finds the plant, but it is eaten by a serpent before Gilgamesh can taste it. He returns to Uruk.

Tablet Twelve: A separate tale of Enkidu in the netherworld.

II. Egyptian

A. Memphite Theology

Approximate Date of Composition
The extant copy was made under Shabaka (25th Dynasty) about 700 B.C. The style of the work has suggested that it dates from the Old Kingdom period (second half of third millennium), though Siegfried Morenz sees the work as suffering from numerous late interpolations.[1] H. A. Schlögel has contended that, based on the use of the compound name Ptah-Tatonen (which is not attested earlier than Ramesses II) and other indications, the work should be dated to the time of Ramesses II.[2]

---

[1]Siegfried Morenz, *Egyptian Religion* (Ithaca, N.Y., 1973), 155.

[2]H. A. Schlögel, *Der Gott Tatonen* (Freiburg/Göttingen, 1980), 110–17. Kenneth Kitchen also accepts this date (private correspondence), and I am grateful to him for bringing this article to my attention.

Manuscript Data

> British Museum 498 (Shabaka Stone) is a rectangular piece of granite about 3 ft. x 4 1/2 ft., and it has 62 columns of text. It was presented to the museum in 1805 by Earl Spencer.

Publication Data

> Text:
>> K. Sethe, *Das "Denkmal memphitischer Theologie," der Schabakostein des Britischen Museums* (Leipzig, 1928; Hildesheim, 1964).
>> H. Junker, *Die Götterlehre von Memphis* (Berlin, 1930).
>> J. Breasted, *Zeitschrift für ägyptische Sprache und Altertumskunde* 39 (1901), 39–50, pls. I–II.
> Translation:
>> AEL, 1:51–57
>> ANET, 4–6 (excerpts).
> Discussion:
>> H. Frankfort, *Before Philosophy* (Harmondsworth, 1949), 65–70.

Content

This work draws from other creation accounts, notably the Pyramid Texts, but inserts Ptah, the god of Memphis, as the supreme deity. Atum is still seen as a creator-god, but Ptah is identified with Nun, the abyss from which Atum came. Ptah is associated with thought and speech and is therefore central in the creative process. This account assimilates the other creation stories but goes further to suggest a "higher truth."

B. Other Creation Texts

The creation accounts originating in Heliopolis and Hermopolis are not separate works but are embedded in larger documents, such as the Pyramid Texts, the Coffin Texts, and the Book of the Dead. The complex nature of these documents prohibits us from going into detail here.[3] In the Hermopolitan version (Coffin Texts), the primeval waters are given four characteristics—depth, endlessness, darkness, and invisibility—each represented by a divine couple. These eight deities or genii formed a primeval egg which, when hatched, brought into being the created order. Thoth, the nome god of Hermopolis, was seen as the head of the eight, though his role is not clear.[4]

In the Heliopolis version,[5] the creator-god Atum emerged on a hill from the primeval waters. Atum's first act of creation was spewing Shu, the god of air, and Tefenet, the goddess of moisture, out of his mouth. From them deities such as Geb (earth) and Nut (sky) were brought forth.[6]

---

[3] Further information may be found in AEL and Morenz, *Egyptian Religion*, 159–82. English translations of the Pyramid Texts and the Coffin Texts may be found in R. O. Faulkner, *The Ancient Egyptian Pyramid Texts* (Oxford, 1969), and *The Ancient Egyptian Coffin Texts*, I–III (Warminster, 1973), 77, 78. For the Book of the Dead, see T. G. Allen, *The Book of the Dead or Going Forth by Day* (Chicago, 1974).

[4] J. M. Plumley, "The Cosmology of Ancient Egypt," in *Ancient Cosmologies*, ed. C. Blacker and M. Loewe (London, 1975), 27.

[5] Pyramid Texts, James Pritchard, ANET, 3.

[6] For more details and discussion, see Plumley, *Ancient Cosmologies*, 28ff.

DISCUSSION

I. Mesopotamia

A. Creation of the Cosmos

One cannot speak of the Mesopotamian view of the creation of the cosmos without speaking of the creation of the gods: in Mesopotamia, cosmogony is intertwined with theogony. Much of what comes under the heading of creation in the literature of Mesopotamia is more properly organization within the cosmos rather than creation of the matter that makes up the cosmos. So in Enuma Elish, the cosmogonic/theogonic material is exhausted after only the first twenty lines of the first tablet, while a large part of tablets IV–VI describe Marduk's acts of organizing the cosmos.

Likewise, a scan of the creation elements incorporated in the various Sumerian works shows a much heavier emphasis on the organizational elements, as the following list shows.

Creation of the Pickax
  Enlil separates heaven and earth.[7]
Gilgamesh, Enkidu, and the Netherworld
  Heaven and earth are separated.
  An is given heaven; Enlil, earth; Ereshkigal is taken to the underworld.[8]
Emesh and Enten: Enlil Chooses the Farmer
  Enlil puts the animal world under the authority of Enten and vegetation under the authority of Emesh.[9]
Enki and Sumer
  Enki decrees the fate of Sumer,
  fills the Tigris and Euphrates with water and fish,
  institutes "rules" for the sea,
  appoints winds to Ishkur's charge,
  causes fields to produce,
  causes houses to be built,
  multiplies plant and animal life in the plain, and
  causes stables and sheepfolds to be built and filled.[10]

As can be seen, then, there really is not much information given concerning the actual creation of the cosmos, and most of what is given is heavily encumbered by a theogonic emphasis. So Thorkild Jacobsen notes in his analysis of Enuma Elish: "World origins, it holds, are essentially accidental: gods were born out of a mingling of the primeval waters and they engendered other gods."[11]

The theogonic element in creation mythology should be seen as distinct from the creative works of a given deity. When cosmological deities are engendered, creation takes place, but the parent deities are not identified as the creators. Our prime interest for comparison with the Old Testament data

---

[7] Samuel Kramer, *Sumerian Mythology* (Philadelphia, 1972), 40, 51ff.
[8] Ibid., 37ff.
[9] Ibid., 49ff.
[10] Ibid., 59ff.
[11] Thorkild Jacobsen, *Treasures of Darkness* (New Haven, 1976), 191. Further discussion of this material can be found in Jacobsen's review of Kramer's *Sumerian Mythology*, "Sumerian Mythology: A Review Article," reprinted in *Toward the Image of Tammuz*, ed. W. L. Moran (Cambridge, 1970), particularly pp. 114–20.

is to examine cosmogonic creative acts of the gods other than theogony. Here we find that the data is very sparse.[12]

> In ancient Mesopotamia there was comparatively little interest in cosmo-
> gony as such. Few texts deal in any detail with the processes whereby the
> physical universe originated and attained its present form. A much
> greater interest was taken in the ancestries of the gods, and these
> frequently have cosmogonic associations. Either a deity is an element in
> the universe, or he controls one.[13]

In the list of the Sumerian data above, there is not one item of the cosmos that is created by a deity. Even in Enuma Elish we are hard pressed to find something created by Marduk. In tablet IV.138, he uses the corpse of the vanquished Tiamat to form the sky. In the same tablet, line 145, he establishes Esharra as a canopy. Third, in V:12 he causes the moon to shine. Each of these could be seen as creative acts, though they do not stress the actual creation aspect so much as the organization aspect.[14] This corroborates the early suggestion that the Babylonians believed in the eternality of matter, as Alexander Heidel finds mentioned in Diodorus Siculus.[15] This constitutes a major difference between Hebrew and Babylonian thinking.

Similarities between Genesis and Enuma Elish have been frequently cited in great detail.[16] While superficial parallels may be noted and do exist, the only substantial similarity occurs in the dividing of the body of Tiamat by Marduk to create the two separated spheres of water. This is comparable to God's dividing the waters of the firmament on the second day of creation. The similarity between Tiamat's name and the Hebrew word for the deep, *tehom*, invites linguistic comparison as well.

In summary, then, it is difficult to discuss comparisons between Israelite and Mesopotamian literature concerning creation of the cosmos because the disparity is so marked. Differences include basic elemental issues such as theogony versus cosmogony, polytheism versus monotheism, and

---

[12] Paul Hanson, "Jewish Apocalyptic Against Its Near Eastern Environment," RB 78 (1971): 41, 42, suggests that theogony has a more central focus in ancient Near Eastern cosmology because "man is an extension of the creative process which produced the gods." In contrast, he notes, "The relation between deity and man in Israelite religion was not a natural outgrowth from theogony and cosmogony. . . . Yahwism finds its basis in election rather than in creation."

[13] W. G. Lambert, "Kosmogonie," RLA 6:219.

[14] Marduk does perform an act of creation when he creates and then destroys a constellation to demonstrate his power to the gods (IV:21–26). But this is not creation of a permanent piece of the cosmos. In a Neo-Babylonian bilingual creation account, Marduk is said to have created the beasts and the plants, but it is difficult to judge how much of that activity is actual creation and how much of it is causing them to reproduce (Alexander Heidel, *The Babylonian Genesis* [Chicago, 1951], 61–63). Lambert comments: "The origin of the basic elements is rarely considered, but spontaneous generation is ascribed to a watery heaven and earth in a bilingual incantation: '[Heaven] was born of its own accord; Earth was born of its own accord. Heaven was abyss; earth was abyss'" (RLA VI:219).

[15] Heidel, *Babylonian Genesis*, 89.

[16] Ibid., 82–140; W. G. Lambert, "A New Look at the Babylonian Background of Genesis," JTS, n.s., 16 (1965): 287–300. These are just two of the scores of treatments of this comparison. Lambert's article contains a short history of the discussion.

emphasis on organization versus emphasis on creative act. Similarities are either linguistic in nature or, as in most cases, due to the fact that the accounts are descriptive of the cosmos of which both are a part.

B. Creation of Man

Below is a summary of the data.

1. Sumerian

Creation of the Pickax
> Man springs up out of the earth.[17]

Cattle and Grain
> Man is given breath.[18]

Eridu Genesis
> Creation of man section is missing, but Enki and Ninhursag may be seen as the responsible deities.[19]

Enki and Ninmaḫ
> Humanity as a whole created from the "clay that is over the abyss."[20]

2. Akkadian

Atraḫasis
> ᵈWe-ila is slaughtered. Nintu mixes clay from his flesh and blood; the *Igigi* and *Anunnaki* spat upon it. Fourteen humans are created (seven male and seven female).
> The purpose of man is to do the work of the gods.[21]

Creation of Man by Mother-Goddess
> Same as Atraḫasis. After the mixture is made, the fourteen humans are birthed from the wombs of the mother-goddess.[22]

Enuma Elish
> Kingu (the god who led the rebellion) is put to death, and his blood is used to create humankind.
> Service of the gods is imposed on new creation.[23]

Trilingual Creation Story
> Two craftsman deities are slain, and their blood is used to create humanity. Humans are created to serve the gods.[24]

The two different perspectives given concerning the creation of man are that either he sprang from the ground (Creation of the Pickax) or that he was formed from a clay mixture using the blood of a slain deity. From these details, it is clear that there are several differences between Mesopotamian and biblical beliefs concerning the creation of man.

---

[17]See Jacobsen, "Review Article," 112.

[18]S. N. Kramer, *Sumerian Mythology* (Philadelphia, 1972), 72ff.

[19]Thorkild Jacobsen, "The Eridu Genesis," JBL 100 (1981): 516.

[20]Kramer, *Sumerian Mythology*, 68–72; see also his discussion in *The Sumerians* (Chicago, 1963), 149–51.

[21]W. G. Lambert and Alan Millard, *Atraḫasis* (Oxford, 1969), 59; ANET, 104, 512.

[22]ANET, 99.

[23]Heidel, *Babylonian Genesis*, 46–47; ANET, 60, 501.

[24]Heidel, *Babylonian Genesis*, 68ff.

a. *Material.*

The Genesis account describes God as creating man from the dust of the earth. This is different from both of the Mesopotamian concepts, though it is similar to both. When Enki wields the pickax to break open the hard surface of the ground, man springs out of the ground.[25] This gives Enki a more passive role than that assigned to YHWH in the Genesis account. On the one hand, when the deities have a more active role in forming man, the material used is a clay mixture rather than simple dust.[26] On the other hand, it should be noted that both the biblical and Mesopotamian accounts view man as being created from that to which he will return in death.[27]

b. *Divine nature.*

The biblical account gives human beings a share in the divine nature by describing them as being created in the image of God. While theologians are still trying to reach a consensus on the meaning and nature of the image, there is nothing that exactly corresponds to it in the Mesopotamian view. The closest correlation is found in the use of the blood of deity in the clay mixture from which man is created. Some see the blood of the deity in these accounts as more comparable to the "breath of life" in the Genesis account; it transfers life to the created form rather than granting the being a share of the divine nature.[28]

Another aspect of the divine image that may exist in Mesopotamia arises in those instances in which it is believed that a human was conceived by a divine father. The most intriguing possibility of this for our purposes is in connection with an individual named Umul who, if A. Kilmer has interpreted properly, is the first baby, sired by the god Enki.[29] Neither the text (Enki and Ninmah) nor Kilmer introduces the image of god as being an issue here. The main drawback is that even if there were some image of god connected to Umul, it would not thereby pass on to all of humanity. Though Umul may have been the first baby, and even may be Atrahasis (as Kilmer speculated), he is not the progenitor of the entire human race.

The only trace of a concept of man possessing the divine nature, then, is if it is included in the blood of the deity used in his creation.

c. *Monogenesis.*

The Genesis account is distinct from the various Mesopotamian perspectives on the creation of man because it insists that God created only one human pair and that all human beings are descended from that pair. While the Mesopotamian accounts are often unclear on the matter of numbers created, there is no instance where monogenesis is claimed. The

---

[25]Jacobsen, "Sumerian Mythology: A Review Article," 112.

[26]See U. Cassuto's discussion, *From Adam to Noah* (Jerusalem, 1961), 104–5.

[27]See Lambert and Millard, *Atraḫasis,* 21.

[28]See H. W. F. Saggs, *Encounter with the Divine in Mesopotamia and Israel* (London, 1978), 165–67; and Lambert and Millard, *Atraḫasis,* 22. Also somewhat similar is the occasional contention that kings are in the image of deity. See, for instance, the claim that Tukulti-Ninurta is in the image (ṣalmu) of Enlil (Epic of Tukulti Ninurta, Ia.18) cited in D. Damrosch, *The Narrative Covenant* (San Francisco, 1987), 74–75.

[29]Anne D. Kilmer, "Speculation on Umul, The First Baby," AOAT 25 (1976): 265.

closest example is found in the trilingual creation story. Heidel's translation suggests that in this account only two humans were created, and he comments accordingly, "On this tablet mention is made for the first time in Babylonian-Assyrian literature of the first two human beings and their names, Ulligarra and Zalgarra."[30] However, Mesopotamian thinking on the whole reflects the idea that man was created en masse. The concept of polygenism is suitable to the purpose for which people were created, according to cuneiform literature; the service of the gods could not be carried out by just one or two individuals.

d. Purpose of humanity.

The cuneiform literature everywhere agrees that people were created to do the work the gods were tired of doing and to provide for the gods' needs. H. W. F. Saggs suggests that this is not so much the reflection of their theology as it is of their society.

> In the Sumerian city-state, . . . the characteristic and most significant organization was the temple-estate, in which thousands of people co-operated in works of irrigation and agriculture in a politico-economic system centered on the temple, with all these people thought of as the servants of the god. The myth of the creation of man, therefore, was not basically a comment on the nature of man but an explanation of a particular social system, heavily dependent upon communal irrigation and agriculture, for which the gods' estates were primary foci of administration.[31]

Whether the concept is social or theological in origin, it resulted in a very important philosophy of human-divine relationships: It was assumed that the gods needed people. It is from this philosophy that the Mesopotamian person derived his dignity and found his metaphysical worth. "In the last resort, man was lord of all: the proper functioning of the universe itself depended upon man's maintaining agriculture, supporting the temples, and providing the gods with their sustenance (sacrifices)."[32] So while Israelites viewed man as created to rule, Mesopotamians viewed him as created to serve. The only hint of a service element in the Genesis narrative is the instruction to Adam to care for the garden.[33]

The fact that the Israelites viewed man as the centerpiece of creation afforded him a certain dignity, undergirded by the fact that he was created in the image of God. In contrast, Mesopotamians did not see man as created with dignity. Human beings achieved their dignity by the function they served. In Israelite thought, the created world was man-centered. This was not the case in Mesopotamian thinking. Rather their attention focused on what J. J. Finkelstein terms the "objective universe":

> The universe of the Mesopotamian was assuredly not a man-centered one; his mode of awareness drew his attention first to the external world,

---

[30] Heidel, *Babylonian Genesis*, 68.

[31] Saggs, *Encounter*, 168. For a revised view of Sumerian temple economy, see B. Foster, "A New Look at the Sumerian Temple State," JESHO 24 (1981): 225–41.

[32] Ibid., 170.

[33] There may be some additional reflection of man's servitude in the naming of Noah in Genesis 5:28–29 as noted by D. Damrosch, *The Narrative Covenant*, 125.

and secondarily, at best, to himself. The understanding of the self—and of the place of man in the cosmic scheme—depended first on the knowledge and comprehension of the environmental universe.[34]

It is this larger entity, the objective universe, that is the main event of creation in the Mesopotamian view. Though humanity was viewed as being created in a barbarous state,[35] cities and civilization were seen to have been created by the gods before humans appeared.[36] Humanity was an unplanned afterthought, created for the sake of convenience. This is contrary to the biblical viewpoint in every way.

C. The Flood

The Mesopotamian literature that gives us the details of the flood has already been introduced in the materials section of this chapter: The Eridu Genesis (columns III–VI), the Atrahasis Epic (tablet III) and the Gilgamesh Epic (tablet XI). The three are literarily related and rarely disagree with one another.[37] A composite account goes as follows:

1. Enlil distraught about the "noise" of humankind.
2. Decision made in the divine assembly to send a flood to destroy humanity.
3. Human king (Ziusudra/Atrahasis/Utnapishtim) warned by Enki/Ea by overhearing the discussion of the assembly.
4. Ea gives the king a plan for a boat.
5. People of the king's city are told that he has to leave because the gods are angry with him.
6. Relatives, skilled workers, animals, and birds all taken on board.
7. Boat has seven stories (either cubical or ziggurat shaped)[38] and is coated with pitch.
8. Storm comes and lasts for seven days and seven nights.
9. Gods lament the great loss of humankind (for their source of provision was gone).
10. Boat lands on Mount Niṣir.
11. Dove and swallow sent out, but both return. Raven sent, does not return.
12. Disembark from boat and offer sacrifices.
13. Famished gods gather around the sacrifice "like flies."
14. Enlil finds out that some mortals escaped.

---

[34]J. J. Finkelstein, "Mesopotamian Historiography," *Proceedings of the American Philosophical Society* 107:6 (1963): 463.

[35]Lambert and Millard, *Atrahasis*, 18.

[36]J. J. Finkelstein, *The Ox That Gored. Transactions of the American Philosophical Society* 71:2 (Philadelphia, 1981): 12.

[37]See Jeffrey Tigay, *The Evolution of the Gilgamesh Epic* (Philadelphia, 1982), 214–31.

[38]The ziggurat shape was well defended in a paper presented at the 1988 Society of Biblical Literature annual meeting by Steven Holloway, "What Ship Goes There: The Flood Narratives in the Gilgamesh Epic and Genesis Considered in Light of Ancient Near Eastern Temple Ideology."

15. Complaint of the gods against Enlil for such a devastating form of punishment.

16. King is granted immortality.

The similarities here are much more discernible than those in the creation accounts.[39] The story line follows a similar route, and the sending out of the birds is a particularly striking parallel.

On the other hand, differences seem to be equally prevalent. These likewise have been noted repeatedly in the literature and include the type of boat, the length of the flood, the people who were saved, the outcome for the hero, and most importantly, the role of the gods. Concerning the latter, it is not only the capriciousness of deity that should be noticed but also the tension that exists between the gods. Whether Ea is betraying the confidence of the city, or Nintur (creatrix and mother-goddess) is lamenting the fate of humankind, or Ea is rebuking Enlil for acting so rashly, we find in the cuneiform literature a view of the gods to which we are not accustomed in the Old Testament.

In the Gilgamesh Epic, no reason is given for the sending of the flood, though it is hinted at when Ea complains to Enlil, "How couldst thou, unreasoning, bring on the deluge? On the sinner impose his sin, on the transgressor impose his transgression."[40] Atraḫasis explains more clearly that the concern of Enlil was the "noise" of humankind. While on the surface this may seem to be another case of pettiness on Enlil's part, recent scholarship has considered this "noise" to be of a moral nature. So J. J. Finkelstein asserts, "There can be little doubt that the noise of mankind which disturbs Enlil's repose is only the metaphoric or mythological guise for what is clearly meant to be the wicked behavior of man."[41] As Finkelstein goes on to suggest, this use of "noise" is not foreign to the Bible, for it is the "outcry" of Sodom that reaches YHWH (Gen. 18:21). In this case, then, while Israelite and Mesopotamian literature both mention a cause related to human behavior, both speak in similar vague or general terms.

Along with the noise factor, we must acknowledge the motif of overpopulation that is clearly a major concern in the Mesopotamian material.[42] The Flood is an attempt to control population growth and is preceded by drought, famine, etc. In contrast, the Genesis account notes the

---

[39]Detailed examination of parallels may be found in Alexander Heidel, *The Gilgamesh Epic and Old Testament Parallels* (Chicago, 1946); and Eugene Fisher, "Gilgamesh and Genesis: The Flood Story in Context," CBQ 32 (1970): 392–403. The latter has a very helpful chart comparison on pp. 402–3.

[40]ANET, 95, lines 179–80.

[41]J. J. Finkelstein, "Bible and Babel," *Commentary* 26 (1958): 437; see also Robert Oden, "Divine Aspirations in Atraḫasis and in Genesis 1–11," ZAW 93 (1981): 197–216.

[42]See Isaac Kikawada and Arthur Quinn, *Before Abraham Was* (Nashville, 1985), 36–40; and A. D. Kilmer, "The Mesopotamian Concept of Overpopulation and Its Solution as Reflected in the Mythology," Or 41 (1972): 160–77. W. L. Moran considers the positions of "noise as moral offense" and "noise as overpopulation" to be "fundamentally opposed" to one another. He gives a good treatment of the evidence to be considered in the discussion without coming to a conclusion between them. See Moran, "Some Considerations of Form and Interpretation in Atra-ḫasis" in *Language, Literature, and History*, ed. Francesca Rochberg-Halton (New Haven, 1987), 251–55.

population growth (6:1) but maintains the perspective of the blessing: "Be fruitful and multiply."[43]

II. Egypt

A. Creation of the Cosmos

As in Mesopotamian cosmology, creation of the cosmos (cosmogony) in Egypt is linked to and explained by birth or formation of the appropriate deities (theogony). While Nun, the god of the primeval waters, is generally seen as the source from which creation takes place, he is not a creator-god. The primary deities who competed for that role were Ptah (Memphite theology) and Atum. In each case the cosmos is created by the gods being formed.[44] Whereas in Mesopotamian cosmology we noted the emphasis on organization rather than on creation, Egyptian literature shows more interest in the creation, particularly of the foundational elements of the cosmos. The gods then function both as creators (often viewed as craftsmen) and as procreators (in the theogonic process gods beget gods). In the more sophisticated Memphite theology, creation takes place, as in Genesis, by the spoken word.

Creation in Egypt proceeds from a condition of watery chaos (Nun) and then is seen to be continually reenacted until a time when chaos will return. Chaos exists as a foundation for the created realm while time, nature, and history are continually involved in re-creation. While Mesopotamian cosmogony was also characterized by creation out of chaos, Egyptian cosmology differs from it in several ways. One of the major distinctions concerns the material that was used in the creation process. S. Morenz presents the contrast as follows:

> According to the great Akkadian creation epic, Marduk fashions the world out of Tiamat, the primeval animal he has killed. Ptah, on the other hand, incorporates the primeval powers into his own substance; he thereby becomes All and creates the world through his word, by his own efforts alone.[45]

Thus, there is no specific material used for the creation of the cosmos in the Egyptian way of thinking, but neither is it creation out of nothing. All matter (existing in chaotic form) becomes part of the creator-god, who then creates, drawing from himself.

As found in the Mesopotamian material to a greater extent and in the Israelite material to a lesser extent, Egyptian cosmogony also offers some information concerning the differentiation aspect (also called "separating" or "ordering") of creation. Particularly, as in both Mesopotamia and Israel, heaven and earth are separated,[46] as are light and darkness and land and water.[47] Both animal and plant life fall into the "evolution" rather than the creation category. Animal life apparently springs from the falcon, who is

---

[43]Kikawada and Quinn, *Before Abraham Was*, 40.

[44]For some details, see John Wilson's contribution in *Before Philosophy*, ed. H. Frankfort (Harmondsworth, 1949), 59–70.

[45]Morenz, *Egyptian Religion*, 173.

[46]Pyramid Texts; cf. Morenz, *Egyptian Religion*, 173–74.

[47]Erik Hornung, *Conceptions of God in Ancient Egypt* (Ithaca, N.Y., 1982), 171.

hatched from a primordial egg.[48] Plants derive from the lotus, which grew on the first primeval hillock that emerged from the waters of chaos.[49]

Some have seen a striking similarity between four basic elements in the Genesis 1 narrative and the four cosmic forces represented by the eight primeval deities in the Hermopolitan version of creation found in the Coffin Texts.[50] It is suggested that the four elements in Genesis, the deep (*tehom*), darkness (*hoshek*), the formless void (*tohu wabohu*), and the Spirit of God/supernatural wind (*ruah 'elohim*) are equatable to Nun, Keku, Hehu, and Amun, respectively. While there is some possibility for common ground here, the connection is highly speculative, and much study would have to be done to determine whether this could be considered a substantial parallel.

B. Creation of Man

There is little data in Egyptian literature concerning the original creation of man. The primary information comes from the Hermopolitan cosmogony.[51] The pertinent section features the creator-god Neb-er-Djer making the following statement: "Now after the creation of Shu and Tefenet I gathered together my limbs. I shed tears upon them. Mankind arose from the tears which came forth from my eye."[52] The connection between tears and the creation of humanity is to be found in the Egyptian preoccupation with wordplay. Since the words for tear (*remeyet*) and for man (*romet*) are similar, it was thought that there must be some kind of connection between them.

The god Khnum also has a role in the creation of man in what is possibly a separate tradition of upper Egypt; but his role seems to involve only the on-going creative process. Each human is fashioned on his potter's wheel, while only the first of humankind was formed by the tears of the creator-god.

Also of interest regarding the creation of man are the statements that speak of his receiving the breath of life from the gods. The following is from the Instructions of Merikare.

> Well tended is mankind—god's cattle,
> He made sky and earth for their sake,
> He subdued the water monster,
> He made breath for their noses to live.
> They are his images, who came from his body,
> He shines in the sky for their sake;
> · He made for them plants and cattle,
> Fowl and fish to feed them.[53]

---

[48]Morenz, *Egyptian Religion*, 177–79.

[49]Ibid., 179–80.

[50]For a recent discussion, see James Hoffmeier, "Some Thoughts on Genesis 1 and 2 and Egyptian Cosmology," JANES 15:4–7.

[51]As found in the ancient work designated *The Book of Knowing How Re Came into Being, and of Overthrowing Apepi*, British Museum papyrus 10188.

[52]Cited from Plumley, *Ancient Cosmologies*, 31.

[53]AEL, 1:106.

This is reminiscent of the details in the Genesis narrative of the "breath of life"[54] and the image of God.[55]

Egyptian sources do not insist on monogenesis, though no source that I have found rules it out. If it was part of their doctrine, we would expect to see it enunciated or promulgated—it is not.

CASES OF ALLEGED BORROWING

The earliest scholarly suggestions of borrowing between Israel and Mesopotamia focused on the area of cosmology. It was the observation of similarities between the biblical and Babylonian flood stories particularly, and creation stories to a lesser extent, that ignited popular interest in the whole area of comparative studies between Israel and the ancient Near East. It is the ever-present curiosity about literary relationships and dependencies that continues to fuel the nonprofessional pursuit of information concerning Mesopotamia. From Franz Delitzsch's "Babel and Bible" lectures in 1902 that set off the "pan-Babylonian" movement, to the moderating responses of scholars such as J. J. Finkelstein ("Bible and Babel"), the question of dependency has held the unabated attention of scholars and laypeople alike for a century. The issue has set further distance between the so-called liberal and conservative biblical scholars, with those on the "liberal" side readily affirming biblical dependence on the older Babylonian culture and those in the "conservative" camp defending the integrity of the Bible sometimes by detailed discussion, more often by ignoring the Babylonian material.

Our examination in the preceding pages has attempted to survey the material and to identify similarities and differences that exist between the Israelite and Mesopotamian cosmological texts. It is on the basis of this study that we may now address the question of literary dependence.

I. Creation

As we have seen above, there is no piece of literature extant from Mesopotamia that presents itself as an account of creation. Therefore, there is nothing comparable to the creation account of Genesis in terms of literary genre. The similarities between Genesis and Enuma Elish are too few to think that the author of Genesis was in any way addressing the piece of literature we know as Enuma Elish. In this case, then, the issue is not one of literary dependence, for literary correlation is vague at best. Rather we need to consider the issue of "tradition dependence." In other words, the question is not so much whether one known piece of literature is dependent on another specific known piece of literature, but whether the creation traditions found in one culture are dependent on the creation traditions of another culture as a source. From a methodological standpoint, we will first consider whether there is sufficient material in common to decide that tradition dependence exists. Then, if tradition dependence does exist, we will consider which tradition served as the source for the other.

The two primary parallels that exist between these two traditions both

---

[54] As Plumley translates (*Ancient Cosmologies*, 36).

[55] Cf. R. J. Williams, "Egypt and Israel," in *The Legacy of Egypt*, ed. J. R. Harris (Oxford, 1971), 288, as well as the discussion in James Hoffmeier, JANES 15:9–10.

involve the goddess Tiamat. It is she who represents the primeval watery chaos in the Babylonian theory that posits water as the primeval element.[56] The word *Tiamat*, representing the primeval body of water, is etymologically equivalent to the Hebrew word for the primeval body of water (*tehom*) mentioned in Genesis 1:2. It cannot be said that the Hebrew term derives from the Babylonian one, for they both are reflections of a common Semitic root. Further, it was Tiamat's corpse that was divided to form the waters above and the waters below. This is parallel to the activity of the second day of creation in Genesis in the sense that waters are divided above and below (though Genesis conveys no knowledge of the "corpse" connection). This dividing of the waters is unique to Enuma Elish in the Mesopotamian literature.[57]

Several other less significant parallels have also been noted in various studies.

A. Creation Through Conflict

Even though the Genesis account is free of this element, scholars such as G. A. Barton, T. K. Cheyne, and Hermann Gunkel at the turn of the century suggested that the conflict element could be discerned in the psalmic creation passages.[58]

B. Separation of Water and Dry Land

In the poetic references to this event, YHWH is pictured as pushing back the cosmic waters.[59] This has a vague parallel in a tale about Ninurta and in Cylinder A of Gudea, though Ninurta's act is postcreation and is therefore a different matter.

C. Rest on the Seventh Day

While the term *sabbath* (Akk. *shapattu*, "fifteenth") has frequently been discussed in this regard, as an explanation for the Israelite institution of Sabbath, the parallel is unconvincing, and allusions to it even as a possibility are less and less frequent. Apart from the term, however, W. G. Lambert has noted that just as YHWH rested after he had completed his creative activity, so the creation of man in the Mesopotamian accounts gives the slaving lower deities occasion for relief from their chores.[60]

Are these parallels enough to establish that tradition dependence did indeed exist? Most have felt that they are, though it is common for scholars to avoid explicit mention of "borrowing" by Israel. Bernhard Anderson, for

---

[56]Cf. W. G. Lambert, "A New Look at the Babylonian Background of Genesis," JTS, n.s., 16 (1965): 293.

[57]Ibid., 295.

[58]Cf. ibid., 287–94. Cf. H. Gunkel, *Schöpfung und Chaos in Urzeit und Endzeit* (1895); T. K. Cheyne's review of Gunkel's work in *Critical Review* 5 (1895): 256–66; and G. A. Barton, JAOS 15 (1893). In Genesis this could at best be considered a minor motif, so I will not enter into this discussion. Some of the most recent treatments may be found in J. Day, *God's Conflict with the Dragon and the Sea: Echoes of a Canaanite Myth in the Old Testament* (Cambridge, 1985); and its review by N. Wyatt in UF 17 (1986): 375–81.

[59]Job 38:8–11; Ps. 104:6–9; Prov. 8:29; cf. Lambert, "A New Look," 296.

[60]Lambert, "A New Look," 297. In both Enuma Elish and Atraḫasis man is created to allow the gods to rest.

instance, speaks of "reminiscences" and "echoes" contained in the Old Testament account.[61] Alexander Heidel's discussion is still the standard in the field and the one most frequently alluded to.[62] He delineates three possibilities to explain the parallels between the biblical and Babylonian accounts of creation: "first, the Babylonians borrowed from the Hebrew account; second, the Hebrews borrowed from the Babylonian; third, the two stories revert to a common fountainhead."[63]

The possibility of the Babylonians having borrowed from the Hebrews is generally considered unlikely on the basis of chronological sequence. Heidel, along with most of his generation, considered Enuma Elish to be a product of the age of Hammurabi (eighteenth century B.C.), which would predate any dating of even Mosaic material. Today Enuma Elish is considered to be some five hundred years later but is also recognized as being a compilation of earlier materials. Furthermore, since Moses is not generally considered the author of the Pentateuch by the scholars working in this field, the date of the material in the Genesis account ends up being placed closer to the Exile; it was therefore compiled long after the Babylonian materials were in place.

Though the chronological argument is considered the strongest and is often the only reason cited before this theory is summarily dismissed, even Heidel was aware of the inherent difficulties in this line of argumentation. "Since priority of publication does not imply priority of existence, this argument must be used with a certain amount of caution. The Hebrew story may have been current in some form or other many centuries before it assumed its present form."[64] The fact remains, that whether one defends something as early as a fifteenth-century Mosaic authorship for Genesis or insists on a date of the P (Priestly) source in the fifth century, both Moses and P are understood by their respective supporters to be compiling material already in circulation. It would not be unlikely to think of Abraham, or depending on one's theory of the origins of Israel, wandering Aramaeans, bringing with them, at least in oral form, accounts of a cosmological nature. Even though the immigrants are most likely coming from Mesopotamia by any theory, we cannot make outright assumptions concerning the possible form of any creation accounts they may have carried. Such an assumption in any direction creates a circular argument.

The point is that we are terribly ill-informed regarding the history of either Mesopotamian or biblical creation accounts. This makes the argument based on chronological sequence null and void. We cannot say for certain that the traditions preserved by the Israelites are any less ancient than the traditions preserved by the Babylonians.

A more convincing line of argumentation points out that the direction of cultural borrowing observable in the ancient world figures against the possibility that the Babylonians borrowed from the Israelites, since the Babylonian civilization itself antedates the beginning of the Israelite civilization. It is unlikely that the Babylonians existed for centuries without a

---

[61] Bernhard Anderson, "Creation," IDB I:726.
[62] Heidel, *Babylonian Genesis*, 130–40.
[63] Ibid., 130.
[64] Ibid.

creation tradition and then, against the direction of the flow of culture, borrowed and corrupted the Israelite version when they encountered it. This argues, not from the date of any piece of literature, but from the date of the civilization as a whole.

The second possibility, that the Israelite account was borrowed from the Babylonians, has enjoyed an overabundance of popularity. In reality, there is nothing that would lend substantiating credence to this belief. The fact that Israel on occasion exhibits cultural characteristics assimilated from Babylon, as did most of the ancient Near East, can in no way serve as independent proof that any given item was borrowed. Each potential case of borrowing must be studied on its own merits, for it is clear that there are several cultural elements from Mesopotamia that Israel rejected.

The only evidence that can be produced to support the case for Israelite borrowing is the similarities we have already identified. These are hardly convincing, in that most of the similarities occur in situations where cosmological choices are limited. For example, the belief in a primeval watery mass is perfectly logical and one of only a few possibilities. The fact that the Babylonians and Israelites use similar names, *Tiamat* and *tehom*, is no surprise, since their respective languages are cognates of one another.

What I am suggesting is that the similarities are *conceptual*, not *specific*. This observation in itself would tend to favor the third option suggested by Heidel—that the traditions stem from a common source. The common source need not be a literary source or even a specific tradition. Common cultural roots could just as easily account for the similarities seen in the creation traditions. What is unfortunate is that we know so little of the cultural roots of ancient civilizations. We know that Abraham came from Mesopotamia, but from which group within Mesopotamia? Amorites? Aramaeans? Some other Semitic stock? We likewise know precious little about the formation of the dominant cultural milieu in Mesopotamia itself. Certainly the Sumerians had much input. But what influence was exerted by the competing Semitic inhabitants?

Since there is little to suggest direct borrowing on the part of the Israelites, we would be inclined to accept a more cautious position. We would tentatively account for the similarities by acknowledging the homogeneity of the cultural roots of the Israelites and the Babylonians and recognizing that this alone, or possibly a common tradition in the past of the roots that these two civilizations hold in common, could be the source from which the similarities are derived. Having come to this, however, we must also state that we have no way of determining the shape of this presumed prototypical source, if such a thing existed. Therefore, aside from a faith statement, we would not be able to determine whether an originally polytheistic account was demythologized or whether a monotheistic account was altered. But such reconstruction assumes an "original account," which is not required by the evidence.

Another possibility that has been suggested is that the Israelite author is making a polemical statement in his presentation of cosmology.[65]

---

[65] Gerhard Hasel, "The Polemic Nature of the Genesis Cosmology," EQ 46 (1974): 81–102.

However, while the Genesis account is, to be sure, nonmythical, it is difficult to demonstrate that it is decisively antimythical.

II. The Flood

The account of the flood presents us with a different situation than the creation accounts. We would expect most cultures to have some tradition or account of how the cosmos came to be. Once the question of origins is addressed, there are a limited number of typical directions that can be followed. Therefore, chance and coincidence may be invoked much more readily as an explanation of similarities.

In contrast, however, Flood accounts are not essential to a complete cosmology (though the pervasiveness of such traditions has been noted);[66] the very existence of such an account in different cultures is suggestive. Furthermore, however, the parallels between the biblical and Babylonian flood accounts are more significant than the parallels found in the creation accounts. Most notable here is the sending out of the birds. This is an action incidental to the main thrust of the story—yet both Noah and Utnapishtim send out birds to determine the situation outside of the ark. This does not appear to be a detail that two different cultures would just happen to include independently of one another.[67] Heidel expresses the consensus: "That the Babylonian and Hebrew versions are genetically related is too obvious to require proof."[68]

We should not be surprised, then, to find that in the flood story, more than in any other literary tradition, it is assumed by scholarship that the Mesopotamian and biblical accounts cannot be thought of as having been independently composed. And again, since even the copies of the flood traditions in Mesopotamia date from the early second millennium (The Eridu Genesis), the biblical account is usually judged to be secondary. So, as stated by Finkelstein, "the dependence of the Biblical story upon the Babylonian to some degree is granted by virtually all schools of thought."[69]

We are faced with essentially the same options for understanding the relationship of biblical and Babylonian materials that were available in our study of the creation accounts, i.e., borrowing in one or the other direction, or a common source. As in the creation accounts, the possibility that Babylon borrowed from the Israelites is usually written off immediately because of the dates of the materials involved.

Borrowing on the part of the Israelites is the position most commonly espoused. The way that the borrowing is explained or described, however, may vary from scholar to scholar. Finkelstein, for instance, chooses the "subconscious" model.

> Nor is there any need to imagine the early Israelite storytellers consciously editing the story they received from Mesopotamia by excising all the "offensive" mythological and polytheistic elements before it might be fit for "local consumption." The Israelite authors, rather, never really "heard" the story in its Babylonian form, for it would have been totally

---

[66] J. G. Frazer, *Folklore in the Old Testament* (New York, 1975), 46–142.

[67] But see Heidel, *Gilgamesh*, 264.

[68] Ibid., 260.

[69] Finkelstein, "Bible and Babel," 435.

incomprehensible to them. If the notions of edition and excision are at all applicable, these processes must be thought of as unconscious; as the basic elements of the original tale were assimilated by Israelite tradition they were naturally and spontaneously harmonized with the Israelite cosmic view.[70]

Heidel is unconvinced by the evidence of Israelite borrowing and in the end chooses the third option, that a common source is responsible for both the Babylonian and the biblical accounts. He acknowledges, however, that proof of such an option is likewise difficult to come by.[71] Despite this admission, there is support for the suspicion that direct borrowing from the Babylonians on the part of Israel was not involved. Most noteworthy is the report of the place where the ark came to rest. The Gilgamesh Epic reports this as Mount Niṣir, generally identified as Pir Omar Gudrun, which is south of the lower Zab in the region of Nuzi.[72] If the Israelites were borrowing directly from the Babylonians, we would expect one of two situations to develop. Either the name of the mountain would remain unchanged and would be reported as Mount Niṣir in the biblical text or the name of the mountain would be changed to one familiar to those in Palestine (e.g., Mount Hermon). Neither of these is the case. The fact that the mountains of Ararat are cited by the biblical text would at the very least suggest that if there was borrowing, it was not direct.

It was this sort of anomaly that led E. A. Speiser to suggest that the Hurrians played a middleman role in the transfer of culture from Mesopotamia to Palestine.[73] Speiser would suggest that the Hurrians, in borrowing the flood story from Mesopotamia at a fairly early date, would have made the change from Mount Niṣir to the mountains of Ararat, which were in their area. The transfer to the Hebrews from the Hurrians would have needed no change. While Speiser's suggestions concerning the Hurrians have not gained wide acceptance in scholarship and are not being endorsed here, they do strongly prove that reconstructing the stream of tradition in our present state of knowledge can be haphazard or even foolhardy. The complexity of the task needs to be recognized.

While most scholars are content to assume that the Mesopotamian account is the ultimate source of flood traditions which eventually are reflected in the Genesis account (readily acknowledging the complexity of attempting to reconstruct the exact path of transfer) there is a minority of scholars who finds this assumption unacceptable. For theologically conservative scholars, it is unacceptable to understand the Genesis accounts as variations of Babylonian myths. The authority of the Bible is a presupposition that needs to be defended and is threatened by theories that suggest that the narratives of Genesis are demythologizations rather than revealed truth. There is then a vested interest of faith that must be considered when examining the relationship of the respective literatures of Israel and Babylon.

---

[70]Ibid., 441.

[71]Heidel, *Gilgamesh*, 267.

[72]Heidel, *Babylonian Genesis*, 250.

[73]E. A. Speiser, "The Hurrian Participation in the Civilization of Mesopotamia, Syria and Palestine," reprinted in *Oriental and Biblical Studies*, ed. J. J. Finkelstein and Moshe Greenberg (Philadelphia, 1967), 266–67.

While scholars who have no such vested interest would be quick to identify special pleading on the part of those who have a faith position to consider, the accusation can also go the other direction, insisting that scholarship at large is too quick to jump to conclusions that cannot be substantiated under close scrutiny. The following statement of A. R. Millard is quoted at length as a good sample of the argumentation.

> However, it has yet to be shown that there was borrowing, even indirectly. Differences between the Babylonian and the Hebrew traditions can be found in factual details of the Flood narrative (form of the Ark; duration of the Flood, the identity of the birds and their dispatch) and are most obvious in the ethical and religious concepts of the whole of each composition. All who suspect or suggest borrowing by the Hebrews are compelled to admit large-scale revision, alteration, and reinterpretation in a fashion that cannot be substantiated for any other composition from the ancient Near East or in any other Hebrew writing. If there was borrowing then it can have extended only as far as the "historical" framework, and not included intention or interpretation. The fact that the closest similarities lie in the Flood stories is instructive. For both Babylonians and Hebrews the Flood marked the end of an age. Mankind could trace itself back to that time; what happened before it was largely unknown. The Hebrews explicitly traced their origins back to Noah, and, we may suppose, assumed that the account of the Flood and all that went before derived from him. Late Babylonian sages supposed that tablets containing information about the ante-diluvian world were buried at Sippar before the Flood and disinterred afterwards. The two accounts undoubtedly describe the same Flood, the two schemes relate the same sequence of events. If judgment is to be passed as to the priority of one tradition over the other, Genesis inevitably wins for its probability in terms of meteorology, geophysics, and timing alone. In creation its account is admired for its simplicity and grandeur, its concept of man accords well with observable facts. In that the patriarch Abraham lived in Babylonia, it could be said that the stories were borrowed from there, but not that they were borrowed from any text now known to us. Granted that the Flood took place, knowledge of it must have survived to form the available accounts; while the Babylonians could only conceive of the event in their own polytheistic language, the Hebrews, or their ancestors, understood the action of God in it. Who can say it was not so?[74]

This suggests that we are not dealing with a literary dependence or even a tradition dependence as much as we are dealing with two literary perspectives on a single actual event. To illustrate from another genre, we expect that the Hittite and Egyptian accounts of the battle of Qadesh will exhibit similarities, for they report about the same battle. Their differing perspectives will also produce some differences in how the battle is reported. The similarities do not lead us to suggest literary or tradition dependence. We accept the fact that they are each reporting in their own ways an experience they have in common.

Our conclusion, then, is that while similarities are recognized, the issue of borrowing is far from settled, and at this point several options are still possible given our current data. The evidence from the literature does not

---

[74] Alan R. Millard, "A New Babylonian 'Genesis' Story," TB 18 (1967): 17–18.

give a clear verdict. One's presuppositions concerning the nature of the respective literatures will still be the determining factor in coming to conclusions.

III. Structure of Primeval History

In the work done by Isaac Kikawada and Arthur Quinn, the suggestion is made that the structure of Genesis 1–11 has a pattern that is also found in the Mesopotamian material.[75] The overpopulation problem that is seen as a major motif of Atraḥasis is paralleled in Genesis by genealogies. Kikawada presents the correlation as in the following chart.

ATRAḤASIS	GENESIS
A. Creation (I.1–351) Summary of work of gods Creation of man	A. Creation (1:1–2:3) Summary of work of God Creation of man
B. First Threat (I.352–415) Humanity's numerical increase Plague, Enki's help	B. First Threat (2:4–3:24) Genealogy of heaven and earth Adam and Eve
C. Second Threat (II.i.1–v.21) Humanity's numerical increase 1. Drought, numerical increase 2. Intensified drought, Enki's help	C. Second Threat (4:1–4:26) Cain and Abel 1. Cain and Abel, genealogy 2. Lamech's taunt
D. Final Threat (II.v.22–III.vi.4) Numerical increase Atraḥasis' flood, salvation in boat	D. Final Threat (5:1–9:29) Genealogy Noah's flood, salvation in ark
E. Resolution (III.vi.5–viii.18) Numerical increase Compromise between Enlil and Enki "Birth Control"	E. Resolution (10:1–11:32) Genealogy Tower of Babel and Dispersion genealogy, Abram leaves Ur

Even Kikawada, however, acknowledges that this parallel does not require literary borrowing on the part of Genesis. Genesis and Atraḥasis may well share a structure which was generally formulaic throughout the Near East. Even if Genesis is mirroring Atraḥasis structurally as a means of responding to it, the integrity of Genesis is not threatened.

D. Damrosch, in a similar yet different vein, sees in this structural similarity a transformation of genre from "historicized poetic epic" to historicized prose.[76] After summarizing the parallels between Genesis 2–11

---

[75] Isaac Kikawada and Arthur Quinn, *Before Abraham Was* (Nashville, 1985). Similar observations had been made previously by Kenneth Kitchen, *The Bible In Its World* (Downers Grove, 1977), 34–36.

[76] D. Damrosch, *The Narrative Covenant*, 119.

and the Gilgamesh Epic that he views as substantiating this transformation, he concludes with what may represent a modern consensus of sorts.

> Each of these parallels shows considerable differences as well as similarities, and there is no need to suppose a direct dependence of Genesis on the Gilgamesh Epic; but it is evident that the two texts are parallel efforts, from roughly the same period, to rework the old mythic material of the creation and flood.[77]

---

[77]Ibid., 120.

FOR FURTHER READING

Damrosch, David. *The Narrative Covenant*. San Francisco, 1987, 88–143.

Finkelstein, J. J. "Bible and Babel." *Commentary* 26 (1958): 431–44.

———. *The Ox That Gored. Transactions of the American Philosophical Society*. 71:2. Philadelphia, 1981, 8–13.

Fisher, Eugene. "Gilgamesh and Genesis: The Flood Story in Context." CBQ 32 (1970): 392–403.

Frankfort, Henri, et al. *Before Philosophy*. Harmondsworth, 1949.

Harrelson, Walter. "The Significance of Cosmology in the Ancient Near East." In *Translating and Understanding the Old Testament*. Ed. H. T. Frank and W. L. Reed. Nashville, 1970, 237–52.

Hasel, Gerhard. "The Polemic Nature of the Genesis Cosmology." EQ 46 (1974): 81–102.

Heidel, Alexander. *The Gilgamesh Epic and Old Testament Parallels*. Chicago, 1946.

———. *The Babylonian Genesis*. Chicago, 1951.

Hoffmeier, James K. "Some Thoughts on Genesis 1 & 2 and Egyptian Cosmology." JANES 15 (1983): 1–11.

Hornung, Erik. *Conceptions of God in Ancient Egypt*. Ithaca, N.Y., 1982.

Jacobsen, Thorkild. "The Eridu Genesis" JBL 100 (1981): 513–29.

———. "Mesopotamian Gods and Pantheons." In Thorkild Jacobsen, *Toward the Image of Tammuz*. Cambridge, 1970, 16–38.

———. "Sumerian Mythology: A Review Article." In Thorkild Jacobsen, *Toward the Image of Tammuz*. Cambridge, 1970, 104–31.

———. *Treasures of Darkness*. New Haven, 1976.

James, E. O. *Creation and Cosmology*. Leiden, 1969, 15–28.

Kikawada, Isaac, and Arthur Quinn. *Before Abraham Was*. Nashville, 1985.

Kilmer, Anne D. "The Mesopotamian Concept of Overpopulation and Its Solution as Reflected in the Mythology." Or 41 (1972): 160–77.

———. "Speculations on Umul, The First Baby." AOAT 25 (1976): 265–70.

Kramer, Samuel N. *Sumerian Mythology*. Philadelphia, 1972.

Lambert, W. G. "A New Look at the Babylonian Background of Genesis." JTS, n.s., 16 (1965): 287–300.

————. "The Cosmology of Sumer and Babylon." In *Ancient Cosmologies*, ed. Carmen Blacker and Michael Loewe. London, 1975, 42–64.

————. "Kosmogonie." In *Reallexikon der Assyriologie*, Band 6.

Lambert, W. G., and Alan Millard. *Atra-ḥasis*. Oxford, 1969.

Mackenzie, John. "The Hebrew Attitude Toward Mythological Polytheism." CBQ 14 (1952): 323–34.

Millard, Alan R. "A New Babylonian 'Genesis' Story." TB 18 (1967): 3–18.

Moran, William L. "Some Considerations of Form and Interpretation in Atrahasis." In *Language, Literature and History*. Ed. Francesca Rochberg-Halton. New Haven, 1987, 245–55.

Morenz, Siegfried. *Egyptian Religion*. Ithaca, N.Y., 1973.

Oden, Robert. "Divine Aspirations in Atraḥasis and in Genesis 1–11." ZAW 93 (1981): 197–216.

Plumley, J. M. "The Cosmology of Ancient Egypt." In *Ancient Cosmologies*, ed. Carmen Blacker and Michael Loewe. London, 1975, 17–41.

Ringgren, Helmer. *Religions of the Ancient Near East*. Philadelphia, 1973.

Saggs, H. W. F. *The Encounter With the Divine in Mesopotamia and Israel*. London, 1978.

Tigay, Jeffrey. *The Evolution of the Gilgamesh Epic*. Philadelphia, 1982.

Waltke, Bruce. "The Creation Account in Genesis 1:1–3." BibSac 132 (1975): 25–36, 327–42.

Chapter 2

PERSONAL ARCHIVES
AND EPICS

In the book of Genesis we have a corpus of material that has come to be designated the patriarchal narratives. While there is no extant literature quite like the patriarchal narratives in the ancient Near East, we have chosen to discuss two types of literature from the ancient Near East that show some similarity to some of the literature comprising the patriarchal narratives: personal archives and epics. I am not suggesting that there is any inherent connection between these two entirely separate genres, nor that either is of the same genre as the patriarchal narratives. The reason for discussing them here is that I feel that they have the most material that has been deemed similar to the material of the patriarchal narratives, despite their generic dissimilarity.

MATERIALS

I. Personal Archives

The patriarchal narratives include numerous instances of personal business transactions. Marriage, inheritance, adoption, employment, and land purchase are just a few of the transactions encountered. In Mesopotamia, at the site of Nuzi, a substantial quantity of tablets identified as archives of individual families was unearthed. While much scholarly discussion has been directed toward the extent or existence of parallels between Nuzi and Genesis, and to what degree the dating of the patriarchal period may be elucidated by the Nuzi material, our concern will be with how the personal archives at Nuzi compare as literature to the archival elements in the patriarchal narratives. Our emphasis centers on Nuzi because many of the comparative studies have focused their attention there, though it is now recognized that Nuzi customs are often reflective of the mainstream of Old Babylonian society.

A. Nuzi Archives

Approximate Date of Composition
    Fourteenth–fifteenth century B.C.

Manuscript Data
    About four thousand tablets found by E. Chiera beginning as early as 1925 (though others had been discovered by local people much earlier) at the modern site of Yorghan Tepe, near Kirkuk.

Publication Data
    Text:
        E. Chiera, *Joint Expedition with the Iraq Museum at Nuzi,* vols. I–VI (vol. VI by E. R. Lacheman) (I–III, Paris, 1927–31; IV–V, Philadelphia, 1934; VI, New Haven, 1939).
        The Harvard Semitic Series (as follows):
            V (E. Chiera, 1929);
            X (R. H. Pfeiffer, 1942);
            XIII (R. H. Pfeiffer and E. R. Lacheman, 1942);
            XIV, XV, XVI, and XIX (E. R. Lacheman, 1950–62).
        E. R. Lacheman, RA 36 (1939): 81–95, 113–219.
        C. J. Gadd, RA 23 (1926): 49–161.
    Transliteration and Translation:
        A fairly complete listing may be found in T. L. Thompson, *The Historicity of the Patriarchal Narratives* (Berlin, 1974), 198, n. 7. Some of the major collections are as follows:
        M. A. Morrison and D. I. Owen, *Studies on the Civilization and Culture of Nuzi and the Hurrians,* (Winona Lake, Ind., vol. 1, 1981; vol. 2, 1987).
        E. M. Cassin, *L'Adoption à Nuzi* (Paris, 1938).
        R. H. Pfeiffer and E. A. Speiser, "One Hundred New Selected Nuzi Texts," AASOR 16 (1936).
        E. A. Speiser, "New Kirkuk Documents Relating to Family Laws," AASOR 10 (1930).
        E. Chiera and E. A. Speiser, "Selected Kirkuk Documents," JAOS 47 (1927): 36–60.

II. Epics

The epic literature involves individuals who are either known from history or whom we have no good reason to suspect did not exist. The epic recounts episodes in the lives of these individuals that generally convey some didactic instruction concerning the gods and their relations with humanity. We will concentrate here on nonroyal epics with the exception of the Keret text.

A. Mesopotamian

1. *Adapa*

Approximate Date of Composition
    Unknown

Manuscript Data
    Four fragments exist: One (B) was found in Egypt among the Amarna tablets (ca. 1360 B.C.); the other three were found at Ashurbanipal's library at Nineveh.

Publication Data
    Text:
        A: A. T. Clay, *A Hebrew Deluge Story in Cuneiform,* Yale Oriental Series, vol. 3, 1922, pls. IV, VI.

B: Otto Schroeder, *Vorderasiatische Schriftdenkmäler*, vol. 12 (Leipzig, 1915), no. 194.
C: R. Campbell Thompson, *The Epic of Gilgamesh* (Oxford, 1930) pl. 31 (K. 8743).
D: S. A. Strong, *Proceedings of the Society of Biblical Archaeology* 16 (1894): 274ff.
The most current edition of the text may be found in S. A. Picchioni, *Il Poemetto di Adapa* (Budapest, 1981).
Translation:
ANET, 101–3.
A. Heidel, *The Babylonian Genesis* (Chicago, 1951), 147–53.

Content

Adapa, a priest of Ea in Eridu known for his wisdom is the main character. When the south wind tips over his boat, he responds (apparently by means of an incantation) by "breaking the wing" of the south wind. For this act, he is summoned before the god of the heavens, Anu. Ea instructs Adapa not to eat food there and tells him how to appease Anu. Adapa does as instructed, but we find that the food was "food of life." Adapa, by his refusal, loses his opportunity to gain immortality.

B. Egyptian

1. The Tale of Sinuhe

Approximate Date of Composition

The setting of the tale is in the mid-twentieth century B.C., and the earliest manuscripts are from about 1800 B.C. This leaves a range of about 150 years when the work could have been composed.

Manuscript Data

The tale is well represented by five papyri and seventeen ostraca. The two primary manuscripts are P. Berlin 3022 (12th Dynasty) and P. Berlin 10499 (end of the Middle Kingdom), respectively designated B and R.

Publication Data

Text:
J. W. B. Barns, *The Ashmolean Ostracon of Sinuhe* (London, 1952).
A. M. Blackman, "The Story of Sinuhe," in *Bibliotheca Aegyptiaca* (Brussels, 1932), 2:1–41.
A. H. Gardiner, "Die Erzählung des Sinuhe und die Hirtengeschichte," in Erman, *Litararische Texte des Mittleren Reiches, Hieratische Papyrus aus den königlichen Museen zu Berlin*, Bd.V/2 (Leipzig, 1909).
Translation:
ANET, 18–22; AEL, 1:222–35.
A. H. Gardiner, *Notes on the Story of Sinuhe* (Paris, 1916).
See also A. Rainey, "The World of Sinuhe," *Israel Oriental Studies* 2 (1972).

Content

In this first-person narrative, Sinuhe, an official in the court of Amenemhet I tells of his flight from Egypt, a long period of self-imposed exile, and his reconciliation to the court. The account opens with the death of Amenemhet I. Sinuhe overhears some information concerning the fight for succession and concludes that he needs to flee for his life. His escape is successful, and he travels through Palestine to Byblos. There he is accepted in good standing into the court and marries the daughter of the prince of Retenu. There is a lengthy description of his many accomplishments, offices, and good deeds. In old age, the pharaoh hears of him and summons him to return. Sinuhe is received with great honor, and a pyramid is constructed for him.

2. The Report of Wenamun

Approximate Date of Composition
Eleventh century B.C., toward the end of the 20th Dynasty or early in the 21st Dynasty.

Manuscript Data
P. Moscow 120 is a Hieratic text on two sheets of papyrus preserving about 142 lines of text. The first page is incomplete, and the end of the story is missing. It was found at el-Hibeh in 1891.

Publication Data
Text:
A. H. Gardiner, "Late Egyptian Stories," in *Bibliotheca Aegyptiaca* (1932) 1:61–76 (hieroglyphic).
V. S. Golenischev, *Recuiel de travaux relatifs à la philologie et à l'archeologie égyptiennes et assyriennes* 21 (1899): 74–102.
Translation:
AEL, 2:224–30.
ANET, 25–29
E. F. Wente, *The Literature of Ancient Egypt*, ed. E. F. Wente, R. O. Faulkner, and W. K. Simpson (New Haven, 1973), 142ff.
See also Hans Goedicke, *The Report of Wenamun* (Baltimore, 1975).

Content
Wenamun was an official of the temple of Amun. This is his first-person account of a trip to Byblos for the purpose of purchasing lumber. Most of the piece reports the negotiations between Wenamun and the king of Byblos. Much insight can be gained from this concerning the extent of Egypt's decline during this period of history. This work is not an epic, but a report. I include it here, again, for some of its similarity, in vague ways, to the patriarchal narratives.

C. Canaanite

1. Keret

Approximate Date of Composition
Unknown. Extant copy was made during the reign of Niqmadu III, ca. 1360 B.C.

Manuscript Data
Three tablets (CTA 14–16) of six columns each (three per side) found in 1930–31 at Ugarit, now kept in the Syrian National Museum in Aleppo.

Publication Data
Text:
J. C. L. Gibson, *Canaanite Myths and Legends* (Edinburgh, 1978).
Cyrus Gordon, *Ugaritic Textbook*, vol. 2. Portion of the text, pp. 328–33; transliteration, nos. 125–28 (pp. 192–96), and pp. 250–53.

Andrée Herdner, *Corpus des tablettes en cunéiformes alphabétiques découvertes à Ras Shamra-Ugarit de 1929 à 1939* (Paris, 1963), 14–16.
Translation:
M. D. Coogan, *Stories From Ancient Canaan* (Philadelphia, 1978), 52–74.
ANET, 142–49.

Content

The three tablets recount three crises that threatened the reign of King Keret, respectively, lack of an heir, illness, and a son's challenge of his competence.

2. *Aqhat*

Approximate Date of Composition

Unknown. Extant copy was made during the reign of Niqmadu III, ca. 1360 B.C.

Manuscript Data

Three tablets (CTA 17–19) found in 1930 at Ugarit.

Publication Data

Text:
J. C. L. Gibson, *Canaanite Myths and Legends* (Edinburgh, 1978).
Cyrus Gordon, *Ugaritic Textbook* (Rome, 1965), 2:245–50.
Andrée Herdner, *Corpus des tablettes en cuneiformes alphabetiques découvertes à Ras Shamra-Ugarit de 1929 à 1939* (Paris, 1963), 17–19.
Translation:
M. D. Coogan, *Stories From Ancient Canaan* (Philadelphia, 1978), 27–47.
ANET, 149–55.

Content

Danel, a leader of some sort, has no son and makes request of the gods for one. Baal takes pity on him, and Aqhat is born. Aqhat is presented with a bow by the craftsman-deity, Kothar-and-Khassis. The goddess Anat covets the bow and makes several unsuccessful attempts to procure it. Her attempts eventually end in Aqhat's death. In this process the bow is broken and lost. Drought comes to the land as a result of the bloodshed. Mourning ensues, and Aqhat's remains are recovered (with the help of Baal) from the eagle that devoured them. Aqhat's sister, Pagat, seeks to avenge his death. The story breaks off here, so the ending is unknown. It is not unlikely that Aqhat is somehow restored to life.

Many other epics exist, including several royal epics from Akkadian literature. Information on these may be gained from A. K. Grayson, *Babylonian Historical-Literary Texts* (Toronto, 1975), and Tremper Longman III, *Royal Akkadian Fictional Autobiography* (Winona Lake, Ind., 1989).

DISCUSSION

I. Personal Archives

From the time that the Nuzi archives were discovered, scholars began to write and lecture on the light that was shed on the patriarchal narratives by the Nuzi material. E. A Speiser was one of the most prolific in this area.[1] As time passed and the material was subjected to repeated and closer scrutiny (both by those enthusiastic about parallels and by those critical of the attempt), many of the parallels identified in the early stages of Nuzi scholarship have been questioned or negated as lacking evidence. Particularly critical evaluation came in the works of Thomas Thompson[2] and John Van Seters.[3] It has generally been conceded that their criticism was not entirely unjustified, though their own conclusions have not succeeded in gaining a strong following. In the thrill of discovery and the rush to make the material available, there was some degree of speculation and misinterpretation of the textual material. But though the Nuzi material may not be as helpful as was initially suggested, the archives still have much to contribute to our understanding of the patriarchal materials.

Profitable studies by M. J. Selman present a balanced and helpful analysis of the Nuzi material and its relationship to the biblical text.[4]

In general, the problems with using the Nuzi archives to inform us about the patriarchs fall into four categories: chronological, ethnic, geographical, and methodological.

Chronological. The archives from Nuzi can be dated by referring to the Hurrian kings of Mitanni named in some of the tablets. The materials cover the time period of the Mitannian Empire, from 1480–1355 B.C.[5] This is several hundred years later than the patriarchs are customarily placed.[6] The problem created here then is that since Nuzi and the patriarchs are so far removed from one another in time, it is dangerous to fill in the details of the patriarchal practices with data found in the Nuzi archives. Even though the Nuzi materials frequently represent typical Old Babylonian customs, such connections need to be established in each case so as not to be extrapolating across centuries.

Ethnic. The population of Nuzi during the time of the archives was largely Hurrian. Not much is known about the Hurrians, but they are an Indo-European rather than a Semitic people and are therefore not even closely related to the Israelites. While they certainly would have assimilated much of the culture around them, in the end it would be difficult to determine whether any particular custom was something the Israelites may have practiced or whether it reflected the Hurrians' ethnic background. Again, this problem can be eliminated if it can be demonstrated that the given Nuzi practice was typical of Semitic Old Babylonian practice.

Geographical. Nuzi was a Hurrian society, representing a form of culture

---

[1]For much of E. A. Speiser's writing concerning light on the biblical text, see the collection of his articles, *Oriental and Biblical Studies*, ed. J. J. Finkelstein and Moshe Greenberg (Philadelphia, 1967).

[2]Thomas L. Thompson, *Historicity of the Patriarchal Narratives* (Berlin, 1974).

[3]J. Van Seters, *Abraham In History and Tradition* (New Haven, 1975).

[4]M. J. Selman, "The Social Environment of the Patriarchs," TB 27 (1976): 114–36; and "Comparative Customs and the Patriarchal Age," in *Essays on the Patriarchal Narratives*, ed. A. R. Millard and D. J. Wiseman (Winona Lake, Ind., 1983), 91–140.

[5]See Thompson, *Historicity*, 199, and the bibliographic data in n. 9.

[6]Cyrus Gordon dated the patriarchs to the fourteenth and fifteenth centuries because of the Nuzi connections that he saw. Cf., e.g., C. Gordon, *The Ancient Near East* (New York, 1965), 115–33.

evident from the Tigris to the Mediterranean. Despite this, it must be recognized that the patriarchs may or may not have had close contact with Hurrian culture. The caution here is that there is some geographical distance between the patriarchs and Nuzi. Where we can *observe* the same customs being practiced, this is immaterial. But the extrapolation of details from Nuzi customs into a patriarchal context must be viewed very suspiciously.

Methodological. In this area, it is the use made of the available textual data that poses potential problems. The fact that any given practice is recorded in a contract from Nuzi does not establish that that practice was a custom in Nuzi. Only a study of Nuzi society as a whole could determine whether any given practice was customary or unusual, and the documentation does not always exist for coming to conclusive decisions. Too frequently the so-called parallels from the Nuzi materials have rested on a single text that is itself unclear. The validity of using isolated material such as this as a window to societal customs must be questioned. Furthermore, even a valid parallel may be limited in terms of the help it gives.

> When all is said, "parallels" prove nothing. At worst, they can be misleading, as additional evidence shows a custom to be local or to be commonplace. At best they show the possibility that the patriarchal narratives exhibit the same practices, so permitting us to conclude that they may tell of the same times.[7]

True parallels can be helpful in various ways, but if the described practice is seen as a custom throughout the second and first millennia B.C., that parallel would not help us date the patriarchal period. Likewise, if the practice was shown to be very local in nature, with variants being observed in other geographical locations, we could never feel certain extrapolating data from the Nuzi material to inform us of the patriarchal custom, for we could not be sure that they would be the same in every detail.

All of these considerations—chronological, ethnic, geographical, and methodological—warn us against jumping to easy conclusions concerning the overlap in customary practices between the patriarchs and the inhabitants of Nuzi. But in the end, it is the nature of the parallel that will determine its acceptability. M. J. Selman[8] has classified the parallels into three categories as follows:

Parallels Giving Additional Examples. Cases in which the Nuzi material simply furnishes additional examples of practices well known from the biblical material. In this category we are only shown that the biblical custom was not an isolated custom but that it was practiced at least in Nuzi also. This does not necessarily help us understand the biblical text any better, but it does help us to see that some phrases or actions which we find unusual were not at all unusual in the ancient Near Eastern culture.

Parallels Providing Supplementary Details. Cases in which the Nuzi material provided more details of a practice than could be gleaned from the biblical material. Here we must exercise some caution, for we can never be

---

[7] Alan Millard, "Methods of Studying the Patriarchal Narratives as Ancient Texts," in *Essays on the Patriarchal Narratives*, ed. A. R. Millard and D. J. Wiseman (Winona Lake, Ind., 1983), 40.

[8] Selman, "Comparative Customs," 97.

certain that the details provided by the Nuzi material give an accurate reflection of the biblical practice. They are helpful, though, insofar as they give an ancient example of the possible elements of the biblical practice.

Parallels Aiding Reconstruction. Cases in which the Nuzi material has been used to provide an explanation of a custom not evident or clearly understood in the biblical material. Here great caution must be used. This is where many of the most controversial parallels can be found. Sometimes it is not even clear that the suggested custom existed in Nuzi. In other cases, the biblical text must be reconstructed to admit the parallel.

At this point we will briefly look at specific parallels from each category that have been identified between the Nuzi material and the patriarchal narratives. In each parallel we will present (1) the initial form of the parallel (generally from E. A. Speiser or Cyrus Gordon), (2) the criticism of the parallel (generally from Thomas Thompson or John Van Seters), and then (3) a modified view of the parallel (frequently in agreement with Selman) that will show an assessment of the validity of the criticism.

A. Parallels Giving Additional Examples

These are parallels in which Nuzi material gives additional examples of practices already known from Genesis.

1. Handmaid given to new bride

Biblical References: Genesis 29:24, 29
Nuzi References: HSS V 67:35–36

Initial Form of Parallel. The practice of giving a handmaid to a daughter at the time of her marriage is attested in Nuzi and is seen to be operative in the biblical cases of Rebekah, Rachel, and Leah.[9]

Criticism of Parallel. Thompson is quick to observe that first, the giving of a handmaid is hardly the norm in Nuzi society, and second, it is amply attested throughout the ancient Near East in many differing time periods. Therefore, this does not constitute a Nuzi parallel and does not give any help regarding the date or authenticity of the patriarchal narratives.[10]

Modified Form of Parallel. In this case the parallel itself can stand, but it cannot be used to validate the authenticity of the patriarchal narratives regarding their chronological placement.

2. Contractual agreement not to take other wives

Biblical Reference: Genesis 31:50
Nuzi References: HSS V 67:17–18; G 51

Initial Form of Parallel. The insistence of Laban that Jacob not take any other wives besides his daughters is consistent with the concern expressed in the Nuzi marriage contracts, where the same practice is often forbidden.[11]

Criticism of Parallel. While there would be a consensus even among the critics that contractual restriction against taking other wives is evidenced

---

[9]Cyrus Gordon, "Biblical Customs and the Nuzu Tablets," in *The Biblical Archaeologist Reader*, 2, ed. D. N. Freedman and E. F. Campbell (Chicago, 1975), 25.
[10]Thompson, *Historicity*, 271.
[11]Gordon, "Biblical Customs," 25.

both in Genesis 31 and in the Nuzi materials, the criticism concerns the reason for the prohibition. In the Nuzi materials one reason for the clause in the contract may be to prevent the adopted son-in-law from passing on the inheritance that he gets from his father-in-law to a son of another wife. This is clearly not the issue in Genesis 31 in that Laban's daughters have already borne children, thereby insuring that any inheritance would remain in the proper family. But even the existence of the problem leading to the inclusion of this clause in the Nuzi contracts is questionable when discussing the case of Jacob. There is no evidence that he was adopted by Laban and therefore no indication that he is to receive any inheritance from him. If there is no inheritance to be passed down from the father-in-law, there is no need for the protective clause in the marriage contract. There are no cases of marriage restriction in Nuzi documents for the same reason that Jacob is so restricted.

Modified Form of Parallel. The observations made above have greatly reduced the value of this parallel. The correlation is now only concerning the most general detail, that occasionally a man was bound by contract not to marry additional wives. This obligation occurs in other periods as well (e.g., the Old Assyrian Cappodocian texts) and does not actually shed much additional light on Genesis 31.

3. Introductory formula for deathbed pronouncements

Biblical Reference: Genesis 27:2
Nuzi Reference: PS 56 (AASOR XVI)

Initial Form of Parallel. In this case, interpreters suggested that the reason that Isaac's blessing on Jacob was binding even though there was a clear-cut case of deception, had to do with the fact that this was considered a deathbed statement that was legally binding. Speiser summarizes,

> In other words, the pronouncement "I have now grown old" was at Nuzi a recognized formula accompanying a solemn final declaration; and such declarations had special standing precisely because they expressed a man's last wish. The phraseology, in short, had definite socio-juridical implications.[12]

Criticism of Parallel. Thompson claims that there is nothing that the Nuzi texts have in common with the patriarchal narratives that cannot be found in the ancient Near East at large. Furthermore, the main text used by those supporting this parallel (PS 56) is claimed to be neither a deathbed testament nor a statement upheld because of the invoking of a formula. Rather it involves witnesses attesting to oral promises made by a dying man.[13]

Modified Form of Parallel. That the phrase "I have now grown old" is a formula for testatory statements is acceptable. But not much other information is available from this parallel. It does not offer any explanation of why Jacob's deception would not invalidate the statements made.

---

[12]E.A. Speiser, "I Know Not the Day of My Death," *Oriental and Biblical Studies*, 91; cf. Gordon, "Biblical Customs," 27–28.

[13]Thompson, *Historicity*, 289–93.

4. Transfer of birthright

Biblical Reference: Genesis 25:33
Nuzi Reference: JEN 204

Initial Form of Parallel. Here the example is adduced of one, Tupkitilla, who exchanges a grove he has inherited for three sheep. The sheep are provided in trade by his brother, Kurpazah. This is viewed as similar to Esau's giving up of his birthright to Jacob in exchange for some food.[14]

Criticism of Parallel. The difficulties here are many. First, it is not a birthright that is sold but property that has already been inherited. Second, the selling of something inherited is somewhat different from the selling of an inheritance. Third, we have no indication in the text which brother is the elder and which is the younger. Thompson has suggested that it is not a sale at all but merely the division of the inheritance and that it is not necessarily disproportionate.[15]

Modified Form of Parallel. The Nuzi material gives no parallel at all for transfer of inheritance rights like that which took place between Jacob and Esau.

B. Parallels Providing Supplementary Details

These are parallels in which Nuzi material provides supplementary details to practices already known from Genesis.

1. Provision of a second wife in cases of barrenness

Biblical Reference: Genesis 16:2
Nuzi References: HSS V 67:19–21

Initial Form of Parallel. It was suggested that Sarah's insistence that Abraham attempt to have children by Hagar is explained by clauses found in Nuzi marriage contracts saying that the barrenness of the wife would allow the husband to take another wife so that children might come from his line. It is often seen to be the responsibility of the wife to provide the "substitute" in these situations. The child of this second union would then be considered a full heir.[16]

Criticism of Parallel. Thompson identifies seven discrepancies between the biblical data and the supposed parallels in the Nuzi material. These discrepancies include (1) whether the wife needed to be barren in order for another wife to be given; (2) whether the husband was restricted by contract from taking other wives; and (3) the status of the resulting children with relation to the first wife.[17] After a detailed review of a vast amount of ancient Near Eastern materials on this subject, Thompson concludes that Genesis reflects the usual situation known throughout the Near East concerning the role of concubines. He sees no direct parallel to the Nuzi material, largely because there is no indication that the husbands in Genesis were restricted by contract from taking a second wife.

---

[14]Gordon, "Biblical Customs," 23–24.

[15]Thompson, *Historicity*, 284–85.

[16]Gordon, "Biblical Customs," 22–23; E. A. Speiser, *Genesis* (Garden City, N.Y., 1964), 120–21.

[17]Thompson, *Historicity*, 256–58.

Modified Form of Parallel. This parallel still provides us with some background to a passage that would otherwise be unclear to the Western reader. Even if cases cannot be cited where Abraham's situation is matched precisely, and even if we are unaware of the nature of the contract stipulations between Abraham and Sarah, the parallel confirms that the procedure they carry out is not unusual in the ancient Near Eastern context.

2. Shepherding contracts

Biblical Reference: Genesis 31
Nuzi References: This parallel is not drawn from Nuzi texts but from Old Babylonian material, particularly a contract from the Yale collection (#5944) dating to the time of Samsuiluna (eighteenth century B.C.), and supported by information drawn from the Code of Hammurabi.

Initial Form of Parallel. J. J. Finkelstein maintained that the Jacob-Laban narratives, particularly Jacob's complaints against Laban, and the nature of the agreements, can be better understood in light of Old Babylonian herding contracts. From those documents it is possible to glean information concerning the responsibilities of the owner and shepherd to one another. The parallel also explains how a shepherd was paid for his service: a proportion of the newborn animals became his property.[18]

Criticism of Parallel. The parallel is not criticized, but it is maintained by critics that the data for correlating the biblical account to ancient Near Eastern practice could be drawn from numerous other periods. This limits the extent to which the parallel can be used to determine the dating of the patriarchal narratives.

Modified Form of Parallel. No modification is necessary. This parallel gives valid insight into the kinds of agreements drawn up between sheep owners and the shepherds and thereby corresponds to some elements that apparently formed part of the relationship between Jacob and Laban.

3. Complaint of Laban's daughters

Biblical References: Genesis 31:14–16
Nuzi Reference: HSS V 11

Initial Form of Parallel. The complaint of Laban's daughters is explained by the information that can be derived from the Nuzi texts concerning the proper handling of the bride price. In the Nuzi documents, the father either gives the bride part of the bride price or reserves it for her use in case her husband dies or deserts her. By using up this money, Laban is accused by his daughters of having reduced the marriage to a sales transaction. As a result, they have nothing more to lose by leaving with Jacob. Laban has no financial security to offer them.[19]

Criticism of Parallel. It is not so much the parallel that is criticized here as it is the argument that the parallel gives evidence for an early dating of the patriarchs. It is claimed that the parallel is not limited to data from Nuzi but could be substantiated in numerous other time periods.

---

[18]J. J. Finkelstein, "An Old Babylonian Herding Contract and Genesis 31:38f," JAOS 88 (1968): 30–36.

[19]Millar Burrows, "The Complaint of Laban's Daughters," JAOS 57 (1937): 259–76.

Modified Form of Parallel. The parallels throughout the ancient Near East illuminate for us the fact that Laban's daughters had some reason to expect a bride gift from their father which clearly was not forthcoming. So again, we are given some background concerning a problem that is being alluded to but not explained by the biblical text.

C. Parallels Aiding Reconstructions

These are parallels in which Nuzi material is used to reconstruct practices unknown in Genesis.

1. Significance of teraphim ownership

Biblical References: Genesis 31:19, 30–34
Nuzi Reference: G 51

Initial Form of Parallel. It was argued that, based on the Nuzi material, the possession of the teraphim was seen to indicate primary rights to the inheritance. As Cyrus Gordon puts it: "The possession of these gods was important for . . . they carried with them leadership of the family on the ancestral estate."[20]

Criticism of Parallel. The definitive criticism of this parallel came from Moshe Greenberg.[21] He indicates that the primary difficulty that exists in trying to substantiate this parallel is that Laban is still alive.

> Whatever the situation be after the death of the father, an adoptee had nothing to gain and everything to lose by making off with the family gods during the adopter's lifetime. That would have been as foolish as the theft, by a king's son, of the crown while his father still lived, in the expectation that possession of the crown would safeguard his claim to the throne. Just as the crown belonged to the king until his death, so the household gods belong to the paterfamilias until his death. We may well imagine a father's outrage if any son—let alone an adoptee!—dared to run off with them during his lifetime. The father-adopter had various means of punishing such trespass, up to and including dishersion. In any event, such an appropriation could hardly have had any legal validity against the express will of a still-living father."[22]

Modified Form of Parallel. At this point there is no viable explanation of Rachel's theft of the teraphim that is provided by the Nuzi material, other than her simple desire to gain the protection of her household deities.

2. Slave adoption

Biblical Reference: Genesis 15:4
Nuzi References: HSS IX 22; HSS V 60

Initial Form of Parallel. It was observed that it was customary in the Nuzi society for childless individuals to adopt an heir. The rights of this adopted heir would become null and void or at least secondary if a true heir should

---

[20]Gordon, "Biblical Customs," 26; cf. Speiser, *Genesis*, 250–51.
[21]Moshe Greenberg, "Another Look at Rachel's Theft of the Teraphim," JBL 81 (1962): 239–48.
[22]Ibid., 245.

later appear. It was proposed that Abraham's relationship to Eliezer was of this sort.[23]

Criticism of Parallel. Thompson engages in a detailed study of the adoption texts from Nuzi and those from the ancient Near East as a whole. He concludes that the particular literary form used in Nuzi is never evident in a situation in which a man adopts his slave and that the terminology is such that it could only refer to a free-born citizen. Contracts outside of Nuzi that do deal with slave adoption use different forms and terminology. As a result, he sees no possibility of correlating Eliezer's situation with anything found at Nuzi.[24]

Modified Form of Parallel. There is little light to be shed on the relationship between Abraham and Eliezer by the Nuzi materials. No paradigm for that relationship is identifiable.

3. Heir adoption

Biblical Reference: Genesis 29:14
Nuzi References: G 51 and many adoption texts

Initial Form of Parallel. The numerous adoption contracts found at Nuzi demonstrate the common practice of adopting an heir when a family had no sons. The adopted heir would often marry the daughter of his benefactor (called an *errebu* marriage) and would take on the obligation of caring for him in old age. When Jacob first becomes acquainted with Laban, it is noticed that no sons of Laban are mentioned. The arrangement agreed upon by Laban and Jacob gives Jacob the right to marry Laban's daughter and includes various statements that have been interpreted to indicate that an adoption is taking place.[25]

Criticism of Parallel. Thompson contends that in the *errebu* marriages in the Nuzi texts, a bride price is not paid. This is clearly contrary to the situation in Genesis where the bride price is clearly delineated in the contract and is later referred to in the complaint of Laban's daughters.[26] Furthermore, the biblical text gives little data that could even be interpreted as a hint of Jacob's being adopted by Laban, and their statements to one another in Genesis 31 seem to preclude any such agreement between them.[27]

Modified Form of Parallel. The criticism has largely been accepted as valid, and this parallel has been abandoned.

4. Wife/sister institution

Biblical References: Genesis 12:13; 20:2; 26:7
Nuzi References: HSS V 80:5–6; 69:1; 25:1

Initial Form of Parallel. E. A. Speiser attempted to clarify the three episodes in Genesis during which Abraham and Isaac each claim that his wife is his sister, by referring to a wife-sister institution among the Hurrians in Nuzi. He summarizes his proposal as follows:

---

[23]Gordon, "Biblical Customs," 22; Speiser, *Genesis*, 112.

[24]Thompson, *Historicity*, 203–30.

[25]Gordon, "Biblical Customs," 24–25.

[26]Thompson, *Historicity*, cf. 274ff.

[27]Ibid., 279–80.

The Hurrian family system contained various fratriarchal features, one of which was the wife-sister concept. Under it, a woman given in marriage by her brother, either natural or adoptive, became legally her husband's sister. Such a wife-sister had the advantage of exceptional socioreligious solicitude and protection which was not enjoyed by ordinary wives. The practice was characteristic of, though not restricted to, the top levels of Hurrian society. It was evidently a mark of superior status.[28]

Criticism of Parallel. Thompson presents evidence that Hurrian society was not fratriarchal, nor would the so-called sisterhood adoption texts support the idea of fratriarchy. Speiser's interpretation is based entirely on his interpretation of the three tablets indicated above, and Thompson joins a line of scholars who dispute the legitimacy of Speiser's interpretation of what is taking place in those contracts. It is difficult to maintain, as Speiser did, that these contracts give any special status to the woman or that they make a husband a brother.[29]

Modified Form of Parallel. There are no suggestions made for a legitimate modified form of this parallel.

The result of this kind of analysis is that we are left with much less information in the form of direct parallels than was previously thought. Despite that situation, the personal archives found at sites such as Nuzi still provide some helpful insight into the patriarchal narratives as authentic literature. Here we are not speaking of the issue of chronology, for we have already seen that very little guidance is provided by the Nuzi materials on that point. What is clear is that the patriarchs and their families were very much a part of the culture of the ancient Near East. Even if we do not identify specific parallels, the similarities between the lifestyle and culture of the patriarchs on the one hand and the lifestyle and culture in centers such as Nuzi on the other hand are patently clear. In this area, as well as in many of the others analyzed here, we see that religious practice was the main element that separated the biblical characters from their Near Eastern counterparts. In the areas of general culture, the similarities are everywhere confirmed by the literature.

II. Epics

We have chosen to use only the nonroyal epics in this discussion. There is a slightly different character to the royal epics (e.g., Sargon, Lugalbanda, Tukulti-Ninurta, or Idrimi of Alalakh) that makes them better suited for discussion in our chapter on historiographical materials. The patriarchs are nonroyal, so we will find the closest match to their stories in the nonroyal data.

---

[28]Speiser, "The Wife-Sister Motif in the Patriarchal Narratives," *Oriental and Biblical Studies*, ed. J. J. Finkelstein and M. Greenberg, (Philadelphia, 1967), 75.

[29]Thompson, *Historicity*, 234–48; see also David Freedman, "A New Approach to the Nuzi Sistership Contract," JANES 2 (1970): 77–85; C. J. Mullo-Weir, "The Alleged Hurrian Wife-Sister Motif in Genesis," *Transactions of the Glasgow University Oriental Society* 22 (1967/68): 14–25; and Samuel Greengus, "Sisterhood Adoption at Nuzi and the 'Wife-Sister' in Genesis," HUCA 46 (1975): 5–31.

A. Similarities

As a genre, the epics match the patriarchal narratives more closely than the personal archives did. As in the patriarchal narratives, the epics recount some episodes of an individual's life to give practical, theological, or political instruction. In both the epics and the patriarchal narratives, biographical data is provided secondarily—but biography is not the primary function of the genre. The element that leads us to study the patriarchal narratives in conjunction with the epics is that both are thought to deal with historical individuals, but in each there is a question concerning the extent to which the details recounted have historical value. There are other similarities between the patriarchal narratives and particular works that we are considering here, but they are minor and more incidental in nature and so would not suggest borrowing of any sort.

B. Differences

Differences exist to varying degrees in these texts. In each area we will categorize each of the five pieces of ancient literature chosen to represent this genre.

1. *Poetry versus prose*

The patriarchal narratives are in prose form along with the two Egyptian works, Sinuhe and Wenamun. (Technically, both the patriarchal narratives and Sinuhe are elevated prose.) Adapa, Keret, and Aqhat are all in an epic poetic form. This is a basic consideration when attempting to compare genres.

2. *Narrative perspective*

In this category, the similarity goes in the other direction. The patriarchal narratives are entirely in the third person, in agreement with Adapa, Keret, and Aqhat. Sinuhe and Wenamun use the autobiographical format of first-person narrative.

3. *Interaction with the supernatural*

This category may be broken down into seven sections.

a. *Prayer.*

Prayer as a petition to God is not so frequent in the patriarchal narratives as one might have guessed. The prayer of Abraham's servant (Gen. 24) and the prayer of a desperate Jacob (Gen. 32) are the only ones evident in the text. There are many more instances, however, of dialogue with deity in a conversation initiated by deity. In the ancient Near Eastern material, Keret and Aqhat are the only two of our test group that evidence petitionary prayer to deity.

b. *Communication by God.*

Communication by God is so frequent in the patriarchal narratives that it could be considered characteristic. It also is evident in various forms in four out of the five test cases from the ancient Near East (all but Sinuhe). In Wenamun the communication is brief and through a prophet. In Keret the communication comes in a dream. In this category there is considerable similarity with the patriarchal narratives.

c. Theophany.

It is not always clear in the texts whether a theophany has occurred when dialogue is taking place between man and God. In the patriarchal narratives there are several theophanies that are clear and a few other contexts in which a theophany may be taking place. We find the same ambiguity in the ancient Near Eastern texts. Ea speaks extensively to Adapa, and every indication is that it is face to face, though the text is not explicit on the matter. In Keret the dream could well be a theophany. In Aqhat there is little distinction between the human and divine realms, so it is difficult to identify theophany per se.

d. Unrealistic elements.

In this category we want to identify situations in which the human characters seem to possess abilities that are usually associated with deity. Jacob's strength may be the only candidate for this in the patriarchal narratives. Some have felt that his moving of the stone in Genesis 29:10 and his success in wrestling the messenger of the Lord in 32:25 are indicators of superstrength. These passages, however, have other alternative interpretations that do not imply any supernatural strength in Jacob. Perhaps the extraordinary lifespans of the patriarchs also should be included in this category. This is not paralleled in any of the ancient Near Eastern epic material.

There are, however, other hyperbolic ascriptions in the ancient Near Eastern material not found in the patriarchal narratives. Sinuhe (immodestly in the first person) describes at length his attributes, successes, prosperity, and good and mighty deeds which, while not divine, seem exaggerated and certainly have no equivalent in the patriarchal narratives. Adapa is described as having a divine measure of wisdom, being the first of the ancient sages.

e. Miraculous occurrences.

Though the presence of deity pervades the patriarchal narratives, the only miraculous occurrence is the birth of Isaac to the aged Abraham and Sarah. This element is also absent from the ancient Near Eastern material. The single exception—the magical healing of Keret—is borderline.

f. Description of occurrences in the divine realm.

The closest the patriarchal narratives approach this is in Genesis 18:17–19 where there is a soliloquy by YHWH. Sinuhe and Wenamun have nothing of this sort, but the other three from the ancient Near Eastern set have extensive scenes of conversations and occurrences in the divine abode. This gives these accounts a mythological tone that distinguishes them from the patriarchal narratives.

g. Elimination of boundaries between divine and human realms.

In this category the patriarchal narratives fall between the two extremes represented in the ancient Near Eastern material. Sinuhe and Wenamun barely include interaction with deity at all, so the boundaries between divine and human realms are left intact. In contrast, Adapa, Keret, and Aqhat show frequent crossing over. Adapa "breaks the wing of the south wind" (probably by incantation) and after receiving advice from the god Ea, has an audience in heaven with the god Anu. So there is free movement between the realms. In Keret, the council of the gods attends the wedding of Keret. In Aqhat a divine bow is fashioned for Aqhat, and he is offered immortality by Anat in exchange for the bow.

The patriarchal narratives do go further than Sinuhe and Wenamun, for there are the three visitors in Genesis 18 and the wrestling match in Genesis 32. But these examples do not go quite so far as Keret and Aqhat and are far from the events that occur in Adapa.

In summary, since interaction with the supernatural is very limited in Sinuhe and Wenamun, and since Adapa evidences many mythological motifs in this category, the Canaanite epics of Keret and Aqhat demonstrate the most similarity to the patriarchal narratives. The primary category of distinction is that discussed in the description of conversations taking place in the abode of the gods. In the other categories, the differences are just a matter of degree.

4. Historical setting

In the patriarchal narratives there is little mention of names of individuals who might be identifiable in history. The major exception is in Genesis 14, which has not provided much help. There are likewise very few chronological references that could help place the patriarchs in a particular historical setting. On the other hand, the patriarchal narratives do include details of a historical nature such as identifiable city names and authentic personal names.

In this category again, the Egyptian materials (Sinuhe and Wenamun) differ from the others. These two include chronological references, and Sinuhe includes the name of the pharaoh. The patriarchal narratives are most like Wenamun on this count. Adapa and Keret use legitimate place names, and Keret and Aqhat use authentic personal names, though none of these are to the extent of that used in the patriarchal narratives.

Beyond these details, however, the patriarchal narratives are differentiated from the rest by their "ordinariness."

> Throughout these narratives, several features are apparent to any reader. They deal almost exclusively with ordinary human beings, men and women, who are born, marry, have children, tend sheep, goats, cattle, and grow a crop or two, who love, quarrel, die and are buried. They worship their God, building simple altars, and have dreams and visions. There is nothing here that is not within the range of known human experience.[30]

5. Range

In this category the patriarchal narratives stand alone. The extension of the patriarchal narratives over three to four generations covering a number of centuries far exceeds the range of the other epic materials in the ancient Near East.

---

[30] Kenneth Kitchen, *The Bible In Its World* (Downers Grove, 1978), 60.

6. Purpose

The purpose of many ancient pieces of literature is difficult to discern. Frequently all that can be done is to identify motifs. Sinuhe and Wenamun, being autobiographical in nature, may have represented an attempt to tell of their adventures for the sake of posterity. Aqhat may have had fertility functions and certainly gives account of great heroes of ages past. Keret addresses some of the difficulties faced by a king. Adapa seems to be most interested in the lost chance at immortality.

Whatever the case may be in each of those individual works, none of them approach the nature or purpose of the patriarchal narratives. It is not as though modern scholarship has definitely agreed upon the purpose of the patriarchal narratives, but certain elements of purpose are clearly identifiable.

1. The covenant and the history of its beginnings is certainly one of the narrative foci. How did it come about that Israel was the chosen people of YHWH and that promises were made to her alone?

2. The possession of the land of Palestine is another of the interests of the narrator, and is, of course, not unrelated to the covenant. A. R. Millard has pointed out that "no other people has left us a family history that explains their occupation of their land."[31]

3. The patriarchal narratives also present the history of the relationship of God with a particular individual and his family.

All of these contribute greatly to the overarching purpose of the patriarchal narratives. YHWH chooses Abraham, makes a covenant with him, and gives him the land. More important is the fact that this is not a story in isolation. It merely serves as a preamble to the history of Israel which builds its foundation on that covenant.

C. Conclusions

A fine technical study of the epic genre was done by A. Berlin, in which she treats three indicators: mode, narrative structure, and contextual aspects.[32] The patriarchal narratives use a "realistic" mode as most epics do. The narrative structure is built on a struggle between the hero and an adversary. The struggle of the patriarchs to lay claim to the promises of the covenant is far removed from the political or mythic struggles common in epics. On the other hand, the smaller struggles over childlessness, inheritance, and status within the family are not unique.

Though the patriarchal narratives do reflect certain similarities with the epic genre and particular similarities with individual epics, the patriarchal narratives do not show sufficient similarity, in my opinion, to be totally identified in this genre.

One of the results of this conclusion addresses the historicity of the patriarchal narratives. It is generally acknowledged that the epic literature is built on historical kernels but cannot be relied upon for accuracy or veracity in every case. Embellishment, distortion, and legendary expansion are not strangers to the genre. If the patriarchal narratives were part of that genre,

---

[31]Millard, "Methods," 42.

[32]A Berlin, "Ethnopoetry and the Enmerkar Epics," in Studies in the Literature of the Ancient Near East, ed. J. Sasson (New Haven, 1984), 17–24.

the historical accuracy of the material would by no means be assured. Since, however, the patriarchal narratives are in a class by themselves (I know of no genre designation that would not be highly controversial), determinations of the historicity need to be made based on internal considerations.[33]

The general similarities in motif and style help us to see the patriarchal narratives as legitimate and authentic products of the ancient Near East and to understand their concerns against that backdrop.

CASES OF ALLEGED BORROWING

The major case I would like to discuss in this genre is the parallel elements of the Adapa epic and the story of Adam's fall from grace. Though Adam is not included in the patriarchal narratives, it seemed best to treat this issue here because the comparison functions within the framework of the epic genre.

William Shea has suggested that three principal parallels are readily apparent:[34]

1. Both subjects were tested by deity based on something to consume.
2. Both failed the test and forfeited a chance for immortality.[35]
3. In each case the failure brought consequences on humanity.

Another interesting similarity occurs in that Ea, the god of wisdom, counsels Adapa not to eat the food because it will bring death. This was apparently deceptive, for the bread was the bread of life. The story of Adam presents the mirror image of this. There the serpent (who also is connected with wisdom) counsels eating something not supposed to be eaten, because eating will not bring death.[36]

Shea adds to these parallels two more that he defends, though they are not readily apparent:

1. Both Adam and Adapa qualify as members of the first generation of humankind. Adapa is the first of a well-known list of sages in Mesopotamia and is the counterpart of the first king on the Sumerian King List.[37] Because of the Mesopotamian view of the creation of man, Adapa is the character most like an Adam figure in Mesopotamia.

2. The names Adam and Adapa can be seen as linguistically related.[38]

---

[33]Kitchen, *The Bible In Its World* (Downers Grove, 1978), 61–65, presents a very plausible defense of the patriarchal narratives as falling between the genres of autobiographical report and historical legend. "In sober content and mode of expression, they are closest to the first category, without being identical with it (not first person). They share their third person narrative form with occasional texts of the first category and all the texts of the second group—but entirely lack the fantasy-embellishments of the second group" (p. 65).

[34]William Shea, "Adam in Ancient Mesopotamian Traditions," AUSS 15 (1977): 28.

[35]Niels-Erik Andreasen disagrees that this is a parallel. He suggests that the test is not failed and that immortality was not really available. See "Adam and Adapa: Two Anthropological Characters," AUSS 19 (1981): 184–85.

[36]Shea, "Adam," 34.

[37]Ibid., 36.

[38]Ibid., 37–38; see also the discussion in Andreasen, "Adam and Adapa," 181–82.

Shea is also careful to point out the divergences between the accounts, even within the areas where general similarity occurs.[39] The major differences are summarized well by Alexander Heidel:

> First of all, it is clear that this story contains nothing to justify the conclusion that the breaking of the wing of the south wind was the first offense ever committed by any human being. Furthermore, it is equally clear that Adapa failed to obtain the priceless boon of immortality not because of any sin or disobedience on his part but because of his strict obedience to the will of Ea, his father, the god of wisdom and the friend of man. And, finally, there is not the slightest trace of any temptation, or any indication whatever that this legend is in any way concerned with the problem of the origin of moral evil.[40]

Shea concludes by arguing that both works are dependent on a common (probably Amorite) source whose function is better preserved in the Genesis account. Niels-Erik Andreasen, on the other hand, suggests that

> In Adam and Adapa we have the representation of two different anthropological characters, perhaps being capable of being illustrated by an actor who plays two distinct roles, but who is clearly recognizable in each.[41]

He explains further,

> On the scene staged by the Mesopotamian artists he characterized man as the noble, wise, reliable, and devoted, but humble hero who is resigned to live responsibly before his god. However, in the biblical tradition, the characterization came through in quite a different way, which has put its lasting mark upon the concept of man in the Judeo-Christian tradition— namely, that before God, man is (or rather has become) basically sinful, failing, ignoble and untrustworthy, bent upon usurping the place of his God.[42]

The Adapa epic is typically Mesopotamian in its attempt to demonstrate that the status quo was foreordained and cannot be changed. Immortality is not available even to the wisest of the ancient sages.[43] This is in direct contrast to the typically Israelite outlook found in Genesis in which the status quo is the result of man's failure that cost him the immortality he once possessed. In Mesopotamian thinking things are as they ought to be and cannot be changed. In Israelite thinking, things are not as they ought to be, and hope exists that one day reversion may take place.[44]

Certainly Shea is right to the extent that he posits a "functional shift" between the biblical material and the Mesopotamian epic. The story of the fall of man in Genesis and the epic of Adapa serve entirely different

---

[39]Shea, "Adam," 28–31.

[40]Alexander Heidel, *The Babylonian Genesis* (Chicago, 1951), 124.

[41]Andreasen, "Adam and Adapa," 192.

[42]Ibid., 193–94.

[43]This is the conclusion of Benjamin Foster, "Wisdom and the Gods in Ancient Mesopotamia," Or 43 (1974): 353. Foster presents an excellent summary of the literature on Adapa and the various interpretations and aspects of the text.

[44]Cf. Andreasen, "Adam and Adapa," 190–91.

functions, have different purposes, and as discussed in the articles already mentioned, have many differences, both large and small.

What is left is to determine whether the similarities are significant enough to suggest that the accounts could not have arisen independently. I do not believe that they are. Let us look at each one again.

1. The so-called test with food has as its presupposition that Adapa is undergoing a test. That presupposition is not supported by the text, and alternative interpretations are more likely.[45] There is no temptation, the foods are different, and as already mentioned, it is likely that Adapa did not fail. This leaves as the only similarity here the fact that food is involved in the story—hardly sufficient to suggest borrowing.

2. Shea attempts to draw a connection between the consequences on humankind in Genesis and the consequences from Adapa by examining the incantation connected to the Adapa epic. The connection between Adapa and the incantation that Shea suggests is far from certain. The use of the Adapa epic may simply be an attempt to invoke the magical powers that had been demonstrated by Adapa.[46]

3. The similarity of the names is intriguing but likewise a dead end for the present.[47] W. G. Lambert has identified the name Adapa as an epithet[48] belonging to Oannes (=ummanu), the first antediluvian sage. This would suggest that the similarity in the names is merely coincidence.

4. While it is possible to see both Adam and Adapa as human archetypes and even prototypes, they are not the only individuals who could be so classed. There are certainly differences in the ways each serves those functions, of which the most significant is that Adam was the first-created man, whereas there was no such occurrence in Mesopotamian belief.

Our conclusion is that the apparent similarities between these two pieces of literature can easily be explained by the fact that they both use general motifs present throughout ancient Near Eastern literature. Immortality is a matter of interest through every period in wide-ranging genres of literature. There is no reason to assume that since it is in some way a major motif of each of these works, they must therefore be organically related to one another. The similarities are incidental and the differences are primary.

---

[45]E.g., Jacobsen's suggestion that Anu's actions are simply those of a hospitable host; Thorkild Jacobsen, "The Investiture and Anointing of Adapa in Heaven," reprinted in *Toward the Image of Tammuz and Other Essays on Mesopotamian History and Culture*, ed. W. L. Moran (Cambridge, 1970), 48–51.

[46]Cf. ibid., 50–51.

[47]The lexical entry of *a-da-ap* = *a-mi-lu* in a syllabary (MSL 12.93) is problematic and cannot be used with confidence to provide a solution. Cf. E. Ebeling, *Tod und Leben nach den Vorstellungen der Babylonier* (Leipzig, 1931), 27, n. a; also, B. Foster, Or 43 (1974): 351, n. 30.

[48]"Wise one"; he compares this to the name "Atraḥasis," which is also considered an epithet. W. G. Lambert, "A Catalogue of Texts and Authors," JCS 16 (1962): 73–74.

FOR FURTHER READING

Andreasen, Niels-Erik. "Adam and Adapa: Two Anthropological Characters." AUSS 19 (1981): 179–94.

Berlin, Adele. "Ethnopoetry and the Enmerkar Epics." In *Studies in the Literature of the Ancient Near East*. Ed. J. Sasson. New Haven, 1984, 17–24.

Finkelstein, J. J. "An Old Babylonian Herding Contract and Genesis 31:38f." JAOS 88 (1968): 30–36.

Foster, Benjamin R. "Wisdom and the Gods in Ancient Mesopotamia." Or 43 (1974): 344–54.

Freedman, David. "A New Approach to the Nuzi Sistership Contract." JANES 2 (1970): 77–85.

Gordon, Cyrus, "Biblical Customs and the Nuzu Tablets." BA 3 (1940): 1–12. Reprinted in *The Biblical Archaeologist Reader*. Ed. D. N. Freedman and E. F. Campbell. Missoula, 1975, 2:21–33.

Greenberg, Moshe. "Another Look At Rachel's Theft of the Teraphim." JBL 81 (1962): 239–48.

Kitchen, Kenneth, *The Bible In Its World*. Downers Grove, 1978, 56–74.

Millard, A. R., "Methods of Studying the Patriarchal Narratives as Ancient Texts." In *Essays on the Patriarchal Narratives*. Ed. A. R. Millard and D. J. Wiseman. Winona Lake, Ind., 1983, 35–52.

Morrison, M. A., and D. I. Owen. *Studies on the Civilization and Culture of Nuzi and the Hurrians*. Winona Lake, Ind., 1981.

Selman, M. J., "The Social Environment of the Patriarchs." TB 27 (1976): 114–36.

———. "Comparative Customs and the Patriarchal Age." In *Essays on the Patriarchal Narratives*. Ed. A. R. Millard and D. J. Wiseman. Winona Lake, Ind., 1983, 91–140.

Shea, William. "Adam in Ancient Mesopotamian Traditions." AUSS 15 (1977): 27–41.

Thompson, Thomas L. *The Historicity of the Patriarchal Narratives*. Berlin, 1974.

Chapter 3

LEGAL TEXTS

In the legal literature we are on much firmer footing than in many of the other categories. There are eight major cuneiform documents that preserve lists of laws for us. These range from pre-Sargonic Sumerian works to Middle Assyrian lists and include a set of Hittite laws. There is no extant legal material from Canaanite sources. Egyptian literature provides a demotic legal code from the Persian period or later and supplementary edicts of pharaohs from earlier periods.[1]

MATERIALS

I. Sumerian

A. The Reform of Uru'inimgina (formerly, Urukagina)

Approximate Date of Composition
Ca. 2350 B.C., sponsored by Uruinimgina, King of Lagash.

Manuscript Data
Cones found at Girsu/Lagash (Telloh) by de Sarzec, late nineteenth century.

Publication Data
Text:
E. Sollberger, *Corpus des Inscriptions "royales" présargoniques de Lagaš* (Geneva, 1956).
E. de Sarzec, *Découvertes en Chaldée* (Paris, 1844–1912).

---

[1]G. Mattha and G. R. Hughes, *The Demotic Legal Code of Hermopolis West* (Cairo, 1975). Thanks to Professor Kenneth Kitchen who brought this and other bibliographic information to my attention.

Translation:
J. Cooper, *Sumerian and Akkadian Royal Inscriptions*, I: Presargonic Inscriptions (New Haven, 1986), 70–74.
S. N. Kramer, *The Sumerians* (Chicago, 1963), 317–22.
M. Lambert, RA 50 (1956), 169ff.
Discussion:
CAH³, I:2, 140–42.
B. Foster, "A New Look at the Sumerian Temple State," JESHO 24 (1981): 225–41.
S. N. Kramer, *The Sumerians* (Chicago, 1963), 79–83.
I. M. Diakonov, "Some Remarks on the Reforms of Urukagina," RA 52 (1958): 1ff.
M. Lambert, "Les 'Réformes' d'Urukagina," RA 50 (1956): 169ff.

Content

While the nature and function of this supposed reform is still disputed, there seemed to be some interest on the part of Uruinimgina to lighten the load of bureaucracy on the general populace; he also tried not to alienate the priesthood in the process. I. M. Diakonov summarized the reforms as follows:

> (1) abolition of certain taxes paid formerly by the higher priesthood; introduction of new rates of rations and payments to certain priests belonging to no definite temples; a slight reduction of payments to priests for some rites (e.g., the funeral rites); (2) abolition of various taxes and exactions, mostly those imposed on well-to-do members of the temple personnel; concession to holders of plots of temple land of the right to sell their houses and moveable property and a guarantee of their right to the inviolable and unlimited possession and use of water on their plots, etc.; (3) declaration . . . that the temple estates are "divine property" thus excluding them from the ownership of the ruler; withdrawal of barley rations issued to priests from the control of the ruler's administration; (4) abolition of law-court duties . . . and of various extortions formerly made to the benefit of the ruler and his administration.[2]

B. Laws of Ur-Nammu

Approximate Date of Composition

The copies date to the Old Babylonian Period. The laws were long thought to be sponsored by Ur-Nammu (2064–2046 B.C.), founder of the Ur III Dynasty, but now have been attributed to his son, Shulgi.[3]

Manuscript Data

Only twenty-two laws are preserved to any extent on the two extant manuscripts found at Nippur (A: Ni 3191, Istanbul) and Ur (B: made up of two fragments, U7739 and U7740, British Museum), and a more recently found fragment (Si 277, Istanbul).

Publication Data

Text:
B: O. R. Gurney and S. N. Kramer, *Assyriological Studies* 16 (1965): 13–19 (Landsberger festschrift).
A: S. N. Kramer, Or 23 (1954): 40ff.
J. van Dijk, F. Yildiz, Or 50 (1981): 87ff.

---

[2] I. M. Diakonov, "The Rise of the Despotic State in Ancient Mesopotamia" in *Ancient Mesopotamia: A Socio-Economic History* (Moscow, 1969).
[3] S. N. Kramer, "The Ur-Nammu Law Code: Who Was Its Author?" Or 52 (1983): 453–56.

Translation:
ANET, 523–25 (Finkelstein).
J. J. Finkelstein, "The Laws of Ur-Nammu," JCS 22 (1968): 66–82.
Discussion:
H. J. Boecker, *Law and the Administration of Justice in the Old Testament and Ancient East* (Minneapolis, 1980), 57–58.

Content

The Ur-Nammu collection begins with a lengthy prologue followed by the first thirty-one laws of the collection, of which only twenty-two are preserved in even fragmentary condition. The laws deal primarily with family matters (e.g., divorce), bodily injury, slavery, false witness, and property case law.

C. The Laws of Lipit-Ishtar

Approximate Date of Composition
Texts date from the first half of the second millennium B.C. and were sponsored by Lipit-Ishtar, king of Isin (1875–1864 B.C.).

Manuscript Data
Six tablets (three large pieces of a single tablet and three excerpts) were found at Nippur by Hilprecht at end of nineteenth century and are now in the University Museum, University of Pennsylvania. A fourth excerpt is in the Louvre.

Publication Data
Texts:
Francis Steele, "The Code of Lipit-Ishtar," AJA 52 (1948): 425–50.
Translations and Discussion:
H. J. Boecker, *Law and Administration of Justice in the Old Testament and Ancient East* (Minneapolis, 1980), 58–60.
ANET, 159–61 (S. N. Kramer).
E. Szlechter, "Le Code de Lipit-Ishtar," RA 51 (1957): 57–82, 177–96.
A. Falkenstein and M. San Nicolo, "Das Gesetzbuch Lipit-Ishtars von Isin" Or 19 (1950), 103–18.

Content

The thirty-eight laws plus prologue and epilogue that make up the collection of Lipit-Ishtar focuses on family, inheritance, property, and slave laws; civil law as opposed to criminal law.

II. Old Babylonian

A. The Laws of Eshnunna

Approximate Date of Composition
Nineteenth century B.C. The sponsor is unknown, though Dadusha, king of Eshnunna is often cited.[4]

Manuscript Data
Iraq Museum texts 51059 and 52614 were found in 1945 and 1947 at tell Abu Harmal (Shaduppum) by Baqir.

---

[4]See J. J. Finkelstein, JAOS 90 (1970): 247; A. Goetze, AASOR 31 (1956): 4–5.

Publication Data
Text:
R. Yaron, *The Laws of Eshnunna* (Jerusalem, 1969).
A. Goetze, "The Laws of Eshnunna," AASOR 31 (1956).
Translations and Discussion:
H. J. Boecker, *Law and the Administration of Justice in the Old Testament and Ancient East* (Minneapolis, 1980), 60–65.
ANET, 161–63 (Goetze).
A. Goetze, "The Laws of Eshnunna," AASOR 31 (1956).
V. Korošec, "Über die Bedeutung der Gesetzbücher von Ešnunna und von Isin für die Rechtsentwicklung in Mesopotamien und Kleinasien," *Proceedings of the 22nd Congress of Orientalists* (Istanbul, 1953), 83–91.

Content
This sixty-paragraph set of laws contains a wide variety of legislation, including civil and criminal law. For specifics see the chart on page 76.

B. Code of Hammurabi

Approximate Date of Composition
Eighteenth century B.C., sponsored by Hammurabi, king of Babylon, 1792–1750 B.C.

Manuscript Data
The diorite stela was found in Susa in 1901 by Jacques de Morgan and is now housed in the Louvre. There are also many copies on clay tablets and a few other fragments of stone stelae.

Publication Data
Text:
G. R. Driver and John C. Miles, *The Babylonian Laws* (Oxford, 1955).
A. Deimel, *Codex Hammurabi* (Rome, 1930).
V. Scheil, *Memoires de la délégation en Perse* 4 (Paris, 1902), 11ff.
Translations:
A. Finet, *Le Code de Hammourabi* (Paris, 1973).
ANET, 163–80 (Meek).
Discussion:
See H. J. Boecker, *Law and Administration of Justice in the Old Testament and Ancient East* (Minneapolis, 1980), 67–133, for discussion and other bibliographic references. Other primary bibliography is listed in ANET, 164.

Content
This is the most extensive of extant law codes, containing 282 laws (remaining), plus prologue and epilogue. It deals with civil matters such as marriage and divorce, inheritance, property, slaves and debt, as well as criminal matters such as murder, theft, and assault.

C. Edict of Ammiṣaduqa

Approximate Date of Composition
Seventeenth century B.C., sponsored by Ammiṣaduqa, king of Babylon, 1646–1626 B.C.

Manuscript Data
The three main texts, A: Ni 632 (Istanbul); B: BM 78259 (London); and C: BM 80289 (London) were all found at Sippar.[5]

Publication Data
Text:
Entire text now published with transliteration and translation by F. R. Kraus, *Königliche Verfügungen in altbabylonischer Zeit* (Leiden, 1984).
C published by J. J. Finkelstein, "The Edict of Ammiṣaduqa: A New Text," RA 63 (1969): 45–64.
Translation:
Above and ANET, 526–28 (Finkelstein).
Discussion:
J. J. Finkelstein, "Ammiṣaduqa's Edict and the Babylonian 'Law Codes'" JCS 15 (1961): 91–104. Kraus, *Königliche Verfügungen in altbabylonischer Zeit*, discusses the whole area of economic edicts in Mesopotamia, as well as a detailed analysis of the Ammiṣaduqa edict and the similar edict of Samsuiluna. For an excellent review of Kraus see Greengus in JAOS 108.

Content
This item could easily be omitted from this listing. It is not a legal collection but a proclamation known as a *mišarum* (an act of justice) and, unlike the collections, was something that was enforced. Its twenty-two laws, therefore, do not address a whole range of legal matters but declare freedom from certain types of indebtedness.

III. Middle Assyrian

A. Middle Assyrian Laws

Approximate Date of Composition
Twelfth century B.C., perhaps representing two hundred years of royal edicts collected by Tiglath-pileser I (1115–1077).

Manuscript Data
Eleven tablets found at Assur, 1903–14 by Koldewey and Andrae.

Publication Data
Text:
Ernst Weidner, AfO 12 (1937): 50ff.
G. R. Driver and John C. Miles, *The Assyrian Laws* (Oxford, 1935).
Otto Schroeder, *Keilschrifttexte aus Assur Verschiedenen Inhalts* (Leipzig, 1920).
Translation:
Above and ANET, 180–88 (Meek).

Content
Over one hundred laws dealing with a variety of civil and criminal matters.

---

[5] Finkelstein, "Ammiṣaduqa's Edict and Babylonian Law Codes," JCS 15 (1961): 92.

IV. Old Hittite

A. Hittite Laws

Approximate Date of Composition

Varied copies and originals, fifteenth–seventeenth centuries B.C., sponsored by either Mursilis I or Ḫattusilis I (both seventeenth century B.C.).[6]

Manuscript Data

Two tablets found at Boghazkoy by Winckler and smaller fragments.

Publication Data

Text:

J. Friedrich, *Die Hethitischen Gesetze* (Leiden, 1959).

F. Hrozny, *Code Hittite Provenant de l'Asie Mineure* (Paris, 1922).

Additional fragments, H. Otten, *Keilschrifttexte aus Boghazköi* (Berlin, 1963), XII, 48–49; AfO 21 (1966): 1–12.

Translation:

ANET, 188–97 (Goetze).

Discussion:

O. Carruba (Review of Friedrich), *Kratylos* 7 (1962): 155ff.

H. G. Güterbock, "Further Notes on the Hittite Laws," JCS 16 (1962): 17ff.

H. G. Güterbock (Review of Friedrich), JCS 15 (1961): 62ff.

O. R. Gurney, *The Hittites* (Harmondsworth, 1954), 88ff.

Content

This collection of approximately two hundred laws involves the updating of older customary laws. It includes both civil and criminal elements.

V. Israelite

A. Biblical Laws

The biblical legal material likewise is presented by means of several distinct compilations as follows:

1. Covenant Code—Exodus 20:22–23:19
2. Decalogue—Exodus 20:2–17; Deuteronomy 5:6–21
3. Ritual Decalogue—Exodus 34:14–26
4. Deuteronomic Law—Deuteronomy 12–26
5. Holiness Code—Leviticus 17–25
6. Priestly Procedures—Leviticus 1–7, 11–16

DISCUSSION

On the basis of an examination of this legal material, we would like to address some of the similarities and differences between the biblical and cuneiform collections. It should be understood that this is not the same as comparing societal taboos or mores.[7] We will focus specifically on the issues of content, form, and function of the literary pieces that serve as collections of legal material. In this we have been given much help by J. J. Finkelstein in his various studies. Finkelstein has suggested that even though the form and

---

[6]See CAH³, II:1, 668.

[7]For a very helpful discussion of Mesopotamian reflections of the mores represented in the Decalogue, see K. van der Toorn, *Sin and Sanction in Israel and Mesopotamia* (Assen, 1986), 13–20.

language of the biblical legal material is similar to that of the Near Eastern material, the similarity does not extend to function, where a different concept about law may be identified.

> The conceptual context of the Mesopotamian statements of these laws [specifically those pertaining to the goring ox] is vastly different from that of the biblical counterpart, and . . . this difference is the most fundamental factor in determining both the inner structure of the laws themselves and the substantive differences in their juridical resolution. The biblical author appropriated a legal theme out of the common ancient Near Eastern heritage, but transposed these laws into a distinctly different framework and in effect transformed them in the most profound sense even while retaining much of their original form and language.[8]

It must be kept in mind that as content, form, and function are analyzed, we are trying to make productive use of both similarities and differences. As Finkelstein notes, we will find areas where the biblical data has drawn heavily from common source material. This should not be perceived as antithetical to the concept of revelation. We are not obliged to think that prior to the revelation of the Decalogue on Mount Sinai, Israelites felt perfectly free to murder, commit adultery, bear false witness, etc. The revelatory nature of the law does not demand that these prohibitions be seen as innovative. The revelation may either provide divine approbation to humans' operation of society or may have as its nucleus the formulation or function of the law. If the latter is the case, those elements of law that constitute Israelite uniqueness would have the first claim for being understood as deriving from divine revelation.[9] Our primary interest is in what we can learn about the worldviews of these respective societies.[10]

I. Content

The content of the legal material can be broken down into subdivisions for the sake of comparison. Already in the listing of the ancient Near Eastern legal literature we have introduced civil and criminal categories. Within each category exist various specific areas that are commonly addressed. The chart on page 76 identifies which of the legal collections deals with each of the major areas.

Most of the laws appearing in these collections fall into these general categories. Exceptions would include miscellaneous dictates such as "No one of the metal workers shall be freed from participating in a royal campaign in a fortress (and) from cutting a vineyard. The gardeners shall render full services."[11]

Turning now to biblical law, the same charting procedure will require the addition of the major category of cultic law. The breakdown is plotted on the chart on page 77.

---

[8]J. J. Finkelstein, *The Ox That Gored*, Transactions of the American Philosophical Society 71:2 (Philadelphia, 1981), 5.

[9]Ibid., 18. Cf. also Moshe Greenberg, "Some Postulates of Biblical Criminal Law," in *Yehezkel Kaufmann Jubilee Volume* (New York, 1960), 5–28.

[10]Ibid., 16.

[11]Hittite Laws #56, James Pritchard, ANET, 192.

	URU'INIMGINA	UR-NAMMU	LIPIT-ISHTAR	ESHNUNNA	HAMMURABI	AMMIṢADUQA	MIDDLE ASSYRIAN	HITTIE
CIVIL LAW								
Marriage/Family		x	x	x	x		x	x
Inheritance		x			x		x	
Property	x	x	x	x	x		x	x
Slaves		x	x	x	x		x	x
Debt		x	x	x	x	x	x	
Taxes/Wages	x		x		x			x
CRIMINAL LAW								
Murder				x	x		x	x
Adultery/Rape		x		x	x		x	x
Theft				x	x		x	x
Sexual Deviation					x			x
False Witness		x			x			x
Assault		x		x	x		x	x
Liability				x	x			

In comparing the chart of ancient Near Eastern law with that of biblical law, there are several items worthy of note.

A. Cultic Law

The mixing of cultic law into the legal genre is a unique phenomenon in Israelite formulation. We would suspect that this would ultimately be significant in determination of the function of these collections, so we will further discuss this idiosyncrasy when function is examined.

B. Shift of Emphasis

Not only is "cultic law" adopted as a new category, but it receives a large proportion of the attention in the biblical collections. The cuneiform collections focused primarily on civil law. While elements of civil law are discussed in the Old Testament, even laws of the same category as the ancient Near Eastern material take on a different perspective. For instance, cuneiform laws concerning property frequently discuss cases involving lost, found, borrowed, or leased property and the principles governing its use or abuse. The biblical discussions of property are much more concerned with issues like fallow year and perpetual ownership of land. J. J. Finkelstein also notices the relative indifferences of the biblical collections to civil law.

> The contrast between biblical and Mesopotamian legal corpora is under-
> scored even further by the almost total absence in the former of normative

	COVENANT CODE	DECALOGUE	RITUAL DECALOGUE	DEUTERONOMIC LAW	HOLINESS CODE	PRIESTLY PROCEDURES
CIVIL LAW						
Marriage/Family				x		
Inheritance						
Property	x			x	x	
Slaves	x			x		
Debt	x			x	x	
Taxes/Wages						
CRIMINAL LAW						
Murder		x		x	x	
Adultery/Rape		x		x	x	
Theft	x	x		x	x	
Sexual Deviation	x				x	
False Witness	x	x			x	
Assault	x			x	x	
Liability	x			x		
CULTIC LAW						
Sacrifices	x		x	x	x	x
Purification	x			x	x	x
Mode/Object of Worship	x	x	x	x	x	
Festival Observance	x	x	x	x	x	

rules, that is, formulations of the proper procedures governing commerce and economic life in general. The legal sections of the Pentateuch betray what amounts to complete indifference to the formalities without which the most elementary social institutions could hardly be said to function. This silence applies not only to contracts and obligations, but also to the normative forms by which family life is ordered, such as marriage, family property rights, and inheritance. The Mesopotamian legal corpora dwell on these themes at great length; biblical law touches upon them only in the most cursory way.[12]

In summary, criminal law is the area of most significant overlap, civil law is the primary focus of the cuneiform collections, and cultic law is the primary focus of the biblical collections.[13]

C. Unclassified Biblical Material

We have already noted that the categories listed on the chart accounted for almost all of the items found in the cuneiform collections. This is not the case with the biblical collections. There are a number of major elements of legislation that defied the established categories. These would include:

Prohibition of mistreating vulnerable classes (widow, orphan, stranger): Exodus 22:22–24; Leviticus 19:9–10, 13–16, 33–36; Deuteronomy 24:17.
Showing respect: Exodus 20:12; 22:28–29; Leviticus 19:32; 20:9.
Prohibition against accepting bribes: Exodus 23:8; Deuteronomy 16:19.
General warning against "perverting justice": Exodus 23:6; Deuteronomy 16:18–20; 24:17; 25:13–16.
Prohibition against magic/divination/sorcery, etc.: Leviticus 19:26, 31; 20:6, 27; Deuteronomy 18:10ff.[14]
Rules of warfare: Deuteronomy 20.
Prohibitions against certain attitudes: Exodus 20:17 (coveting); Leviticus 19:17 (hating); Leviticus 19:18 (bearing a grudge).

For the most part, these topics are absent from cuneiform collections and, again, we will expect to find an explanation of the difference in our study of function.

Having observed the general characteristics and nature of the respective collections, we should now examine how the Bible and the cuneiform collections each treat the material found in both. Similarities can occur in the formulation of the specifics of the case and sometimes even extend to the punishment meted out. S. Greengus has presented a helpful selection of these similarities divided into the following categories:[15]

- Offenses and penalties described in identical fashion.
- Identical or nearly identical formulations.
- Close but not identical formulations.
- Same subject, differing formulation.

While we cannot examine in detail all of the examples Greengus provides for us, we can benefit from the extensive analysis that J. J. Finkelstein has done

---

[12]Finkelstein, Ox, 42.
[13]Ibid., 41.
[14]Middle Assyrian Laws #47 (ANET, 184) and Hammurabi #2 (ANET, 166).
[15]Samuel Greengus, "Law in the Old Testament," IDB Supp., 533–34.

on the laws of the "goring ox" (Exod. 21:28–32) in which formulations are nearly identical. From Finkelstein's work we can establish a paradigm for understanding the relationship between biblical and cuneiform law.

On the basis of the nearly identical formulations in the goring ox legislation, Finkelstein has concluded that there must be either a legal or literary dependence of the biblical material on its ancient Near Eastern forerunners. The former would suggest that as societies facing similar problems, they are bound to develop laws governing identical situations. The latter would insist that the legal documents of the ancient Near East, or something descended from them, were being used as a literary source for the biblical laws. Finkelstein opts for the latter because he feels that many of the situations dealt with do not commonly recur;[16] he particularly mentions Exodus 21:22 in this connection.

Despite this alleged literary dependence (which has some rather convincing support), Finkelstein suggests that the two societies (Israelite and Mesopotamian) gave totally distinct meanings to the law as evidenced by the reaction to the offense of the goring ox. In both the Eshnunna and Hammurabi formulations, the ox, though the actual offender, is ignored, while the owner of the ox is fined. Thus, even though human death has occurred, the crime "constitutes an economic trespass against the dependent kin of the victim, and is to be made good as such once liability is properly established."[17]

In the biblical formulation the ox is stoned to death and the owner (of the habitually goring ox) is subject to capital punishment as well. Stoning is only used in Scripture as a penalty for certain types of offenses. Finkelstein thereby concludes that the biblical laws classify this as a crime that is religious in nature.

> The real crime of the ox is that by killing a human being—whether out of viciousness or by an involuntary motion—it has objectively committed a de facto insurrection against the hierarchic order established by Creation: Man was designated by God "to rule over the fish of the sea, the fowl of the skies, the cattle, the earth, and all creatures that roam over the earth" (Gen. 1:26, 28).[18]

Concerning the owner now accused with culpable negligence—though he is subject to death, his life may be ransomed. Even if he is ransomed, though, there still exists a distinction with the cuneiform material. In the latter, appropriate restitution to the deceased's survivors is the focus. In the former, bloodguilt must be absolved. It is not simply a case of reimbursement for an economic loss; rather, it is for the owner's life that the money is being paid.[19]

In summary, comparison of the content of the cuneiform and biblical legal connections shows a high degree of similarity in material covered[20] and

---

[16]Finkelstein, Ox, 17–20, esp. n. 11.

[17]Ibid., 24.

[18]Ibid., 28.

[19]As Finkelstein points out, this can be seen even more clearly in the case of the unsolved homicide in the countryside, Deuteronomy 21:1–9; Code of Hammurabi, 22–24; Ox, 29–30.

[20]See also the treatment concerning the similar views of societal ethics in Mesopotamia and Israel by van der Toorn, Sin and Sanction, 10–39.

even in formulation within the area we have designated criminal law. Penalties within criminal law, however, seem to indicate a shift in thinking concerning the significance of the offense and what redress is necessary. We feel that this can be further substantiated from the fact that Israel supplements its criminal law primarily with cultic law, whereas cuneiform collections supplement criminal law with civil law. Based on these observed foci, we might suggest a civil bias in all cuneiform law and a cultic bias in Israelite law. Put another way: no matter which category of law is under consideration, in Mesopotamia, offense is ultimately viewed in relation to society; while in Israel, all offense is ultimately against God. Finkelstein views this as the "barbaric" element in ancient society.

> It is rather the all but universal primitive practice of treating physical assaults, including homicide, as private civil invasions remediable by pecuniary satisfaction, which, far from perceiving any moral—and therefore criminal—issue in such acts, is the truly "barbaric" situation.[21]

This explanation would account for the different directions pursued through the common criminal material but at this point can only be accepted tentatively. We will return to this matter in our discussion of the function of the legal collections and of the law itself.

II. Form

Another important element for understanding the function of the collections is the form in which the dicta are expressed. The two standard forms of expression have been identified since Albrecht Alt as apodictic and casuistic.[22] Casuistic law is identified primarily by its use of conditional clauses. Thus each case is presented by means of an "if . . ." formulation with the verdict presented as the apodosis, "then. . . ." R. MacKenzie enlarges on this type of law with the following description: "It is strictly pragmatic; that is, it is quite independent, *per se* of any religious doctrine or ethical principle. No general principles are appealed to, no axioms laid down. The situation described calls for such and such action or has such and such consequences."[23] He further notes that it is remedial, not preventive. It does not prohibit; it threatens. It places no obligation on the individual. In turn, Alt identifies as apodictic any formulation that did not make use of the conditional clause. In the Old Testament there are four classes of apodictic law in Alt's classification system.

- The *mot yumat* series (Exod. 21) (he shall be sentenced to death).
- The *'arur* (curse) series (Deut. 27:15–26).
- The sexual prohibitions of Leviticus 18:7–17.

---

[21]J. J. Finkelstein, "Ammiṣaduqa's Edict and the Babylonians 'Law Codes,' " JCS 15 (1961), 98.

[22]A. Alt, "The Origin of Israelite Law," in *Essays on Old Testament History and Religion* (Oxford, 1966), 81–132. (Originally published in 1934). For a summary and critique of Alt, see R. Sonsino, *Motive Clauses in Hebrew Law* (Chico, Calif., 1980), 2–13.

[23]R. A. F. MacKenzie, "The Formal Aspect of Ancient Near Eastern Law," in *The Seed of Wisdom*, ed. W. S. McCullough (Toronto, 1964), 35–36. On casuistic forms see also H. W. Gilmer, *The If-You Form in Israelite Law* (Missoula: 1975).

● The Decalogue (Exod. 20; Deut. 5).

Since Alt's pioneering work in the field, it has seemed necessary to further subdivide Alt's apodictic category. It has been noticed that the first two series (*mot yumat* and *'arur*) use the third-person address and are directed toward individual cases; both characteristics are usually connected to casuistic formulation. The latter two series are formulated in the second person and make no reference to specific cases.[24] These latter two are most strictly apodictic in nature, for they place an obligation to comply squarely on the individual. MacKenzie notes: "In its pure form, apodictic law does not contemplate the hypothesis of disobedience or contumacy. Its enunciation, unlike that of casuistic law, makes no provision for the statement of a penalty; this must be added, if at all, in a separate clause."[25]

MacKenzie prefers to classify apodictic law into two categories: jussive formulation—which he finds even in Hammurabi (par. 36, 40); and command or prohibition—which he sees as uniquely Israelite.[26]

Regardless of which system of classification seems best suited to the data, certain observations remain true:

1. Cuneiform law is almost entirely composed of casuistic law. The few exceptions are only apodictic in a very limited sense.[27]

2. Israelite law, while enunciated and expanded by casuistic law, has a foundation in prohibitive apodictic law.

So while there is great similarity demonstrated in using casuistically formulated law, Israelite law distinguishes itself by its use of apodictic law.

Following are the primary examples of apodictic formulation in cuneiform law:

Eshnunna 11. The wages of a hired man are one shekel of silver; his provender is one pan of barley. He shall work for one month.[28]

Eshnunna 16. To a joint heir or a slave a mortgage cannot be furnished.[29]

Eshnunna 51. A slave or a slave girl of Eshnunna who is marked with a *kannum*, a *mashkanum*, or an *abuttum*, shall not leave the gate of Eshnunna without [his or her] owner's permission.[30]

Hammurabi 36. In no case is the field, orchard, or house belonging to a soldier, a commissary, or a feudatory salable.[31]

Middle Assyrian A40. Neither wives of seignors nor [widows] nor [Assyrian women], who go out on the street [may have] their heads

---

[24] See especially Hans J. Boecker, *Law and the Administration of Justice in the Old Testament and Ancient East* (Minneapolis, 1980), 191–207.

[25] MacKenzie, "The Formal Aspect," 39. Professor Kitchen kindly reminded me that apodictic prohibition also occurs in Egyptian texts such as "Instruction According to Ancient Writings," in which every entry begins, "Do not. . . ."

[26] Ibid., 41–42. For another suggested classification system, see Sonsino, *Motive Clauses*, 13–17.

[27] Finkelstein has suggested that the apodictic sections may perhaps have *mišarum* edicts as their source, JCS 15 (1961): 102.

[28] ANET, 162.

[29] Ibid.

[30] Ibid., 163; cf. par. 52.

[31] Ibid. 167; cf. pars. 38–40.

[uncovered] . . . (proceeds to discuss situation for virgin daughters, concubines, prostitutes, etc.).[32]

Hittite 56. No one of the metal workers shall be freed from participating in a royal campaign in a fortress [and] from cutting a vineyard. The gardeners shall render the full services.[33]

These can be easily differentiated from the Israelite Decalogue in that they do not lay down moral principles. However, we must determine whether the Decalogue may actually be considered a part of Israel's legal collection. Should we identify it as a different kind of literature? Is there anything comparable to the Israelite Decalogue in other types of cuneiform literature?

George Mendenhall has provided an affirmative answer to the latter question in his suggestion that the closest parallel to the Decalogue in ancient Near Eastern literature is to be found in treaty stipulations.[34] As an example, he cites the stipulation from a treaty between the Hittite king Mursilis and Kupanta-kal, "Thou shalt not desire any territory of the land of Hatti." This leads naturally to the possibility of the Decalogue being considered technically part of the treaty formulation rather than a part of the legal formulation per se. Or, put differently, because of the inseparability of covenant and law in Israel, it is difficult to determine which type of formulation belongs to each genre. This discussion more properly belongs under the heading of "function," which will be discussed below.

Another formal element of Israelite law that has been studied against the background of Near Eastern law is the use of motive clauses.[35] These are clauses appended to the laws to give a reason why the law ought to be observed. Of the 1,238 legal prescriptions that R. Sonsino identifies in the law collections of the Pentateuch, 375 include motivation clauses.[36] In contrast, among the ancient Near Eastern collections, only Hammurabi and the Middle Assyrian Laws contain motivated formulations.[37] Sonsino identifies several points of comparison including:[38]

1. Motivated laws are much rarer in the ancient Near Eastern collections.
2. Motive clauses appear only in conditional formulations in the ancient Near East, while in the Bible both conditional and unconditional laws are motivated.
3. Motive clauses in the ancient Near Eastern material achieve their aim by underscoring the key element in the case. In contrast, the

---

[32]Ibid., 183.

[33]Ibid., 192. R. Sonsino, *Motive Clauses*, 61, nn. 316–19, also provides a list that suggests a few additional possibilities (Eshnunna 15, 52; Hammurabi 38–40; Hittite 48, 50–51).

[34]George Mendenhall, "Ancient Oriental and Biblical Law," in *Biblical Archaeologist Reader*, 3, ed. E. F. Campbell and D. N. Freedman (Garden City, N.Y., 1970), 7. (Article first published in 1954.)

[35]Sonsino, *Motive Clauses*.

[36]Ibid., 98.

[37]Ibid., 155. Eighteen examples in Hammurabi, seven in the Middle Assyrian Laws.

[38]Ibid., 173–75.

biblical motive clauses almost always add new information and identify some of the presuppositions of the law.

III. Function

Having discussed the issues of content and form, we are now ready to address the question of function. To begin we must distinguish between the function of the legal collections and the function of law in general. These two areas overlap and are certainly interrelated to a large extent, but the legal collections cannot be synonymous with the "law," for not all of the "law" is covered by the legal collections.[39] S. E. Loewenstamm cites a good example of this in biblical law. Deuteronomy 25:1–3 legislates a limitation on the number of times a man can be flogged by the court, yet only once in the Pentateuch is flogging the sentence prescribed for a crime (Deut. 22:18). The necessity for the limitation coupled with the rarity of the crime for which flogging is prescribed suggest the existence of other laws in which flogging was a more prominent sentence. This having been noted, however, our determination of the function of the law will derive, for the most part, from the observations made concerning the legal collections. These observations will include the elements of content and form that have already been introduced. The function of the legal collections may be addressed through an examination of statements of purpose in prologues and epilogues and by the use made of the collections.

A. Observations on the Function of Cuneiform Legal Collections

We are fortunate to have preserved for us the prologues and epilogues of several cuneiform collections that address the idea of function. Some of the more salient features include:

1. Ur-Nammu prologue

The orphan was not delivered up to the rich man, the widow was not delivered up to the mighty man; the man of one shekel was not delivered up to the man of one mina.[40]

2. Lipit-Ishtar prologue

I . . . [estab]lished [jus]tice in [Su]mer and Akkad in accordance with the word of Enlil.[41]

3. Hammurabi prologue

When lofty Anum, king of the *Anunnaki*, and Enlil, lord of heaven and earth, the determiner of the destinies of the land, determined for Marduk, the first-born of Enki, the Enlil functions over all mankind, made him great among the *Igigi*, called Babylon by its exalted name, made it supreme in the world, established for him in its midst an enduring kingship, whose foundations are as firm as heaven and earth—at that time Anum and Enlil named me to promote the welfare of the people, me Hammurabi, the devout, god-fearing prince, to cause justice to prevail in

---

[39]Cf. S. E. Loewenstamm, "Law," in *Judges: The World History of the Jewish People,* (New Brunswick, N.J., 1971), 3:232–34; and Boecker, *Law and Administration,* 55ff.
[40]ANET, 524.
[41]Ibid., 159.

the land, to destroy the wicked and the evil, that the strong might not oppress the weak. . . . When Marduk commissioned me to guide the people aright, to direct the land, I established law and justice in the language of the land, thereby promoting the welfare of the people.[42]

4. Hammurabi epilogue

I wrote my precious words on my stela, and in the presence of the statue of me, the king of justice, I set (it) up in order to administer the law of the land, to prescribe the ordinances of the land, to give justice to the oppressed.[43]

Let any oppressed man who has a cause come into the presence of the statue of me, the king of justice, and then read carefully my inscribed stela, and give heed to my precious words and may my stela make the case clear to him; may he understand his cause.[44]

In the days to come, for all time, let the king who appears in the land observe the words of justice which I wrote on my stela; let him not alter the law of the land which I have enacted, the ordinances of the land which I prescribed.[45]

We can see from these that the promulgators of these collections saw them as intimately connected with the performance of their kingly duties. The primary concern of society was to insure its own well-being;[46] the king had the major contribution to make in that process by maintaining justice.[47] The law collections seem to be his way of maintaining justice, promising that justice will be maintained, or showing how justice has been maintained (or some combination of the three).[48] Therefore, they could be considered to have propagandistic or apologetic value.

While it may be argued that these collections had primarily political functions, we cannot ignore the statements of Hammurabi concerning the public display of the stela. Certainly he could have been using the medium to attempt to persuade the gods that he was worthy of his commission or to persuade the people that he was faithfully fulfilling his obligations to society—but these do not exclude a more practical legislative or prescriptive usage. With regard to this aspect, D. J. Wiseman makes the following observations:

The laws were set up in the temple before the god in Babylon and in the epilogue the king makes it clear that it was a record of the royal wisdom (emqum) and that it was also meant for the benefit of his successors for he made the plea that they, as he had, would continue the same legal practices. The statement that the laws were available for general consultation probably implies no more than that copies were made both for later kings and lawyers. Indeed, copies of these laws and other earlier collections, were made down to the late Babylonian times. In addition to

---

[42]Ibid., 164–65, lines I:1–39, V:12–21.

[43]Ibid., 178.

[44]Ibid.

[45]Ibid.

[46]Finkelstein, "Mesopotamian Historiography," 463.

[47]E. A. Speiser, "Authority and Law in Mesopotamia," JAOS Supp. 17 (1954): 13.

[48]Cf. Finkelstein, JCS 15 (1961): 100ff., for discussion of connections between legal collection and mišarum acts.

its value in providing a reference work, the requirement to copy and preserve the law and order was necessary for the preservation of the living and continuing tradition. This need for the king to demonstrate the wisdom with which he had been endowed on taking office led to his final report to the god, including a selection of the most erudite cases. It is not surprising that among a large body of extant legal cases there is scant reference or allusion to any of the laws of Hammurabi.[49]

Though the ancient citizen's right to base a claim on a given point of an ancient collection is clearly enunciated in the epilogue, Finkelstein argues that the collections had no real influence on daily jurisprudence.

Whatever might have been the proportions of realism, idealism, hyperbole, and scholasticism in the amalgams that took the shape of the "law corpora" of ancient Mesopotamia, they left no palpable traces in the substantive law (as distinct from the forms in which the law could be made manifest) of subsequent civilizations. . . . Consideration of the absurd and the offensive in Mesopotamian legal expression . . . thus results in a sharp difference in historical balance. Mesopotamian legal experience was never translated into action.[50]

Finkelstein comes to the conclusion that the penalties of Mesopotamian law (he would also include biblical law, which we will discuss elsewhere), "were not *meant* to be complied with literally" but rather served an "admonitory" function.[51]

H. J. Boecker, on the other hand, suggests that the practical use was much more extensive. Quoting F. R. Kraus, he agrees that the laws of Hammurabi are "exemplary decisions, models of sound legal judgments,"[52] but he then concludes: "This means that they were intended to influence future judgements, that they were intended to be taken seriously as legal patterns, that judges had to abide by them . . . and therefore that they approximate what we call laws."[53]

Finkelstein's evaluation makes it clear that Boecker's conclusions fail to take account of legitimate alternatives. This does not mean that Boecker is wrong, but the point-blank statement, "This means that . . . ," is unacceptable without supporting evidence. Likewise, the true function of the collections could fall somewhere between Finkelstein's presentation as "apologia" and Boecker's as law. At this point, however, Finkelstein has developed the more persuasive argument and has garnered much convincing evidence in support of his cause. For an example, let us take a brief look at his treatment of Hammurabi paragraph 230, which stipulates that if a newly built house collapses and kills the owner's son, the son of the builder

---

[49]D. J. Wiseman, "Law and Order in Old Testament Times," *Vox Evangelica* 8 (1973): 9–10; for supporting statement by Finkelstein, see JCS 15, p. 103: "It is significant that never is there any adjuration of judges and officials to pay any heed to these 'codes.' " This indicates that the collection would have carried moral rather than legal force.

[50]Finkelstein, *Ox*, 35.

[51]Ibid.

[52]Boecker, *Law and Administration*, 77.

[53]Ibid. *See also*, R. Westbrook, "Biblical and Cuneiform Law Codes" RB 92 (1985): 247–64.

is to be put to death. Finkelstein points out that while this makes "logical sense within the Mesopotamian categorical universe," it constitutes a legal absurdity. On the theoretical side, his defense is as follows:

> One must first remember that Mesopotamian society is structured by status, each status being translatable into a corresponding "value" with reference to other statuses on the scale. . . . Status implies a certain standard of quality for persons. . . . Hence, to require that a negligent builder should be put to death for the *loss* of a minor person would, in Mesopotamian terms, amount to gross imbalance of justice: a relatively minor economic loss to the houseowner (and one that might be presumed to be replaceable without cost by procreation) would be "remedied" by the killing of a head of household, an economic loss of major proportions, and a catastrophic one for his family.[54]

In addressing the legal aspect, Finkelstein asks the simple questions: "What . . . would the 'law' do in the event that the builder had no minor son, or even a son of any age? Would his daughter do instead? And supposing he had no daughter either?"[55]

He therefore again concludes that "this paragraph states a kind of ideal principle rather than a literal rule."[56] It is a document of theory, not of practice—perhaps of justice, not of law. It could be seen as a detailed development of some of the forms "justice" would take.

This would, of course, support the "apologia" model for the function of these collections. Further support may be found in the connection of deity with the collections. In the epilogue of Hammurabi's laws, he does not hesitate to use the first person: "*I* wrote *my* precious words on *my* stela . . . *I* set it up . . . the law of the land which *I* have enacted, the ordinances of the land which *I* prescribed."[57] It can be seen that these laws are not considered to be divine pronouncements.[58] Again, it is Finkelstein who cites the pertinent distinction: "The famous laws of Hammurabi . . . are *not* received

---

[54]Finkelstein, *Ox*, 34.

[55]Ibid. A suggestion other than apologia, yet still in the realm of the ideal, is that the law collections are part of the Mesopotamian scholastic tradition. This seems particularly likely in the case of the laws of Eshnunna that do not contain the prologue and epilogue to set them in the apologia context. B. L. Eichler's analysis of literary structure in the laws of Eshnunna would give further evidence of that. "This revealed structure, with its presentation of polar cases and juxtaposition of legal cases to create legal statements would seem to exclude the Laws of Eshnunna from the realm of legislated statutory law or exemplary legal verdicts based on actual court cases. This structure would rather seem to add further support for placing the Eshnunna law compilation within the orbit of Mesopotamian scholastic tradition. The features of the structure suggest a legal textbook featuring a 'socratic' methodology, designed for the teaching of Mesopotamian legal thought and the appreciation of the complexities of legal situations" ("Literary Structure in the Laws of Eshnunna" in *Language, Literature and History*, ed. Francesca Rochberg-Halton [New Haven, 1987], 79). Eichler goes on to suggest a similar structure in Hammurabi's code.

[56]Ibid., 35. Even as a guiding principle, however, it may have given a framework for the appropriate penalty to be assigned.

[57]ANET, 178.

[58]Cf. G. R. Driver and John C. Miles, *The Babylonian Laws* (Oxford, 1952), 1:39.

from Shamash, the god of justice. This god is conceived of as approving and demanding just action on earth, but he does not 'reveal the Law' itself."[59]

Shamash, then, is the one to whom Hammurabi would be expected to have to give a report—demonstrating that his duties have been properly executed.

W. G. Lambert finds a solution between the positions of Finkelstein and Boecker. Obviously not providing a comprehensive set of rules for society, the law codes, according to Lambert,

> presume a fixed body of accepted norms and proceed to legislate for those cases where growth and change of society gave rise to circumstances for which no traditional ruling existed. In particular the very complex commercial life with the inherent dangers of the profit motive needed regulating, and for that reason the Mesopotamian laws seem to the modern reader to have a very secular flavour.[60]

This leads him to the following conclusion about Mesopotamian law:

> It is a combination of two very diverse elements. On the one hand it offers precise regulations for specific needs of society, and incorporates some old traditional rulings. On the other hand it offers an ideal of legal decisions to be taken as a pattern rather than a working manual. Behind this structure the true nature of Mesopotamian social behaviour stands out very clearly. Despite the advanced and complicated commercial life, morals were still very much in the "tribal" stage. Everyone knew the basic requirements in social life, and there was no need to have them put in writing. All citizens, but especially the rulers, were guardians of the standards demanded and were presumed to uphold them in their respective spheres.[61]

B. Observations on the Function of Law in Mesopotamia

This leads us finally to an examination of the concept of "law" itself in Mesopotamia. E. A. Speiser has stated that "law is an aspect of the cosmic order and hence ultimately the gift of the forces of the universe."[62]

This observation can be supported from the occurrence of truth, goodness, and justice in the list of the divine decrees (ME) which is given in the Sumerian myth of "Inanna and Enki: The Transfer of the Arts of Civilization from Eridu to Erech."[63] In the reform text of Uruinimgina we are told that "Urukagina was chosen by Ningirsu, the tutelary deity of the city, out of the whole multitude of Lagash citizens and enjoined to re-establish the 'divine laws' (*namtar*) which had been abandoned and neglected by his predecessors."[64] So while the legal collections were the work of kings, the law that they embodied and the justice that they sought to enforce were built into the cosmic system. Speiser further makes the distinction that Shamash,

---

[59]J. J. Finkelstein, "Bible and Babel," *Commentary* 26 (1958): 442.

[60]W. G. Lambert, "Morals in Ancient Mesopotamia," JEOL 15 (1958): 187.

[61]Ibid.

[62]E. A. Speiser, "Cuneiform Law and the History of Civilization," *Proceedings of the American Philosophical Society* 107:6 (1963): 537.

[63]S. N. Kramer, *Sumerian Mythology* (Philadelphia, 1972), 64–66; cf. also discussion in Kramer, *The Sumerians* (Chicago, 1963), 116, 160–62.

[64]Kramer, *Sumerians*, 82; cf. 318.

the god of justice, likewise, "was not the source of *kittum* (truth) but only its guardian, for that boon, being eternal and universal, could not originate with gods, let alone mortals."[65] We have already mentioned that the Mesopotamian ideal was a well-ordered, smoothly running society.[66] It was the decrees (ME) that accomplished this. Law is thereby descriptive of how the system works best. It is prescriptive only to the extent of requiring a person to conform his actions to what is necessary for civilized society. It is amoral, i.e., there is no moral absolute that serves as the foundation for behavior.[67] The gods are not moral, and the system does not require morality per se, only justice, though the two obviously overlap. So the function of law is to insure a well-ordered society. It is the jurisdiction and obligation of the king to monitor and administer society's adherence to that cosmic order on a day-to-day basis. Both the content and form of cuneiform law lend support to this concept of the amoral nature of law, though they do not prove it. It will be recalled that the content focuses on what might be called "social" legislation and makes no reference to general moral principles. It is strictly secular. The form is primarily casuistic, not apodictic. R. MacKenzie has observed that "the casuistic laws do not formally express any obligation laid upon the individual . . . he is not forbidden, for example, to steal or to commit adultery; at most he is warned that if he does these things, certain consequences are likely to follow."[68] The Mesopotamian worldview had no absolutes upon which categorical prohibitions could be based. The distinction between *wrong and right* could not be made in any absolute way. Something could be pleasing or displeasing to the gods, but one had no measure by which to determine what would be pleasing to deity or to which deity it might be pleasing. Finkelstein pursues this further: "Taken as a whole, the evidence strongly indicates that Mesopotamian legal thinking was not conscious of any *categorical* gulf between various classes of wrongs."[69]

The offenses were all against *civilization*—that is, society's norms built into the cosmic system. These norms were administered by the gods but were not revealed by the gods and frequently not adhered to by them. They were norms for the proper and successful functioning of society.

> It is noteworthy that, unlike biblical laws, no cuneiform law is ever motivated by reference to a historic event; a promise of well-being; or, for that matter, a divine will. In fact, in these laws the deity is completely silent, yielding its place to a human lawgiver whose main concern is economic rather than religious. Biblical law, on the other hand, ascribed in its totality to God both in terms of source and authorship, displays a concern that goes beyond the economic, enveloping all aspects of community life, whether past, present, or future, and incorporating both the strictly cultic/sacral and that which remains outside of it.[70]

[65] Speiser, "Cuneiform Law," 537.

[66] Lambert, "Destiny and Divine Intervention in Babylon and Israel," OTS 17 (1972): 67.

[67] Cf. MacKenzie, "Formal Aspect," 35; Speiser, "Authority and Law," 14.

[68] MacKenzie, "Formal Aspect," 35.

[69] Finkelstein, *Ox*, 41.

[70] Sonsino, *Motive Clauses*, 174.

C. Observations on the Function of the Biblical Legal Collections

Finkelstein suggests that like cuneiform law, biblical law was never intended to be taken literally but served an "admonitory" function.[71] While this may be a possible understanding of the casuistic sections, we feel that it could hardly be applied to the apodictic sections. D. J. Wiseman, for instance, sets forth many passages from the historical literature in which a king's measure is taken by how he adhered to the law, or the commandments of Moses.[72] He does not allow that this is a general comment but rather finds that it "refers to specific legal action taken by the king."[73] First Kings 15:5, for instance, comments concerning David that he "did what was right in the sight of the LORD, and had not turned aside from any thing that He commanded him all the days of his life, except in the case of Uriah the Hittite" (NASB).

Finkelstein's concern is not to demonstrate that the biblical laws are impractical or irrational, but rather that they are not sufficiently comprehensive to serve as a legal foundation for administering a society. The question, then, is not whether people strove to keep "the Law"—it is clear that some at least did and that that was a standard against which one could be measured (cf. Ps. 119:133; Deut. 5–6). The question is what the intended function of the legal collections was.

Finkelstein finally suggests that the intended function was covenantal[74] and further that "the Law of Moses served only as a most general guide and as the moral underpinning for the arrangement of real social institutions."[75] The observation earlier made by George Mendenhall (that apodictic statements find their Mesopotamian equivalent in treaty stipulations) now takes on great significance. If the Decalogue (as the major representative of apodictic law) is considered *not* a legal collection, but a set of treaty stipulations, we would have much closer alignment of the form and function of the legal collections in Israel and Mesopotamia. The Mesopotamian collections used casuistic formulations to demonstrate the king's fulfillment of his contractual obligations. Those obligations were connected with justice and a well-ordered society and were built into the cosmic order. Israelite collections used casuistic formulations to demonstrate the community's fulfillment of its contractual obligations. These obligations were connected with the moral behavior built on the covenant they had with YHWH. Deuteronomic law, for instance, presents Moses as citing precedent or sample cases of how the Decalogue is to be worked out in various legal situations.[76] Notice, though, that there is still a vast difference (and a very significant one) in the *basis* of law. Concerning the Mesopotamian collections, it was suggested that they were a detailed development of some of the forms "justice" would take. The biblical collections differ in that they represent a

---

[71] Finkelstein, *Ox*, 35.

[72] Wiseman, "Law and Order," 6.

[73] Ibid., 6.

[74] Finkelstein, *Ox*, 42.

[75] Ibid., 45.

[76] Cf. especially S. A. Kaufman, "The Structure of the Deuteronomic Law," *Maarav* 1/2 (1978–79): 105–58. See also J. H. Walton, "Deuteronomy: An Exposition of the Spirit of the Law," GTJ 8 (1987): 213–25.

detailed development of some of the forms *morality* or *holiness* would take. This leads us into the function of law in Israelite society.

D. Observations on the Function of Law in Israel

In Israel, law represents the demands of Deity on his people. It is important to realize that while morality was considered universally applicable, the law was not. This again suggests that the law is very much bound up with the covenant. The law is not YHWH's demands of anyone else—only of Israel. This law, however, was based on absolutes, for the standard was YHWH himself—"You are to be holy, for I am holy" (Lev. 19:2). In Israelite law, then, all legislation is, at heart, religious, for morality has its ramifications in every aspect of society. So, biblical law seeks to answer the question, What does *morality* require in this situation? or How can the holiness of God be upheld in the community? In contrast, Mesopotamian law asked, How do we maintain order and prevent chaos? How can civilization be preserved?

In Mesopotamia, legal collections did not contain religious legislation. This is not to say that such legislation does not exist in Mesopotamia. There are documents that give lengthy descriptions of how special days are to be observed,[77] how rituals are to be performed,[78] details concerning festivals,[79] etc. Furthermore, historical texts give information about how particular kings made decrees concerning worship of particular deities.[80] What is significant is that these things do *not* make their way into the legal collections. In the Israelite collections, on the other hand, religious expression is the intended subject matter; social conduct is a form of religious expression.

YHWH's revelation to Israel, then, does not present itself, for the most part, as a new mode of conduct. Israel had laws before to insure the smooth functioning of society, and it is logical to believe that they would have been heavily dependent on other cultures of their day for those guidelines. The revelation, though, had to do with providing a foundation for those norms (the covenant) and establishing YHWH as the source of those norms. One does not refrain from adultery merely because adultery disrupts society. Rather, adultery is prohibited because it goes against an absolute standard of morality by which YHWH himself is characterized.

In conclusion, we have found some degree of similarity in all three areas—content, form, and function. We would have to suggest, however, that the similarities are largely superficial, while the differences are substantive. Acknowledging the danger of overpolarization, perhaps the chart on page 91 can help highlight some of the comparisons in summary fashion.

---

[77]E.g., Stephen Langdon, *Babylonian Menologies and Semitic Calendars* (London, 1935).

[78]E.g., W. G. Lambert, "A Part of the Ritual for the Substitute King," AfO 18 (1957–58): 109–12; or cf. any of the *bit rimki* rituals.

[79]E.g., Svend Pallis, *The Babylonian Akitu Festival* (Copenhagen, 1926).

[80]E.g., Adad-Nirari III, cf. D. D. Luckenbill, *Ancient Records of Assyria and Babylonia* (Chicago, 1926), 260–65.

COMPARATIVE SUMMARY OF BIBLICAL AND MESOPOTAMIAN LAW

	SIMILARITIES	DIFFERENCES	
		Biblical	*Mesopotamian*
CONTENT	Civil and criminal law contained in both	Very light on civil law, heavy emphasis on religious law	No religious law, focus on civil law
	Both cover similar topics using similar wording	Penalties show different elements of concern, even when formulation of problem is the same	
FORM	Casuistic formulations	Apodictic basis for casuistic form	Very little apodictic formulation
FUNCTION	Both serve "admonitory" function	Morality is goal	Justice is goal
	Both seek to demonstrate adherence to contractual obligations	More prescriptive	More descriptive
		Adherence to covenant	Adherence to cosmic order
		God reveals	God's monitor
		Maintain holiness	

EXCURSUS: LAW IN EGYPT

As was mentioned at the beginning of this chapter, the legal material in Egypt is not in the same style as found in Mesopotamia, though reasons for this are not hard to identify. The Egyptian king, unlike the Mesopotamian king, was considered partially divine; he did not have to justify himself to the gods. Thus there was no need for the genre of apologia to which the Mesopotamian collections belong. Discussion of Egyptian law does not focus so much on collections of legal data, as on the concept of *ma'at*. Morenz defines the term: "Maat is right order in nature and society, as established by the act of creation, hence means, according to the context, what is right, what is correct, law, order, justice, and truth."[81]

It thereby has some similarity to the Mesopotamian ME. This similarity exists in the manner in which both ME and *ma'at* constitute a world order. *Ma'at*, however, seems to have more extensive ramifications in its relation to the divine realm. Mesopotamian gods are wielders of the ME,[82] whereas the

---

[81]S. Morenz, *Egyptian Religion* (Ithaca, N.Y., 1973), 113.
[82]Cf. "The Adoration of Inanna," ANET, 579.

Egyptian pharaoh and gods exist by *ma'at*.[83] It therefore would appear to have constituted a standard by which behavior could be measured and to which conformance was required. This would come as close to the Israelite concept as a polytheistic structure could. John Wilson identifies *ma'at* as belonging to the "religious order"—"a spirit which properly pervaded the civil carrying out of government and justice for the ends of religion."[84] It is not surprising, then, that R. J. Williams makes the connection that *ma'at* "has its counterpart in the Hebrew belief in a similar order established by YHWH."[85] Israel expresses this world order as the commands of deity embodied in both apodictic and casuistic formulations. It also addresses adherence to a world order in the genre we identify as wisdom literature. Thus law and wisdom could be considered two sides of the same coin. In Egyptian thinking, it would be presumptuous to even consider codifying law while deity incarnate sat on the throne;[86] so the expression of *ma'at* is addressed through other genres. The "Eloquent Peasant" is perhaps the most important of these. This tale speaks of a peasant who has been robbed by a lower eschelon official. The peasant appeals for justice to a higher authority and presents his case so eloquently that the one to whom he is appealing does not pass judgment because he wishes to hear further appeals.[87] A second work speaking about *ma'at* is "the installation of the Vizier Rekhmire."[88] (the vizier was "the prophet of *ma'at*"[89] and thus administered justice on a day-to-day basis).

At the risk of being simplistic or of overgeneralizing, we might contrast the Mesopotamian, Israelite, and Egyptian ideas in the following way.

Israel. Law represents absolute standard of behavior prescribed by God: "You will behave in this way because I am holy and you are to be holy as well," thus placing demands on the people.

Mesopotamia. Law represents royal apologia and requires no response by people. It does not reflect an absolute standard of behavior. The gods are not characterized by any consistent behavior, and the people are provided no guidelines for their own behavior from the gods. In the legal collections the king is merely stating, "I was a *šar mišarim* (just king), and here is my evidence."

Egypt. Law represents an absolute standard that is built into the universe and is adhered to by deity and pursued by mortals. It is not prescribed but is the basis on which the universe operates and therefore must be maintained to achieve success.

---

[83]Cf. Henri Frankfort, *Kingship and the Gods* (Chicago, 1978), 158, 278; Frankfort, *Ancient Egyptian Religion* (New York, 1948), 55.

[84]John Wilson, "Authority and Law in Ancient Egypt," JAOS Supp. 17 (1951): 7.

[85]R. J. Williams, "A People Come Out of Egypt," VT Supp. 28 (1974): 245.

[86]Cf. Wilson, "Authority and Law," 6; cf. also John Wilson, *The Culture of Ancient Egypt* (Chicago, 1951), 49–50.

[87]"Vizier Rekhmire," AEL, 2:21–24; ANET, 213. Another text of interest in this matter is the so-called "Negative Confession" in the Book of the Dead, ch. 125.

[88]AEL, 1:169ff.; "Eloquent Peasant," ANET, 407–10.

[89]Wilson, "Authority and Law," 3.

FOR FURTHER READING

Alt, Albrecht. *Essays on Old Testament History and Religion*. Oxford, 1966, 79–132.

Boecker, Hans Jochen. *Law and the Administration of Justice in the Old Testament and Ancient East*. Minneapolis, 1980.

Borger, R., et al. *Texte aus der Umwelt des Alten Testaments*. 1.1. Rechtsbücher: Gutërsloher, 1982–85.

Clark, W. Malcolm. "Law." In *Old Testament Form Criticism*. Ed. John Hayes. San Antonio, 1974, 99–139.

Driver, G. R., and John C. Miles. *The Babylonian Laws*. Oxford, 1952.

Eichler, B. L. "Literary Structure in the Laws of Eshnunna." In *Language, Literature and History*. Ed. Francesca Rochberg-Halton. New Haven, 1987, 71–84.

Finkelstein, J. J. *The Ox That Gored. Transactions of the American Philosophical Society*. Philadelphia, 1981, 71:2.

Greengus, Samuel. "Law in the Old Testament." In *Interpreter Dictionary of the Bible Supplement*. Nashville, 1976, 532–37.

Lambert, W. G. "Destiny and Divine Intervention in Babylon and Israel." OTS 17 (1972): 65–72.

Loewenstamm, S. E. "Law." In *Judges—World History of the Jewish People*. Vol. 3. New Brunswick, N.J., 1971, 231–67.

MacKenzie, R. A. F., "The Formal Aspect of Ancient Near Eastern Law." In *Seed of Wisdom*. Ed. W. S. McCullough. Toronto, 1964, 31–44.

Mendenhall, George. "Ancient Oriental and Biblical Law." BA 17 (1954): 26–46.

Morenz, Siegfried. *Egyptian Religion*. Ithaca, N.Y., 1973.

Sonsino, Rifat. *Motive Clauses in Hebrew Law: Biblical Forms and Near Eastern Parallels*. Chico, Calif., 1980.

Speiser, E. A. "Authority and Law in Mesopotamia." JAOS Supp. 17 (1954): 8–15.

————. "Cuneiform Law and the History of Civilization." *Proceedings of the American Philosophical Society* 107:6 (1963): 536–41.

Theodorides, Aristide. "The Concept of Law in Ancient Egypt." In *The Legacy of Egypt*. Ed. J. R. Harris. Oxford, 1971, 291–322.

Van der Toorn, K. *Sin and Sanction in Israel and Mesopotamia*. Assen, 1986.

Westbrook, Raymond. "Biblical and Cuniform Law Codes." RB 92 (1985): 247–64.

Wilson, John. "Authority and Law in Ancient Egypt." JAOS Supp. 17 (1954): 1–7.

Wiseman, D. J. "Law and Order in the Old Testament." *Vox Evangelica* 8 (1973): 5–21.

Chapter 4

COVENANTS AND TREATIES

The 1920s saw the publication of the Hittite treaties that had been unearthed from Boghazkoy, but it was some decades before scholars began to notice the similarity between the forms of those treaties and the covenant formed at Sinai between YHWH and Israel. As we have already discussed, there is certainly some overlap between the issues of law and covenant. Both treaties and covenants contain stipulations that take the form of law. In this chapter we will examine the formal similarities between the covenant of Sinai and the treaties of the ancient Near East. Our discussion will be limited to form and structure because the content of Israel's covenant is admittedly quite distinct from the political treaties of the ancient Near East.

MATERIALS

There are fifty-seven treaties currently extant from the ancient Near East, and almost a dozen of these are fragmentary. The chart on pages 96–99 summarizes the parties of the various treaties and their general time period.[1]

Publication Data
There is no single source that will provide the researcher with text, transliteration, or translation of even a majority of these treaties. Each treaty has its own list for publication data, and I have not found any published source that gives a comprehensive listing.

---

[1] I am indebted to Professor Kenneth Kitchen for providing me with a comprehensive bibliography of ancient Near Eastern treaties.

ANCIENT NEAR EASTERN TREATIES

	Anatolia	Egypt	Syro-Palestine	Mesopotamia
3RD MILLENNIUM				
1.				Eannatum/LAGASH–UMMA
2.				Hita/AWAN –
3.			EBLA–ABARSAL	Ñaram-Sin/AKKAD
EARLY AND MIDDLE 2ND MILLENNIUM				
4.			Abba-AN/YAMHAD–Yarimlim/ALALAKH	Ilum-gamil/URUK–?
5.			Niqmepa/ALALAKH–IR.ÍM/TUNIP	
6.			Idrimi/ALALAKH	
7.	Pilliya/KIZZUWADNA—.............			
8.	Arnuwandas (I?)/ḪATTI–Ishmerikka people			
9.	ḪATTI—Šunaššura/KIZZUWADNA			
10.	Telepinu/HATTI—Ishputaša/KIZZUWADNA			
11.	Zidanza/HATTI—Pilliya/KIŽZUWADNA			
12.	ḪATTI—Paddatissu/KIZZUWADNA		HABIRU	
13.	ḪATTI			
14.	ḪATTI—?			

ANCIENT NEAR EASTERN TREATIES (continued)

Anatolia	Egypt	Syro-Palestine	Mesopotamia
29. Ḫattusil III/ḪATTI		Benteshina/AMURRU	
30. Ḫattusil III/ḪATTI	Ramesses II/EGYPT		
31. Ḫattusil III/ḪATTI	Ramesses II/EGYPT		
32. Tudhalia IV/ḪATTI		Šaušgamuwa/AMURRU	Sausgamuwa/AMURRU
33. Tudhalia IV/ḪATTI Ulmi-Tešub/DATASSA			
34. ḪATTI		Labu & Elders/TUNIP	
35. Ḫattusil III/ḪATTI–TILIURA			
36. Šuppiluliuma II/ḪATTI		Talmi-Tešub/CARCHEMISH	
37. (Šuppiluliuma II)/ḪATTI		ALAŠIA (CYPRUS)	
38. (Šuppiluliuma II)/ḪATTI–Ehli-Sarruma/ISUWA			
39. Arnuwandas (III?)/ḪATTI–KASKEANS			
40–2. Parts of three treaties with the Kaskeans			
43. ḪATTI—KIZZUWADNA			
44. ḪATTI–KURUSTAMA (?)			
45. ḪATTI		Mukish	

46. Bar-Ga'yah/KTK–
    Matiel/ARPAD

47. Bar-Ga'yah/KTK–
    Matiel/ARPAD

48. Bar-Ga'yah/KTK–
    Matiel/ARPAD

49. Matiel/ARPAD .... Aššur-nirari/
    ASSYRIA

50. Marduk-zakir-šumi/
    BABYLON–
    Šamši-AdadV/ASSYRIA

51. Sennacherib/
    ASSYRIA-?

52. Esarhaddon/
    ASSYRIA–

7 Median Rulers

53. Baal/TYRE
    Esarhaddon/ASSYRIA

54. (Esarhaddon)/
    ASSYRIA-?

55. Aššurbanipal/ASSYRIA–
    Samaš-sum-ukin (?)
    BABYLON

56. Abiate/QEDAR .... Aššurbanipal/ASSYRIA

57. Sin-šar-iskun/ASSYRIA (?)

James Pritchard's *Ancient Near Eastern Texts* translates only thirteen of the treaties,[2] and D. J. McCarthy translates four more.[3] While that will provide the reader with a good representation, it is far from covering the territory.

Perhaps the one work that provides more information than any other is E. Laroche's *Catalogue des Textes Hittites*, which lists the cuneiform copies of thirty-five of the thirty-nine treaties involving the Hittites.[4] Ten of the Hittite treaties are given in transliteration and German translation in E. F. Weidner, *Politische Dokumente aus Kleinasien* (1923).[5] One of Weidner's texts is revised and five other Hittite treaties are presented in transliteration and German translation in J. Friedrich, *Hethitische Staatsverträge* (vol. 1, 1926; vol. 2, 1930).[6] This means that approximately one half of the Hittite treaties are covered by either ANET, McCarthy, Weidner, or Friedrich. This includes all of the major ones; many of those not treated in these sources are quite fragmentary.

Of the eighteen treaties that do not involve the Hittites,[7] seven are translated by ANET[8] and one by McCarthy.[9] Six more of these are fragmentary.[10] The remaining four have been published as follows:

#1. E. Sollberger, *Studi Eblaiti* 3:9–10 (1980): 129–55. See review of discussion as well as reference to several other likely Eblaite treaties in L. M. Muntingh, "Second Thoughts on Ebla and the Old Testament," in *Text and Context*, ed. W. Claassen (Sheffield, 1988), 157–75.

#2. Transliteration:

Thureau-Dangin, *Die Sumerischen und Akkadischen Königsinschriften* (1907)—(Stela of Vultures).

Translation:

J. S. Cooper, *Sumerian and Akkadian Royal Inscriptions* (New Haven, 1986), 33–39.

S. N. Kramer, *The Sumerians* (1963): 310–13.

#3. F. W. König, *Die Elamischen Königsinschriften* (1965), no. 2; W. Hinz, ZA 58 (1967): 66–96.

#50. E. F. Weidner, AfO 8 (1932): 27–29.[11]

DISCUSSION

There are two basic issues to be discussed in the remainder of this chapter. First, we will present the similarities and differences between the formats used in ancient Near Eastern treaties and those used in the biblical covenant. Second, we will discuss how much evidence for the dating of the biblical covenant can be drawn from the results of the format comparison.

---

[2] Nos. 6, 7, 16, 19, 22, 30, 31, 46–48, 49, 52, 53.

[3] Nos. 5, 11, 23, 33; D. J. McCarthy, *Treaty and Covenant* (Rome, 1978): 301–8.

[4] Nos. 8–11, 14–30, 32–45.

[5] Nos. 15–19, 22, 27, 29, 30, 34.

[6] No. 22; nos. 20, 24–26, 28.

[7] Nos. 1–6 and 46–57. The Neo-Assyrian Treaties have been published in a new edition by S. Parpola and K. Watanabe, *New-Assyrian Treaties and Loyalty Oaths*, State Archives of Assyria, Vol. 2 (Winona Lake: 1988).

[8] Nos. 6, 46–48, 49, 52, 53. Nos. 46–48 are the Aramaic Sefire treaties. These have been published by J. Fitzmyer, *The Aramaic Inscriptions of Sefire* (Rome, 1967), and more recently updated by A. Lemaire and J.-M. Durand, *Les Inscriptions Araméennes de Sfiré et L'Assyrie Shamshi-Ilu* (Geneva and Paris, 1984).

[9] No. 5; some would not consider this a treaty. See the discussion in McCarthy, *Treaty and Covenant*, 86ff.

[10] Nos. 4, 51, 54–57.

[11] I am indebted to the bibliographic information supplied to me by Professor Kenneth Kitchen for many of the details of this summary.

I. Format

The formats of the ancient treaties, particularly the Hittite treaties, have been treated in great detail;[12] and what I present here is a summary of the results of the research thus far.

The basic elements characteristic of treaties as a genre include:
- Introduction of the speaker
- Historical prologue
- Stipulations
- Statement concerning the document
- Divine witnesses
- Curses and blessings

These elements do not all occur in every treaty, and certain elements appear to be characteristic of either particular time periods, particular geographical locations, or particular types of treaties. The analyses that have been conducted have attempted to determine whether there is sufficient consistency within any given group and wide enough diversity between various groups to be able to distinguish convincingly between, for instance, a "late second-millennium Hittite format" and a "first-millennium Neo-Assyrian format."

Early studies insisted that a clear distinction was evident,[13] and this distinction is still emphasized in more recent treatments.[14] However, there are those who insist that while some differences may be identified, there is a basic unity found in the treaties as a whole that precludes confident classification into clear subgroupings regarding form.[15]

Even the dissenters must admit, however, that there are certain basic elements that distinguish the Hittite group from the other categories. There are at least two basic, identifiable subgroups. (1) The Hittite family of treaties is characterized by the use of historical prologue to an extent not found elsewhere; (2) the treaties from Syria and Assyria show a much greater emphasis on the curses that are used to enforce the treaty.

To better comprehend what differences and similarities exist, we will now examine each characteristic element of the treaty genre and discuss the cases in which it is either present or absent in the known treaties of the ancient Near East and the biblical covenants (i.e., the Exodus–Leviticus complex, the book of Deuteronomy, and Joshua 24).

A. Introduction of the Speaker

Description. Generally this identifies the author of the treaty, the suzerain. His various titles and attributes and, occasionally, genealogical data comprise this element. This section emphasizes the suzerain's greatness and his right to proclaim the treaty.

---

[12]E.g., especially McCarthy, *Treaty and Covenant*.

[13]George Mendenhall, "Covenant Forms in Israelite Tradition," *Biblical Archaeologist Reader 3*, ed. E. F. Campbell and D. N. Freedman (Garden City, N.Y., 1970), 31.

[14]Kenneth Kitchen, *The Bible in Its World* (Downers Grove, 1977), 79–85.

[15]McCarthy, *Treaty and Covenant*, 122ff. and Moshe Weinfeld, JAOS 93 (1973): 190–99. McCarthy does acknowledge the possibility of structural subgroups (p. 124), which is the major distinction pressed by Kitchen. See also McCarthy's discussion of the historical prologue, pp. 144ff.

Ancient Near East Occurrence. This section is attested in all periods in all locations and, as would be expected, always comes first. One distinction is that in the parity treaty (no. 30–31), where there is more equality between the parties, the rhetoric is somewhat toned down, and titles, etc., of both parties are given.

Old Testament Occurrence. Exodus 20:1; Deuteronomy 1:1–5; Joshua 24:1–2. In all three cases YHWH is identified as the covenant's author and the suzerain who has a right to make certain demands.

B. Historical Prologue

Description. This section reviews the relationship between the two parties prior to their entering into the present agreement. Frequent emphasis is placed on the kind acts of the suzerain on behalf of the vassal as well as on the suzerain's power. The vassal is expected, as a result, to be grateful in accepting the terms and fearful of violating them. In light of this function, McCarthy identifies the historical section as more hortatory than objective.[16]

Ancient Near East Occurrence. While George Mendenhall insists that "such a narrative is never lacking in texts that have been completely preserved,"[17] D. J. McCarthy avers that the treaty between Mursilis II and Niqmepa of Ugarit (no. 23 above), while badly broken, can be sufficiently reconstructed to show that it moves from preamble right into stipulations.[18] It is certainly true that treaties from all periods and locations *except* the Hittite treaties generally lack any historical prologue.[19]

Old Testament Occurrence. The historical prologue is readily recognizable in the biblical covenants. It is most limited in Exodus 20:2 but quite pronounced in Deuteronomy 1:6–3:29 and Joshua 24:2–13.

C. Stipulations

Description. Mendenhall summarizes the basic elements of the stipulations section:

> This section states in detail the obligations imposed upon and accepted by the vassal. They include typically the prohibition of other foreign relationships outside the Hittite Empire. Second, there is the prohibition

---

[16]McCarthy, *Treaty and Covenant*, 53. McCarthy cites the work of G. Kestemont as having demonstrated that the historical prologue is very consistently organized: "It is careful and selective argumentation to establish the rights to be claimed in the document," p. 37.

[17]Mendenhall, "Covenant Forms in Israelite Tradition," 33.

[18]McCarthy, *Treaty and Covenant*, 54. As pointed out to me by Professor Kenneth Kitchen, there does, however, appear to be a short historical paragraph after the preamble in this treaty. It mentions Mursilis's patronage of Niqmepa in helping him secure the throne. McCarthy also makes mention of eight other Hittite treaties that do not have historical prologues, largely because they are made with groups instead of individuals, p. 55 and n. 21.

[19]McCarthy, *Treaty and Covenant*, 123, contends that the historical prologue, while certainly a more major characteristic of the Hittite treaties, is not unique to them. The examples he gives are the "Vulture Stela" treaty (no. 2 above) from the early period and the treaty between Ashurbanipal and Qedar (no. 56 above) from the Neo-Assyrian period. However, the limited extent of the so-called historical section of these two makes it arguable that they could be categorized with the Hittite series.

of enmity against anything under the sovereignty of the great king. . . . Third, the vassal must answer any call to arms sent him by the king. . . . Fourth, the vassal must hold lasting and unlimited trust in the king; he must not entertain malicious rumors that the king is acting disloyally toward the vassal, nor must he permit any evil words against the king, for this is the beginning of rebellion. Fifth, the vassal must not give asylum to refugees, whatever their origin. Sixth, the vassal must appear before the Hittite king once a year, probably on the occasion of annual tribute. Last, controversies between vassals are without exception to be submitted to the king for judgment.[20]

The stipulations can be presented in several grammatical varieties. They may be formulated in the precative ("Let no man do . . ."), the imperative ("Thou shalt not do . . ."),[21] or most commonly, it may be placed in a conditional phrase ("If such and such occurs . . .").

Ancient Near East Occurrence. Stipulations are the core of the treaty and occur in all examples. If there were no stipulations, it would be difficult to defend the document as a treaty.

Old Testament Occurrence. Likewise, if the biblical examples did not have stipulations, there would be very little basis for comparing them to the ancient treaties. In Exodus–Leviticus, stipulations comprise the Decalogue, the covenant code, and the ritual instructions in Leviticus 1–25. In Deuteronomy, certainly chapters 12–26 are stipulations, and many find reason to include 4–11 also. In Joshua 24, verses 14–15 are the core of the stipulations, with 16–25 also containing the repetition of some of them.

D. Statement Concerning the Document

Description. This clause provides for the periodic public reading of the treaty so that all may remember their obligations. It also occasionally spells out requirements for the storing of the document.

Ancient Near East Occurrence. This type of clause is only characteristic of the Hittite treaties, but even in that group it is often missing. Some of the treaties are broken at the point where this clause would normally be placed, so it is difficult to discern whether or not the clause was originally present. McCarthy suggests that since there are only two cases where it is clear that a public reading is demanded (nos. 16/17, 28 above), and only one additional case where instructions for the deposit of the document are included (no. 33), perhaps this should not be considered a separate element of the format.[22]

Old Testament Occurrence. Exodus 25:16 (cf. Deut. 10:1–5) speaks of the tablets being deposited in the ark, but this does not have the appearance of a separate clause dictating the proper handling of the document. Deuteronomy 31:24–26 has Moses commanding the Levites to put the Law in the ark, but this comes from Moses, not the Lord, and therefore would not be seen as

---

[20]Mendenhall, *Biblical Archaeologist Reader* 3, 34.

[21]This category is of interest to those studying the various types of law in the ancient Near East and was treated in our chapter on law. McCarthy, *Treaty and Covenant*, 62, and his chart on 82–83, discusses the use of these apodictic statements and makes observations concerning how they are grouped together and in what geographical locations they occur.

[22]McCarthy, *Treaty and Covenant*, 63.

a clause of the covenant itself, though certainly the concept of deposition is here. Deuteronomy 31:10–13 includes instructions from Moses that the Law be read every seven years at the Feast of Booths. This also seems to be in an epilogue section apart from the covenant document. In Deuteronomy 27:2–3 (a section most like a document clause), the people, just prior to hearing the blessings and curses, are commanded to set up stones when they arrive in the Promised Land and to write the Law on them. This is carried out in Joshua 8:30–32. Joshua 24:26 is the document clause in that covenant and again involves the writing of the words in a book and depositing them by a large stone.

E. Witnesses

Description. In this section it is generally the gods who are called to witness the agreement that is being made. Gods of both parties are included, and it is intended that the gods would be the ones who would enforce the terms of the treaty if need arose. Mendenhall points out that there are also instances of the "Mountains, rivers, springs, sea, heaven and earth, the wind and the clouds" all being called to witness.[23]

Ancient Near East Occurrence. The list of witnesses is a standard part of the ancient Near Eastern treaties.

Old Testament Occurrence. The witness section of the Deuteronomic Covenant is the most evident. In Deuteronomy 31 the Lord instructs Moses to compose a song and teach it to the Israelites so that it may function as a witness (Deut. 31:19–22). Also in that chapter the Book of the Law as well as the heavens and earth are identified as witnesses (31:26–28). The Song of Moses, which is recorded for us in Deuteronomy 32, fits into the witness category, for it affirms YHWH's ability to enforce the terms of the covenant. Of particular significance are verses 39–43, in which YHWH takes an oath to exact vengeance on behalf of his people.

In Joshua 24:22 the people are called to be witnesses against themselves, and as in Deuteronomy 32, their witness status is established by entering into an oath. Joshua 24:27 also indicates that the stone by which the Law was deposited would act as a witness against the people. There does not appear to be a witness clause in Exodus–Leviticus.[24]

F. Curses and Blessings

Description. This section entails not the specifics of what the suzerain will do in the event of either faithfulness to or violation of the treaty, but rather, the actions of the gods either for or against the vassal.

Ancient Near East Occurrence. Curses are a standard feature of treaties irrespective of time or location. Blessings are not so prevalent. As mentioned above, the curse sections in the treaties from Assyria and Syria are much more extensive than the short, formulaic curses characteristic of the Hittite

---

[23]Mendenhall, "Covenant Forms in Israelite Tradition," 35.

[24]Kitchen (*Bible in Its World*, 82) lists Exodus 24:4 as a witness clause with the thought that the pillars mentioned there were to be witnesses, similar to what was found in Joshua 24:27. But this function of the pillars is not made explicit in the text, so it is difficult to consider this a witness clause, though it may very well be that the pillars were thought to be witnesses.

treaties. McCarthy comments about the curse section in the Assyrian treaties: "It is long, emphatic, colorful, of a spirit far different from the sober Hittite tradition."[25]

Old Testament Occurrence. In the Exodus–Leviticus complex, the blessings and curses come respectively in Leviticus 26:1–13 and 14–33. In Deuteronomy, the well-known blessings and curses are found in chapter 28, with blessings occupying verses 1–14 and the longer curses section in verses 15–68. Joshua 24 is the least distinctive in this section. Blessings must be inferred from the text, and the only curse is very briefly stated in verse 20.

II. Order

In the Hittite treaties the order is generally that followed in the above treatment. One of the most consistent deviations from this order observable in treaties from other areas and periods is the placement of the witnesses section. In the first-millennium treaties from Syria and Mesopotamia, the witnesses section generally precedes the stipulations. In the Syrian treaties it is common to find the curses also preceding the stipulations.

In the biblical covenants, there is likewise some variation in order.

Exodus–Leviticus	Deuteronomy	Joshua 24
Introduction of Speaker	Introduction of Speaker	Introduction of Speaker
Historical Prologue	Historical Prologue	Historical Prologue
Stipulations	Stipulations	Stipulations
Blessings and Curses	Document Clause	Curses
	Blessings and Curses	Witnesses
	Epilogue	Document Clause
	Witnesses	

It should be noted, however, that while they do not each use the Hittite format exactly, they are closer to that format than they are to the formats found in any other area or period. They all contain the historical prologue, and the stipulations come immediately after the prologue in each case. The Exodus–Leviticus complex deviates from the Hittite form the most because of what it lacks (document clause and witnesses). Of the absent elements, the document clause is often missing from the Hittite treaties. The witnesses section may not be in Israelite ones because of Israel's distinctive view of deity and YHWH's role as suzerain of the treaty. It is still more like the Hittite treaties than the other types that are extant because of the inclusion of the historical prologue. Minor departures in order may be the result of having both law and treaty forms to comply with.[26]

III. Date

There has been considerable controversy over whether the similarity in form that exists between the biblical covenants and the Hittite treaties of the late second millennium is sufficient to date the biblical covenants with confidence to the later second millennium B.C. Kenneth Kitchen has been

---

[25]McCarthy, *Treaty and Covenant*, 121.
[26]Kitchen, *Bible in Its World*, 83.

persuaded that form analysis can delineate a range within which the covenants must be dated.

> We have, therefore, no warrant factually to date the basic Sinai covenant and its two renewals any later than the time of the data to which they are most closely related, i.e. to the thirteenth century down to c. 1200 BC at the very latest. The present books of Exodus, Leviticus, Deuteronomy and the data of Joshua 24 would necessarily stem from about 1200 BC or not long afterwards, on the same basic criterion.[27]

Others have felt that the data are too incomplete and that there are sufficient similarities between eras to rule out using form correspondence as a dating criterion. D. J. McCarthy says:

> While we can distinguish two groups within the single treaty tradition, it is possible that the fact that the two belong to different epochs is due to a lacuna in our evidence. . . . In view of the many points of continuity between first and second millennium it would be dangerous to conclude a total break between the two sets of treaties and then use this break as a criterion of date.[28]

As is frequently the case in the discussion of the dating of the Pentateuchal materials, there is much more involved here than simply the form of the covenant. Both Kitchen and McCarthy had opinions about the dating of the Pentateuch when their analyses began, and both find the covenant/treaty comparison supportive of their respective positions. This can hardly be avoided and does not in any way discredit the inductive nature of the research of either of these men or the dozens of others who have done work in this area.

In summary, there are three questions that can help us determine the extent to which form analysis can serve as a criterion for dating the covenant.

1. *Is the Hittite treaty form sufficiently unique to distinguish it from other forms?* Based on the data that has been presented above, I think that we could conclude that there are some clear distinctions, particularly in the presence of the historical prologue.

2. *Does the biblical data conform closely enough to the Hittite treaty form?* In our study above we found that while there is not total conformity, there is more similarity to the Hittite form than to any other known form, and the major elements do conform.

3. *Is there enough material from other periods to eliminate the possibility of dating the covenant to another period?* This question is the most problematic. Our first-millennium data is very limited in time, space, and number. While it is significant to observe that the first-millennium examples from Syria and Assyria do not contain a historical prologue, we do not have positive evidence that other geographical areas also stopped using a historical prologue. We know that the Assyrians greatly expanded the curses section, but we do not know that that was true of all first-millennium treaties. Furthermore, one should note the striking similarity between the Esarhaddon treaties and the curses of Deuteronomy.[29]

---

[27] Ibid.

[28] McCarthy, *Treaty and Covenant*, 153.

[29] See M. Weinfeld, "Covenant Terminology in the Ancient Near East and Its Influence on the West," JAOS 93 (1973): 190–99.

While evangelicals would be happy to have evidence that would further support beliefs about the early dating of the Pentateuch, at this stage in our knowledge of the ancient treaties, the data is only suggestive, rather than conclusive. The mid-late second millennium does seem a more likely placement of the covenant form when compared to the treaties that are available for study. But it must also be admitted that if that kind of data suggested that the Pentateuch was a late document, evangelicals would be the first to point out that there was not enough information to decide the matter.

The fact that the biblical covenants most closely resemble the Hittite treaty form certainly gives some credibility to the placement of the covenant documents in the second millennium B.C. and gives some good arguments against the composition of those documents in the mid-first millennium. So, given our present state of knowledge, the form used in the biblical covenants is an authentic form attested most closely in the Hittite treaties of the late second millennium B.C. The formal similarities are striking and undeniable. Differences in content, length, emphasis, theology, and the way in which law and covenant are combined in the Bible all ought to be recognized and considered. This could well be a case of borrowing a form, though no one suspects borrowing of a particular piece of literature.

FOR FURTHER READING

Baltzer, K. *The Covenant Formulary*. Oxford, 1971.

Craigie, P. C. *The book of Deuteronomy*. Grand Rapids, 1976, 20–44.

Frankenah, R. "The Vassal Treaties of Esarhaddon and the Dating of Deuteronomy." In *OTS*, Issue 14, 1965, 122–54.

Kalluveettil, Paul. *Declaration and Covenant*. Rome, 1982.

Kitchen, Kenneth. *Ancient Orient and Old Testament*. Downers Grove, 1966, 90–102.

————. *The Bible in Its World*. Downers Grove, 1978, 79–85.

Knutson, F. Brent. "Literary Genres in PRU IV." In *Ras Shamra Parallels*. Vol. 2. Ed. Loren Fisher. Rome, 1975, 155–98.

Korošec, V. *Hethitische Staatsverträge*. Leipzig, 1931.

McCarthy, D. J. *Old Testament Covenant*. Atlanta, 1972.

————. *Treaty and Covenant*. Rome, 1978.

Mendenhall, George. "Covenant Forms in Israelite Tradition" in *Biblical Archaeologist Reader 3*, Ed. E. F. Campbell and D. N. Freedman. New York, 1970, 25–53.

de Vaux, Roland. *The Early History of Israel*. Philadelphia, 1978, 439ff.

Weinfeld, Moshe. "Covenant Terminology in the Ancient Near East and Its Influence on the West." JAOS 93 (1973): 190–99.

————. "Berith." In *Theological Dictionary of the Old Testament*. Vol. 2. Ed. G. J. Botterweck and H. Ringgren. Grand Rapids, 1975, 253–79.

————. *Deuteronomy and the Deuteronomic School*. Oxford, 1972, 59–157.

Chapter 5

HISTORICAL LITERATURE

When dealing with the historical literature of the ancient Near East, we cannot list all of the documents that provide historiographic information or even all of those that would be considered to be part of a historiographical literary genre. There are hundreds of documents that would fall into this literary genre. Our approach, therefore, will be to classify by type the various pieces of literature that could be called historiographic and then to discuss each type and major representatives of the category where feasible. Our discussion will cover the three areas of (1) historiography (the writing of history), (2) the role of deity in history, and (3) the concept of history.

MATERIALS

The Mesopotamian historical literature has been thoroughly and conveniently summarized for us in an article by A. K. Grayson.[1] Grayson classifies the historical texts into three categories: royal inscriptions, chronographic texts, and historical literary texts.

---

[1] A. K. Grayson, "Assyria and Babylonia," Or, n.s., 49 (1980): 140–94. Bibliographic information is discussed in that same article, pp. 143–48. Deserving specific mention is Professor Grayson's own work in the publication of historical texts, including: *Assyrian and Babylonian Chronicles*, Texts from Cuneiform Sources V (Locust Valley, N.Y.: J. J. Augustin, 1975); *Babylonian Historical-Literary Texts* (Toronto, 1975); and his editions revising D. D. Luckenbill's "Ancient Records of Assyria and Babylonia": *Assyrian Royal Inscriptions* (Wiesbaden, 1972, 1976). Historical texts in ANET: 227–319, 553–64.

I. Royal Inscriptions

Royal inscriptions are records of royal achievements, focusing primarily on military exploits and secondarily on building projects. They could be intended for the royal archives, for public display (generally inside the palace), or for address to deity. Assyrian annals found in foundation deposits intended to inform future kings of a predecessor's deeds. So various kinds of royal inscriptions served different functions.[2]

II. Chronographic Texts

Chronographic texts are texts that give us data in sequence and likewise can take many different forms. This category includes date lists and eponym lists that identify a year by the main event or by an honored official. King lists, of which nearly twenty are extant, are also in this group. Chronicles are also included here; they usually have political or religious agendas and, to that end, present a narrative of events over a given period of time. The events are chosen by the editor to make his point. The data are usually derived from secondary sources. The Babylonian Chronicles share some information with astronomical diaries, while the Chronicle of Early Kings[3] leans heavily on omen texts and the Weidner Chronicle. The chronographic texts are important for helping to establish a sequence of events and rulers. At times they also provide valuable information for making sychronisms. On other occasions, however, such as in many of the king lists, overlapping elements are presented in a single line of succession. This can cause some confusion with regard to absolute chronology.[4]

III. Historical Literary Texts[5]

The primary texts of the Historical-Literary category are the Historical Epics, defined by Grayson as "lengthy poetic narratives about the activities of kings."[6] Among the most famous of these, the following might be mentioned:

A. King of Battle (about Sargon the Great)

Publication Data
Kouyunjik Fragment—Lambert, AfO 20 (1963): 161–62.
Old Babylonian version—Nougayrol, RA 45 (1951): 169–83.
Amarna Fragment, C. Gordon, Or, n.s., 16 (1947): 13–14; 20–21.
H. Güterbock, ZA 42 (1934): 86–91; ZA 44 (1938): 45–48.

---

[2]See H. Tadmor, "History and Ideology in the Assyrian Royal Inscriptions," and A. K. Grayson, "Assyrian Royal Inscriptions: Literary Characteristics," both in *Assyrian Royal Inscriptions: New Horizons*, ed. F. M. Fales (Rome, 1981), 13–33, 35–47.
[3]ANET, 266–67.
[4]This is an understatement. See P. Michalowski's comment, "The text (Sumerian King List) should forever be banished from reconstruction of early Mesopotamian history," in "History as Charter: Some Observations on the Sumerian King List," in J. Sasson, ed., *Studies in Literature of the Ancient Near East* (New Haven, 1984), 243.
[5]Grayson includes the so-called "Akkadian Prophecies" in this category, but we will discuss them in a separate chapter.
[6]Grayson, "Assyria and Babylonia," 184. For a discussion of the Sumerian Enmerkar epics, see A. Berlin, "EthnoPoetry and the Enmerkar Epics" in Sasson, *Studies in Literature*, 17–24.

Discussion:
CAH³ I:2, 425–30.

Content
The epic tells of Sargon's venture into Asia Minor to redress injustices done against Mesopotamian merchants by Nur-Daggal in the colony of Purushkhanda.

B. Tukulti-Ninurta I (1243–1207 B.C.)

Publication Data
> G. Ebeling, "Brüchstücke eines politischen Propagandagedichtes aus einer assyrischen Kanzlei," MAOG 12/2 (1938): 1–2 (transliteration).
> R. C. Thompson, *Archaeologia* 79 (1929): 127–33; pls. 47–52.
> Additional fragments: Lambert, AfO 18 (1957–58): 38–5l, pls. 1–4; Weidner, AfO 7 (1931–32): 280–81.
> P. Machinist, " 'The Epic of Tukulti-Ninurta I'': A Study in Middle Assyrian Literature," Ph.D. diss. (New Haven, 1978).

Content
This epic tells of Tukulti-Ninurta's defeat of Babylon and its Kassite king, Kashtiliash IV.

C. The Verse Account of Nabonidus

Publication Data
> ANET, 312–15.
> B. Landsberger, T. Bauer, ZA 37 (1926–27): 88ff.
> S. Smith, *Babylonian Historical Texts* (London, 1924), 83ff.

Content
This account is an indictment of Nabonidus by the priests of Marduk for his irresponsibility, not only with regard to his royal obligations, but in his religious duties as well.

These texts deal with historical figures by means of lengthy poetic discourse. While they are frequently considered to have some historical basis, they are also thought to have been subjected to aggrandizement. Thus, as historical documents, they must be handled with a keen, critical sense. John Van Seters gives the following summation:

> The features common to all epics are an elevated poetic style of narration and a strongly tendentious political or religious character. But even within one category of epic, the historical epic, there is a wide diversity in form, structure, and sources utilized by the past.[7]

IV. Omen Texts

A fourth literary form that has been considered a resource for historiography is the omen texts. These preserve centuries of observation of omens and their presumed consequences. When the same omens recur, their significance may be predicted and the consequences avoided. J. J. Finkelstein suggests that "the omen texts, and the historical information imbedded in

---

[7]John Van Seters, *In Search of History* (New Haven, 1983), 96.

them, lie at the very root of all Mesopotamian historiography"[8] and gives these texts "precedence both in time and in reliability over any other genre of Mesopotamian writing that purports to treat the events of the past."[9] He concludes that other historiographic forms (e.g., the Chronicles) were derived from the omen texts. Recent study of the historical omens has cast doubt on Finkelstein's confidence in the historiographical value of the omens,[10] and his conclusions about the foundational position of the omen texts in history writing have long been disputed.[11]

DISCUSSION

I. Historiography

A. The Ancient Near East

In discussing historiography, we are attempting to discover what purpose these ancient authors had in writing the documents we have termed historical. We must take care not to assume that their idea of writing history was the same as our Western idea. The writing of history is going to reflect the *concept* of history.

W. W. Hallo comments rightly that "historiography is a subjective enterprise in which each culture ultimately defines the ethnic parameters of its own past for itself."[12] Granting this subjectivity, we are not passing judgment on whether a particular historiography is right or wrong but rather how it compares to our own ideas of historiography. Only in this way can we properly understand the literature.

When Westerners write history, it is often intended to be history for history's sake. There is value in recording and preserving events of the past. While many pragmatic purposes may be considered, it is deemed theoretically desirable to preserve details just for the record. Western historiography attempts to achieve objectivity, though it is realized that perhaps the only objectivity that can be reached is a collection of many subjective perspectives. We seek to present what "really happened" and to identify accurately the

---

[8]J. J. Finkelstein, "Mesopotamian Historiography," *Proceedings of the American Philosophical Society* 107:6 (1963): 463.

[9]Ibid. Reliability remains a concern for historians despite some of the valid philosophical objections raised by those who would question anyone's ability or right to conduct that analysis. See P. Michalowski, "History as Charter," 237–38.

[10]There is disagreement over the historical worth of the omen apodoses. Cf. I. Starr's suggestion: "Historical accuracy in the apodoses of omens may not have been the major concern of the scribes. The purpose of the apodoses was prediction (favorable or unfavorable, as the case may be), and the choice of subject matter was subservient to that end" ("Notes on Some Published and Unpublished Historical Omens," JCS 29 [1977]: 162).

[11]Ibid., 470. Cf. A. K. Grayson, "Divination and the Babylonian Chronicles," in *La Divination en Mesopotamie Ancienne* , RAI 14 (1966): 69–76; and Van Seters, *In Search of History*, 77–81, where Finkelstein's conclusions are contested. More recently see I. Starr, "The Place of the Historical Omens in the System of Apodoses" BO 43 (1986): 628–32.

[12]W. W. Hallo, "Biblical History in Its Near Eastern Setting: The Contextual Approach," *Scripture in Context*, ed. C. D. Evans, W. W. Hallo, and J. B. White (Pittsburgh, 1980), 6.

elements of cause and effect. If the writing of history entailed merely a catalog of events, objectivity would not be as elusive. It is the cause/effect analysis that creates the greatest variables, and these variables exist whether objectivity is primary or not.

With this idea of Western historiography in mind, we now proceed to ancient Near Eastern historiography.[13] Finkelstein has suggested that

> all genres of Mesopotamian literature that purport to deal with past events, with the exception of the omens and chronicles, are motivated by purposes other than the desire to know what really happened, and the authenticity of the information they relate was not in itself the crucial point for their authors.[14]

If, then, objectivity or accuracy were not of prime importance, what was the purpose of writing about the past? A. K. Grayson suggests that the past was used commonly for "propagandistic or didactic purposes."[15] While few would disagree, this does not entirely solve the problem. "Objective" history can also be used propagandistically or didactically. It should also be realized that the existence of propagandistic or didactic value does not necessarily nullify or even distort the historical credibility. A problem occurs only when historical data is changed or embellished to enhance the propagandistic or didactic value. In these cases, not only has objectivity been abandoned in the selection of material to be presented, but history per se has been abandoned to suit an independent agenda.

Propagandistic and didactic agendas are readily identifiable in ancient historiography. When accounts of a particular battle are available from both contestants (as they are for the battle of Qadesh between the Egyptians and the Hittites, 1275 B.C.), and both sides claim victory (as they do), it is not difficult to see propaganda at work. When past kings' names are replaced in records of his accomplishments by his successor's name (as when Sargon II attempts to claim credit for his predecessor's achievements), or a monarch's record is presented in only glowing and exaggerated terms with no negative elements supplied, again we see propaganda in action.[16]

Didactic elements may be a little more difficult to identify but are less likely to occasion departure from accurate historical data. Frequently the instruction concerns religious matters: cultic, ethical, or ritualistic. Another common theme is nationalism.

Among Mesopotamian documents, Finkelstein isolates omens and

---

[13]Discussion of Western historiography has of course been greatly simplified here. It will be further treated when "Concept of History" is considered but still will not be treated in detail.

[14]Finkelstein, "Mesopotamian Historiography," 469.

[15]Grayson, "Assyria and Babylonia," 189.

[16]For a treatment of propaganda in the Hittite historical literature, see Harry Hoffner, "Propaganda and Political Justification in Hittite Historiography," in *Unity and Diversity*, ed. Hans Goedicke and J. J. M. Roberts (Baltimore, 1975), 49–62. Western historiography is by no means immune to these, as any presidential campaign speech will attest. This similarity is highlighted in Tadmor's comment concerning royal inscriptions that "their purpose was not so much to relate what the king did; they rather indicate the way he aspired his image to be portrayed" ("History and Ideology," 13–14).

chronicles as the least self-serving. Of the Chronicles, the Babylonian Chronicles come nearest to some standard of objectivity. They range from the eighth to the third century B.C. The fact that they present victories and defeats that are not embellished or slanted in such a way that an agenda is evident differentiates them from most other ancient Near Eastern historiographical material. It is for that reason that they are identified as being "objective."[17]

Though some may disagree with Finkelstein's assessment of the historical value of the omen texts, their significance for understanding historical thinking in Mesopotamia is unquestioned. The omen texts are founded on the premise that "ultimate understanding of the universe would, in theory, require nothing but the painstaking accumulation of as much detail as possible about literally everything. . . . A moment of time was apprehended and defined as the sum total of the occurrences and events known to be in temporal conjunction."[18] The omen texts selected and compiled divination information from many areas, including the various events of history. This was thought to provide empirical data for gaining knowledge of how various omens could be understood in the present. While we might think, as Finkelstein has maintained, that historical accuracy would be mandatory for this system to function, such was not always the case. Starr suggests that the historical omens were didactic only in the sense that "they came to serve as a reflection of the fears and aspirations of the people of Mesopotamia, rather than as statements of reality."[19]

B. Israel

Through the centuries, there has always existed a segment of society that considered the Bible, including its record of Israel's history, to be accurate in every way. Many have assumed that accuracy demanded similar principles of historiography as those found in Western civilization. Scholarship less encumbered by doctrinal restraints, on the contrary, has not hesitated to see in Israelite historiography the same self-serving premises that characterize the ancient Near East at large. The documentary hypothesis of Julius Wellhausen itself was formulated on the basis of a belief that the Pentateuch was, not objective history, but a mixture of events and legends of the past being used didactically. Others have not hesitated to suggest propagandistic purposes of the Davidic dynasty, the Aaronic priesthood, or the Josianic reformers.

Likewise, the work of the Deuteronomistic historian is considered historiography subjected to a definite editorial agenda. Again, it should be mentioned that purposes other than preservation of "objective history" do not necessarily suggest historical inaccuracy. It is only when a particular agenda and historical accuracy are at cross-purposes that objectivity is jeopardized.

The premise of Israelite historiography is that Deity has formed history

---

[17] Grayson likewise identifies the Babylonian Chronicles as the earliest examples in Mesopotamia of history being written for history's sake. See *Assyrian and Babylonian Chronicles*, 11.

[18] Finkelstein, "Mesopotamian Historiography," 463.

[19] Starr, "Place of the Historical Omens," 630.

around them, his chosen people; that they have, in Wright's words, a "God who acts"; and that history is the account of the acts of this benevolent, sovereign Deity on their behalf. This is not to say that God's initiative is the most prominent factor in all of Israelite historiography. Rather it is primarily in the early stages (that some have hesitated to even identify as historiography—Genesis through Joshua) that God's initiative is the central focus. Here it is a history of YHWH's election of his chosen people. Examination of the historical writings from the Judges period onward show that they are much more like the sort of history we are used to. YHWH's role is now more one of reacting rather than acting. The covenant is in place as the major result of his initiative, and we now find human history that makes sense geopolitically.[20]

> In other words, we are always shown how one thing led to another, on the human level. The question why it did so is invariably answered by the assertion that it was the Lord's just and reasonable decision. The historian always finds an explanation using terms of reward, punishment, or mercy. A general theory of theodicy has been developed in the process into a very subtle and flexible tool, which is effectively used to solve all kinds of problems. Its result is to make Divine initiative rather rare and marginal. God has sent Samuel to anoint David. The choice was entirely his own and rather surprising in human eyes (1 Sam. 16). It was, however, the outcome of the Lord's decision to reject Saul, a decision based on Saul's disobedience. It is man who sets divine theodicy in motion by his behaviour, deserving reward or punishment, it is not God's business to push him along. So we cannot truly say that God acts in history; He reacts in most cases, though neither automatically or arbitrarily: He takes His time, and pursues His policy. Nevertheless, if it were not for Israel's sins they would be secure in the enjoyment of their land, living in a perfect society based on the Lord's laws and commandments. Such contemplations, however, are not the ancient historians' concern. They reconstruct what has actually happened in the past, in terms of geopolitics, and they explain it by theodicy.[21]

The term *Heilsgeschichte* has been used by Gerhard von Rad (and since his work, by many others) to describe the particular way the religious experience of Israel is expressed through the use of historical narrative—whether the initiative is Israel's or YHWH's. This term is certainly accurate as a description of the perspective of the biblical writers. It does not imply that the history contained therein is accurate, but neither does it preclude that possibility. J. Licht has rightly observed, however, that

> its events . . . are as real to the narrators as anything else, and we have no grounds to doubt the actual occurrence of these events on the human level. It provides down-to-earth background for its sublime subject, presenting it as realistically as possible. The most important thing about it is that it tries to solve theological (or existential) problems by the methods of historical narration; this alone makes it a rather emphatic sort of history.[22]

---

[20] Cf. Jacob Licht, "Biblical Historicism," in *History, Historiography and Interpretation,* ed. Hayim Tadmor and Moshe Weinfeld (Leiden, 1983), 111–12.

[21] Ibid., 112.

[22] Ibid., 114.

It cannot be denied that the potential for propaganda value exists. But propaganda cannot legitimately be viewed as the primary moving force for this history. The one major criterion used for identifying propaganda as the primary element is whether there are any negative elements presented. This test biblical history passes with flying colors. From Noah to Abraham to Moses and Aaron to David, Hezekiah, or any other figure whom the material serves, negative elements are not avoided. This shows us that there has not been an overall intentional violation of accuracy for the sake of propaganda.

In conclusion, then, while the purpose may be viewed as didactic, and while the data could have been used for propaganda purposes, I see nothing that suggests that those concerns have brought about intentional falsification.

In summary, historiography shows numerous similarities and few but significant differences between Mesopotamia and Israel. The types of sources available are generally similar but different in proportion. Mesopotamia evidences royal inscriptions, chronographic texts, and historical literary texts.[23] While the Israelites do have chronographic texts[24] and a few items that show some similarity to royal inscriptions,[25] most of Israelite historical writing is of a type rarely seen in Mesopotamia. J. R. Porter refers to it as "authentic narrative, reflecting the customs, relationships, and, particularly, the speech of real life and what may be called ordinary people."[26] The literature that seems to catch the flavor closest to the "authentic narrative" mentioned by Porter is some of the Egyptian heroic literature such as the "Tale of Sinuhe"[27] and the "Journey of Wenamun."[28]

D. Damrosch affirms the uniqueness of the Israelite genre but is anxious to maintain that it does not develop in a vacuum. Continuity with Mesopotamian genres is observable, though a genre transformation has occurred.

> The origins of Hebrew historical prose can be traced in Mesopotamian literature of the second millennium, but not through a direct comparison of historical writings alone. Rather, the Bible's historical writing can best be understood as the result of a far-reaching transformation of earlier genres, resulting in a combination of many of the values, themes, and formal properties of historical chronicle with those of poetic epic.[29]

Damrosch sees this transformation as a complex process.

> Even once the earlier materials have been examined together, there remains a pronounced novelty to Hebrew historical writing. Biblical

---

[23]Grayson says that the category of historical epic is unique to Akkadian literature, for he sees nothing similar in Sumerian, Hittite, Hebrew, or Egyptian literatures.

[24]Chronicles, Deuteronomic histories, and Genesis genealogies all fall into this category.

[25]For instance, some of the first-person passages in the Solomon narratives, 1 Kings 8:15–21, 23–53. Royal decrees and proclamations would also fit into this category.

[26]J. R. Porter, "Old Testament Historiography," in *Tradition and Interpretation*, ed. G. W. Anderson (Oxford, 1979), 131.

[27]ANET, 18–22.

[28]ANET, 25–29. These have been discussed in chapter 2.

[29]D. Damrosch, *The Narrative Covenant* (San Francisco, 1987), 41.

narrative cannot simply be understood as a translation of epic into prose, an analogy that has occasionally been made with unconvincing directness. In periods when revolutionary transformations of existing genres are undertaken, the older forms are subverted even as they are renewed, and biblical narrative is the product of a rich mixture of direct use, through adaptation, and outright polemical rejection of earlier narrative practices.[30]

With regard to purpose, Israel does share a didactic use of history with her neighbors but does not evidence anything like the propagandistic intention visible in the royal annals.[31] The fact that some of the narrative may be used in a self-serving way is not denied, but neither does that make a conclusive case. It is also certain that the historiographers of Israel were selective in what they presented (notice, for instance, the chronicler's omission of David's sin with Bathsheba), but selectivity is expected when there is a didactic agenda. This is different from distortion or embellishment.

A final significant difference is that only in Israel was there compiled a single corpus arranging their various documents in an orderly form with an overarching purpose in mind.[32] Even this distinction can be seen as being theological in nature, for it is covenant related. "Israel has developed a historiography because it was conscious of its Lord's policy throughout the ages. The policy is simple: To establish and to maintain Israel as His people."[33] Van Seters says it this way:

> Dtr's (The Deuteronomist) purpose, above all, is to communicate through this story of the people's past a sense of their identity—and that is the *sine qua non* of history writing. No other historical work of the ancient Near East reveals so broad a purpose as this.[34]

Israel's historiography focuses on the nation as a whole; the king is secondary. After noting all of the different forms that historiographic information can take and all the varying genres that yield historical information, Van Seters again observes:

> Yet for the Egyptians, the Hittites, and the nations of Mesopotamia these historiographic genres did not lead to true history writing. Insofar as the king, his dynasty, or even kingship itself was the focus of such texts, they did not develop into a form of tradition encompassing the people as a whole. To be sure, the king was both public and political, and his deeds were of great significance to the nation. But only when the nation itself took precedence over the king, as happened in Israel, could history writing be achieved.[35]

---

[30] Ibid.

[31] See also the attempt to parallel the propagandistic nature of the Tukulti-Ninurta Epic with the value the Yahwistic material had for David and Solomon; P. Machinist, "Literature as Politics: The Tukulti-Ninurta Epic and the Bible," CBQ 38 (1976): 455–82.

[32] Porter, "Old Testament Historiography," 130–31. This is accomplished by the Jewish canon at the latest but most likely much earlier in historical collections like the one designated the Deuteronomistic history.

[33] Licht, "Biblical Historicism," 115.

[34] Van Seters, *In Search of History*, 359.

[35] Ibid., 354–55, though this may be considered a very narrow view of history writing.

II. Role of Deity in History

The role of deity in history is one of the primary areas of distinction between Israel and her neighbors. Israel's view of deity was unique in her world, a view that profoundly affected her concept of history. The nature of this distinction has been a primary issue in scholarship of the last few decades. The controversy was crystallized in Bertil Albrektson's book, *History and the Gods*,[36] which attacked the prevailing opinion that he found expressed most clearly by Sigmund Mowinckel: "While other peoples experienced the deity in the eternal cyclic process of nature, the Israelites experienced God in history."[37] Albrektson, in contrast, suggests that purposeful action by deity in history is not unique to Israel and that the divine plan that had been considered unique in Israel cannot really be found there after all (with the exception of apocalyptic literature).[38] He concludes that there is some uniqueness, however, in the view of God's saving acts: "The idea of historical events as divine manifestations has marked the Israelite cult in a way that lacks real parallels among Israel's neighbors."[39]

While Albrektson's work has been appreciated for precipitating much needed reevaluation, it has not been universally accepted as the final word. W. G. Lambert[40] and H. W. F. Saggs[41] have added other perspectives and evidence. Lambert summarizes his own position as follows:

> Thus the Sumerians, Babylonians and Assyrians shared with the Hebrews what can conveniently be called the Deuteronomic view of divine intervention in human affairs: that divine power is used to maintain standards imposed from above. In other respects the two civilizations were different. Israel conceived of itself as a chosen nation, and that God worked among the nations to create and sustain this nation with future purposes in view. No similar idea is known from ancient Mesopotamia, where it was held that the gods had taught all the arts of civilization at the beginning, and nothing further was to be expected.[42]

Saggs disagrees with both Albrektson and Lambert. He suggests that both Israel and Mesopotamia show evidence of a divine plan in history,[43] therefore that it is not uniquely Israelite thinking that deity works in history toward future purposes. He sees the Israelite uniqueness expressed, not in new concepts added to deity by Israel, but in rejection of certain Near Eastern concepts of deity.[44]

The reevaluation of material presented in these studies has been helpful for bringing data to the surface. It has been shown that it is no longer

---

[36] Uppsala, 1967.

[37] Ibid., 11.

[38] Ibid., 76–88.

[39] Ibid., 115.

[40] W. G. Lambert, "History and the Gods: A Review Article," Or, n.s., 39 (1970): 170–77; and "Destiny and Divine Intervention in Babylon and Israel," OTS 17 (1972): 65–72.

[41] H. W. F. Saggs, *Encounter with the Divine in Mesopotamia and Israel* (London, 1978), 69ff.

[42] Lambert, "Destiny and Divine Intervention," 72.

[43] Saggs, *Encounter*, 81ff.

[44] Ibid., 92.

possible to retain the simplistic distinction of Mesopotamian gods working through nature while YHWH worked in history. The differences are far more subtle. Mere intervention is clearly discernible in both. The question concerns whether a "plan" exists for history and the ability of deity to carry out a plan successfully.

Saggs has suggested that there is sufficient evidence (at least in the Neo-Assyrian period) that Mesopotamian thinking did posit a divine plan.[45] W. G. Lambert, however, claims that any intervention as adduced "is not concerned with a movement in history."[46] He continues, "The intervention could be entirely whimsical, but if purposeful it was intended to maintain the norms or destinies."[47] In this sense, we see nothing in Mesopotamia that suggests a plan for any more than retaining the status quo, or, at best, reinstituting a previous, more desirable status quo. Many Israelite examples contain no more than this and are therefore similar. Similarity also exists in the instruments of deity used in the intervention process.[48] The preeminence of the Davidic dynasty, for instance, is a status quo to be maintained. But there is also in Israel the idea of a goal that has not yet been achieved and toward which history is moving. While this is largely discernible in prophetic rather than historical literature, it entails a view of history and YHWH's role in that history. YHWH's acts are not whimsical, and any ad hoc intervention still focuses on the final goal. All intervention works toward his plan in history. In the Israelite literature where this view is present, it certainly represents a major departure from ancient Near Eastern thought, for this theology could never survive in a polytheistic setting.

This brings us to the second part of the issue—the ability of deity to carry out a plan. Polytheism has its inherent limitations: deity can be foiled by deity. The "plan" of one god can be overridden by the intervention of another. Even destinies decreed by the divine council from the beginning can be jeopardized.

> The lack of absolute authority on the part of any one god led to uncertainty about the actions of the divine powers combined. Nothing was settled for all time, nothing could be taken for granted; hence the anxiety and the insecurity of the mortals, who must forever be intent on propitiating the gods in order to obtain a favorable decision. The view that nothing was permanent and that the gods were unpredictable brought with it a fitful and dramatic conception of the universe, one that called for constant watchfulness and elaborate ritual.[49]

It is commonplace, then, that divine intervention in history in a polytheistic setting must by its nature be primarily ad hoc—one god responding to the moves of another as in a chess match. In this realm lies the uniqueness of the Israelite concept. No Mesopotamian god is seen as having

---

[45] Ibid., 81ff.

[46] Lambert, "Destiny and Divine Intervention," 71.

[47] Ibid.

[48] Moshe Weinfeld, "Divine Intervention in War in Ancient Israel and in the Ancient Near East," in Tadmor and Weinfeld, *History, Historiography and Interpretation*, 121–47.

[49] E. A. Speiser, "Ancient Mesopotamia," in *The Idea of History in the Ancient Near East*, ed. Robert Dentan (New Haven, 1955), 43–44.

total sovereignty over history. It is granted that the realm of deity is the controlling force in history, but with individual deities at loggerheads, any possibility of sovereign control is eliminated. There may then be divine planning in history, but no overall, achievable divine plan. Paul Hanson views the absence of this as a natural result of the Mesopotamian perspective that the real world simply copies what happens in the cosmic realm, the human realm having no independent status.

> An historical sequence spanning centuries in an unbroken development could not be recognized, for in reflecting cosmic events, history was reflecting timeless episodes. The rise and fall of empires reflected decisions in a divine assembly which was not bound by any historical sequence. One decision leads to the rise of Akkad to hegemony over the city states, another to its fall. The same pattern leads to the rise of Ur, and then to its fall; again to the rise of Babylon, and its fall. No common line connects these separate phases in an unbroken development. They are but separate episodes reflecting isolated decisions in the divine assembly.[50]

It is in this latter context that we identify the saving acts of YHWH on Israel's behalf and the election of Israel as unique witnesses to a unique view of history. It is not that Mesopotamian deities were considered incapable of delivering their patrons from distress nor that they were uninterested in choosing particular groups for special favors. In Israel, however, these contributed to an overall scheme in history that could not be frustrated, for YHWH was in sovereign control of every possible contingency.

III. Concept of History

The concept of history concerns how the past is seen as relevant to the present and future. Our Western mode of thinking sees history as linear. The constant is the abstract concept of time along which history moves. Causality is posited in many factors including nature, chance, human decision, and depending on one's religious persuasion, divine acts. The past is seen as instructive in helping us avoid similar mistakes. In the discussion of ancient concepts of history, much emphasis has been laid on a linear versus cyclic dichotomy. It is a frequently maintained distinction that the Israelite concept of history was linear, whereas that of her neighbors was cyclic.[51] This dichotomy, however, is inadequate for discussion of the ancient concepts and is inappropriate insofar as there are cyclical and linear elements in both Israelite and Mesopotamian perceptions. It is more preferable to speak in terms of constants and causality.

In Mesopotamian perception, it was the omen mentality that provided their historical constant; i.e., series of events X, as often as it may occur, will inexorably be followed by something like event Y. It is uncertain whether "series X" here would be considered as the actual cause of event Y or whether series X is the result of some unseen cause which also leads to Y. In

---

[50] Paul Hanson, "Jewish Apocalyptic Against Its Near Eastern Environment," RB 78 (1971): 38–39.

[51] A "cyclic" concept is the idea that historical phenomena pass through several set stages in a fixed sequence, eventually returning to the original point, a pattern seemingly derived from the cycles of nature.

either case, series X was thought to be inextricably related to event Y. Our hypothetical series X here could consist of numerous elements, including astronomical positions, behavior of animals or insects, configurations of entrails of sacrificed animals, or any number of other things. Event Y, on the other hand, would frequently be a historical event.

So, for instance, from the Old Babylonian Omen Texts comes the example: "When the liver is formed in such and such a way [form described], this is the omen of the king of Apishal whom Naram-sin took captive when he tried to break through the wall of his city."[52] So history was not seen as being caused by other historical events. From the fact that the gods are seen to be movers of history even when omenological elements were present, we can probably conclude that the events of series X were considered to be constant side effects of the *divine* act that was bringing about event Y.

> We have here the following idea of history, . . . Every situation or kind of time has already existed once in the incomprehensible sequence of situations; every one comes back again, although the sequence as such cannot be determined; the symptoms can only help us to determine which situation is about ready to appear again. We have here no thought of the development of one condition out of another in the course of time, let alone the idea that history has a goal and purpose.[53]

It was possible, and even likely, that history would repeat itself, but the purposes of the gods were indiscernible. The omen mentality gave the people some help in trying to figure out *when* history might repeat itself. There was ignorance concerning where history was going (if anywhere), and the inscrutable acts of the gods were only faintly divulged by the readable effects in the omens.

For Israel, YHWH is the constant and the all-pervading cause. YHWH was defined by his attributes, which were constant, and he had obligated himself in various ways (the covenants). The cycles of judges demonstrate the constancy of YHWH, for as often as Israel acts in rebellion, YHWH will respond with judgment. YHWH is the cause of every historical event. Human decision and activity are his instruments.

Mesopotamia and Israel are alike in seeing deity as the cause behind historical effect. For Israel, this produced a constant, for YHWH had revealed his demands, desires, and some of his intentions. For Mesopotamians, this still left everything uncertain. The only control possible came from gaining knowledge of what the gods intended to do, and this was achieved by omens. Both societies used the past to learn about deity—since it was deity who controlled the present. For Mesopotamia, they did this by looking for patterns in how the omens accompanied the acts of the gods and attempting to deduce acceptable and unacceptable behavior. They met with only partial success at discerning what actions pleased or displeased deity. For Israel, a study of the past revealed more about YHWH's attributes, demands, and self-imposed obligations. Our Western philosophy is that the key to history lies in human nature and human behavior. The Israelites were convinced

---

[52]Cf. A. Goetze, "Historical Allusions in Old Babylonian Omen Texts," JCS 1 (1947): 253–58.

[53]H. Gese, "The Idea of History in the Ancient Near East and the Old Testament," *Journal for Theology and the Church* (1965): 53.

that the key to history was knowing YHWH and being familiar with how humanity had interacted with him in the past. The difference, then, both between ancient Near Eastern and modern Western concepts, as well as between Israelite and Mesopotamian concepts, is the relative theological significance of history.[54]

If we think in terms of models, it is the "Historical Recurrence" model suggested by G. W. Trompf[55] that logically explains both Israelite and Mesopotamian concepts of history. Recurrence can be seen either in reenactment or in the notion that common events are regularly followed by consequences in a way that creates a general pattern of history.

> Thus the Deuteronomist's work was a history of the recurring execution of appropriate recompenses, and Israel's past was viewed as if the same principles operated time and time again. Implicitly the nature of rewards and punishments was in accordance with the degree of merit or of incurred guilt, but these operations were ultimately dependent on Yahweh and not upon natural or "mechanical" laws.[56]

The model of recurrence accounts for both linear and cyclic qualities and allows for the differences already noted. The actual stimulation of recurrence in history is brought about by the cause/effect perspective and the nature of the constants that are responsible for the real differences in how history was viewed in Israel and Mesopotamia.

A. Egyptian Historiography

Again we have focused primarily on Mesopotamia for comparison with the Israelites. Egyptian records feature many of the same elements as the Mesopotamian records. A propagandistic agenda is even more discernible in Egyptian practices, as the frequent obliteration of predecessors' names and ignoring of negative elements attests.[57] In regard to a concept of history, H. Frankfort has observed:

> Egyptians had very little sense of history or of past and future. For they conceived their world as essentially static and unchanging. It had gone forth complete from the hands of the Creator. Historical incidents were, consequently, no more than superficial disturbances of the established order, or recurring events of never-changing significance. The past and the future—far from being a matter of concern—were wholly implicit in the present . . . only the changeless is truly significant.[58]

---

[54]See J. J. M. Roberts, "Myth Versus History," CBQ 38 (1976): 1–13.

[55]G. W. Trompf, "Notions of Historical Recurrence in Classical Hebrew Historiography," VT Supp. 30 (1979): 213–29.

[56]Ibid., 223.

[57]For political propaganda present in Egyptian literature in general, see R. J. Williams, "Literature as a Medium of Political Propaganda in Ancient Egypt," in The Seed of Wisdom, ed. W. S. McCullough (Toronto, 1964), 14–30.

[58]H. Frankfort, The Birth of Civilization in the Near East (Garden City, 1951), 9. Similar conclusions are drawn by Ludlow Bull, "Ancient Egypt," in The Idea of History in the Ancient Near East, ed. Robert Dentan (New Haven, 1955); see especially his conclusions on pp. 32–33. S. Morenz adds to that the perspective that "Egyptian history is written as a dogma of sacrosanct monarchy," Egyptian Religion (Ithaca, N.Y., 1973), 11. Professor Kitchen warns, however, that this can be misleading. The present

Of course, this does not mean that the Egyptians had no historical records or no historiographic forms of literature. King lists, annals, royal inscriptions, and other forms are all ways in which the Egyptians demonstrated their interest in preserving records of the past. Van Seters accepts the opinion of E. Otto that Egyptian historiography takes a form unlike that of other ancient Near Eastern civilizations in that there is a very evident tension between the world of facts and a historical ideal. "No Near Eastern society was more meticulous in its record keeping . . . and yet more ideological in its presentation of past events as they centered upon the king."[59]

So again we find that Egyptian concepts are not on a comparable level with Israelite concepts, for a unique royal ideology heavily influenced Egyptian thinking.

B. Hittite Historiography

"The Hittites were more interested in using the past than in recording it."[60] Whether we speak of the royal annals in general, the "Apologies," or the first-person accounts of the king's "manly deeds," history is the tool of the king and is used to justify, legitimize, magnify, and if need be, embellish his rule and his person.

Annals provide the major type of historiography found in use among the Hittites. The oldest annals date from the reign of Ḫattusili I (ca. 1650–1620 B.C.), but the primary examples of the class are the three works from the time of Mursili II (ca. 1345–1310 B.C.): Ten-Year Annals of Mursili, the Detailed Annals, and the Deeds of Šuppiluliuma I. Harry Hoffner identifies these as "Narratives of military campaigns with prominent division into years and with standard stylistic format."[61] They generally are presented in the first person as if the king himself is relating the information.

A second category contains narratives of military campaigns within a single year. A third is comprised of court histories descriptive of either officials or family members, generally with the purpose of discrediting them (e.g., The Political Testament of Ḫattusili I; The Palace Chronicle).

A fourth and very significant category is that often referred to as "Royal Apology." Hoffner identifies these as documents "composed for a king who had usurped the throne . . . in order to defend or justify his assumption of the kingship by force."[62]

They have the form of royal edicts with a historical prologue that often

---

is measured by comparison with the past (an idealized golden age). The changelessness mentioned by Frankfort is in many ways a "convenient fiction" (private correspondence). See also P. Hanson, "Jewish Apocalyptic Against Its Near Eastern Environment," RB 78 (1971): 37.

[59] Van Seters, *In Search of History*, 129.

[60] Ibid., 122.

[61] H. Hoffner, "Histories and Historians of the Ancient Near East: The Hittites," Or 49 (1980): 332. Even earlier Hittite historiography is found in "The Deeds of Anittas" (E. Laroche, *Catalogue des Textes Hittites*, 1971, p. 2, no. 1). Thanks to Professor Kitchen for bringing this to my attention. More recently, see H. G. Güterbock, "Hittite Historiography: A Survey," in *History, Historiography and Interpretation*, ed. Tadmor and Weinfeld, 22–25.

[62] Hoffner, "Propaganda and Political Justification in Hittite Historiography," in *Unity and Diversity*, ed. H. Goedicke and J. J. M. Roberts (Baltimore, 1975), 49.

goes far back in time. The two examples identified by Hoffner are The Apology of Ḫattusili III and the Telepinu Proclamation.[63]

A final category identified by Hoffner[64] is made up of historical sections in literature of other genres, i.e., prologues to treaties and edicts, and sections of the royal prayers.

The Royal Apologies, particularly that of Ḫattusili III, have drawn a significant amount of attention as the potential forerunners of works known in the other ancient Near Eastern cultures. Herbert Wolf did his dissertation at Brandeis comparing the Apology of Ḫattusili with other ancient Near Eastern works of political self-justification, including a comparison with the succession narratives concerning David.[65] More recently, Hayim Tadmor has attempted to demonstrate that numerous examples of autobiographical apology occur in Royal Assyrian literature and down into Neo-Babylonian and Achaemenid times as parts of longer royal inscriptions.[66] Tadmor contends that at least in the Assyrian literature these sections were "composed not so much in order to reflect apologetically upon the past but rather to serve certain imminent political aims in the present or some particular design for the future."[67] He sees the primary aim to be in conjunction with the appointment of a successor.

Whatever parallels may exist in the other areas of the ancient Near East, the apology category (whether or not it can be identified as a separate genre), shows again by its use of history that the Hittites' primary use of historiography was for propagandistic purposes, although didactic purposes may also be identified in some works.[68]

Much has been made of what has been viewed as a heightened sense of divine causality in the Hittite view of history.[69] However, there is nothing that distinguishes the Hittite understanding found in the plague prayers of Mursili II from the view found anywhere else in the ancient Near East. The gods are seen to have intervened in history because of actions that displeased

---

[63]Hoffner makes a strong case for the inclusion of the Telepinu Proclamation in this category in "Propaganda and Political Justification" and in his survey in "Histories and Historians," para. 9. H. Güterbock disagrees with the placement, considering it rather "an account that serves the purpose of showing reason for political action. The purpose is the regulation of the dynastic succession and the establishment of jurisdiction over the royal family" ("Hittite Historiography," 28).

[64]These categories have all been taken from Hoffner, "Histories and Historians," 332.

[65]H. M. Wolf, "The Apology of Ḫattusilis Compared with Other Political Self-Justifications of the Ancient Near East," unpublished diss., 1967. Reviewing Wolf's work, M. Tsevat (JBL 87 [1968]: 458) rightly objects that even given an acceptable list of similarities between the Apology of Ḫattusilis and other ancient Near Eastern works, there are no other pieces of literature that can be placed in the genre of "Apology" from a form-critical perspective if such a genre exists.

[66]Hayim Tadmor, "Autobiographical Apology in the Royal Assyrian Literature," in Tadmor and Weinfeld, History, Historiography and Interpretation, 36–57.

[67]Ibid., 37.

[68]See Hoffner, "Histories and Historians," 331. Professor Kitchen identifies Egyptian royal apology in divine birth legends and compositions concerning the appointment of the king by gods or previous kings (private correspondence).

[69]A. Malamat, "Doctrines of Causality in Hittite and Biblical Historiography," VT 5 (1955): 1–12.

them. As John Van Seters points out, this is not significantly different from the perspective found in the Weidner Chronicle.[70] A. Malamat seeks to demonstrate that a similar situation occurred in Israel in the incident of the famine during David's time, which was oracularly determined to be caused by Saul's violation of the treaty with the Gibeonites (2 Sam. 21). But as we have already noted above, Israel and the ancient Near East at large had in common the notion that divine intervention in the course of history was not unusual.

Not much can be said concerning the "concept of history" among the Hittites, for it cannot be determined whether they had one or not. Of interest but insufficient for further analysis is the statement from a magical text cited by Hoffner that reads, "When the former kings shall return and look after the law of the land, then only may this seal be broken!"[71] Only further texts can help us to understand whether this represents a hope or a developed eschatology.

C. Conclusion

As in previous genres, the distinction between Israel and her neighbors has largely and ultimately to do with her view of deity. In all three areas discussed, the fact that YHWH, the sole God of Israel, was the sovereign of history, directing it unwaveringly in a predetermined direction, is the premise that dictates the distinctions. This element is initially evident in the covenant and in that way becomes a mainstay in the agenda of the Deuteronomist. Through the period of prophetic literature, it eventually is expressed in a distinct eschatology.

> The doctrine of Israel's election as the chosen people of Yahweh set the nation apart from other peoples. It was a special feature of its identity. All other callings and elections, whether to kingship, priesthood, or prophecy, were viewed in association with the choice of the people as a whole. Many of the Near Eastern historiographic documents that have to do with kingship deal with the special election of the king to rule, and even recount the divine providence by which he gained the throne and was victorious over his enemies. But nowhere outside of Israel was the notion of special election extended to the nation as a whole, such that the complete history of the people should be viewed in this way.[72]

CASES OF ALLEGED BORROWING

I. Antediluvian Sumerian King List and Genesis 5

The only occurrence of suspected borrowing between historiographic sources is found in the close relationship between Genesis 5 and the antediluvian section of the Sumerian King List. Genesis 5 presents a list of ten patriarchs in genealogical format that bridges the gap from creation to the flood; i.e., Adam to Noah. The ages attributed to these men are unusually high, many being in the 900s. The Sumerian King List[73] preserves the names

---

[70] Van Seters, *In Search of History*, 123, n. 96.
[71] Hoffner, "Histories and Historians," 329.
[72] Van Seters, *In Search of History*, 360–61.
[73] Here we make reference to the Weld-Blundell prism 444 ascertained by Jacobsen's

and length of reign of eight Mesopotamian kings bridging a similar gap—from the time "kingship descended from heaven" until the flood. If the length of life in Genesis 5 is unusual, the length of reign in the Sumerian King List is incredible, ranging from 18,600 to 43,200.

Based on the date of the Sumerian King List (Isin-Larsa period—early second millennium B.C.) and the generally assumed priority of Mesopotamian sources, it has been standard to consider the Genesis 5 genealogy to be in some way dependent on the Sumerian King List tradition. These criteria, however, are inconclusive and require reevaluation. It is true that whether the editor of Genesis 5 be Moses or P (priestly editor), the final editing of Genesis came well after the Sumerian King List. But almost any theory on Genesis posits early material that was used in the editing process. Therefore, neither Moses nor P provides for us a date of *composition* of the Genesis 5 genealogy.

Concerning the priority of Mesopotamian sources, we would have to admit that, of course, Hebrew sources cannot be earlier than the mid-second millennium, for that is when the Hebrews as a nation originated. If Abraham brought written documents with him to Palestine, they must have been Mesopotamian. Since the Hebrews derived from Mesopotamia, then, their early sources would have been Mesopotamian. Our concern, then, is not a geographical one (where the information developed) but a critical one, which form of the data has more of a claim to be original.

In the case of Genesis 5 and the Sumerian King List, we cannot rule out a priori the possibility that Genesis 5 derives, in either written or oral form, from a date older than the Sumerian King List. If it is that old, it too would have been Mesopotamian (by Mesopotamian we allow either Sumerian or Semitic, such as Amorite, Aramaean, etc.). Our obligation is to judge between the documents.

I have previously undertaken a comparison of a very specific element of these lists: the totals.[74] I will here summarize those findings and discuss what implications they may have. It is important to emphasize the speculative and limited nature of this comparison. There are still many differences between the lists that this analysis does not explain, and the identified similarity may well be coincidental, though it is curious.

The comparison was conducted by eliminating the superficial elements that characterized the two lists so that true comparison could be made. Three differences were identified as follows:

Genesis 5	Sumerian King List
Genealogy	King List
10 names	8 names (in WB 444)
Decimal number system	Sexagesimal number system

---

critical study as preserving the most original form. See Thorkild Jacobsen, *The Sumerian King List* (Chicago, 1939), 70ff. Other texts of the Sumerian King List preserve different names and numbers and a different number of names.

[74]John Walton, "The Antediluvian Section of the Sumerian King List and Genesis 5," BA 44 (1981): 207–8.

A. Genealogy Versus King List

The difference here is that in a genealogical listing the numbers will overlap while in a king list they will not. If these two lists are related, we must assume one of the forms is secondary.[75] Since we would not be able to recreate what the King List would have looked like as a genealogy, this difference was neutralized by treating the genealogy like a king list. So for comparison's sake, the ages in Genesis 5 were treated as lengths of reign.

B. Number of Names

This is a minor difference, but it cannot be ignored. We must ascertain that we are dealing with the same span. The Sumerian King List (in this eight-name version) does not include the name of the flood hero. I felt justified, then, in not counting Noah in Genesis 5. As previously noted, the Sumerian King List begins "when kingship descended from heaven." There is no Mesopotamian figure comparable to Adam, because monogenesis was not a Mesopotamian concept. Therefore, I also felt justified in eliminating Adam from Genesis 5. It should also be noted that in Genesis 5 eight names are used to connect Adam and Noah—they are included in the genealogy but not in the same formal style. We can thus reduce the specifically genealogical material of Genesis 5 to eight names in order to be able to compare with the Sumerian King List. This is not intended in any way to devalue the significance of Adam or Noah in the narrative. It simply recognizes that their role is more connected to the narratives than to the genealogy. The genealogy connects the narratives.

C. Number Systems

It was common among Semitic peoples to use a decimal system, and the Hebrews are no exception. The Sumerians, on the other hand, used a combination base 6/base 10 system called the sexagesimal system. This difference must also be neutralized for comparison to be made.

D. Results

If we add up the eight totals of the names in Genesis 5, the total comes to 6,695. Using 6,700, if we convert this to a sexagesimal number, we get 241,200, the exact total of the Sumerian King List ($6,700 = 6 \times 1,000 + 7 \times 100$, the equivalent places in the sexagesimal system would be $[6 \times 36,000] + [7 \times 3,600] = 241,200$. The choice of using 36,000 and 3,600 was not arbitrary. The early notation for 3,600 was $\bigcirc$; this symbol is also found in nonsexagesimal systems equaling 100).[76]

E. Conclusion

The similarity of the total may suggest that the two lists share a common link somewhere in their heritage. The numerical situation suggests that if such a relationship exists, the Genesis 5 list would be earlier. In the

---

[75]For a form-critical study comparing the genealogies of Genesis 1–11 with their ancient Near Eastern counterparts, see R. Hess, "The Genealogies of Genesis 1–11 and Comparative Literature," *Biblica* (forthcoming, 1989).

[76]P. E. van der Meer, "Dix-Sept Tablettes Semi-Pictographiques," RA 33 (1936): 185–90.

above example we move from decimal to sexagesimal, and as we saw, correlation became immediately evident. If we started with sexagesimal and moved into decimal, no such results would occur.[77] Therefore, if we assume that the sexagesimal account came first, our comparison would show no correlation, and we could not assume any connection. If we assume that the decimal came first, the correlation occurs and connection is more plausible (at least from a mathematical standpoint). A scenario that would explain the situation would be that a Sumerian scribe had access to a decimal record that he mistook for a sexagesimal record.[78] The Sumerian King List was the result. One of Thorkild Jacobsen's observations is that the antediluvian section of the list was only secondarily appended to the list and that the author was uncertain of how to handle it.[79] He concludes that the author was appending this information culled from a different kind of source.

Of the possible borrowing scenarios (if this is sufficient to suggest borrowing), this leaves as most probable that the Semitic genealogical form was primary (similar to Genesis 5) and that the Sumerian King List version came about in a three-step process (over a long period of time): (1) reduction of genealogy to include only names and total age (dropping age when son was born), (2) misreading of the decimal numbers as sexagesimal, and (3) interpreting the resulting ambiguous list as a king list.

We can in no way prove that this took place; it is only hypothetical. At present, however, it suits the known data well, though it is true that it still gives no explanation for the variations between individuals, numbers, or the variations between the names.

F. Implications

If the above process or something like it is accurate, the implications are far-reaching. First, it gives a precedent for the concept of Israelite traditions reflecting older traditions more accurately than our extant Mesopotamian sources. While this would in no way ascertain that the biblical record therefore *always* represented more original forms, it would certainly necessitate that in each case the evidence be examined with the possibility that the biblical record represents the older tradition. As we have already seen in our cosmological study, this would greatly alter the current view of creation and flood accounts. In those cases, neither Mesopotamian nor biblical data can claim very strong literary support for preserving an earlier form. Because of date factors, however, Mesopotamian forms have frequently been granted priority. With the existence here, however, of an example of an earlier tradition being demonstrated as preserved in the biblical text, previous presuppositions of Mesopotamian priority would have to be considered simplistic.

Second, we would now have somewhat stronger evidence that the

---

[77] The difference between 36,000 and 3,600 is a 10 factor, but the difference between 3,600 and the next digit, 600, is a 6 factor. This would be equivalent to the 10's place in the decimal numbers, so every time the 10's place exceeded 5, a numerical distortion would occur in conversion. So 960 converted to sexagesimal = 9 x 3,600 + 6 x 600 = 36,000, whereas 36,000 sexagesimal converts back to 1,000 in decimal.

[78] This can easily happen, for the Sumerian notation is used in both systems.

[79] Jacobsen, *The Sumerian King List*, 60ff., esp. 64, n. 119.

accounts of Genesis have a long tradition behind them. If a misreading took place, as we have suggested, the material that ended up in Genesis 5 would have to have been available in written form, in cuneiform, even before the time of Abraham. This would be the first evidence of such an ancient written tradition of the Israelite materials.

Finally, the biblical accounts would now need to be taken a bit more seriously in the history of traditions approach. They cannot simply be written off as late based on the date of their final editing.

FOR FURTHER READING

Albrektson, Bertil. *History and the Gods*. Uppsala, 1967.

Bull, Ludlow. "Ancient Egypt." In *The Idea of History in the Ancient Near East*. Ed. R. C. Dentan. New Haven, 1955, 1–34.

Damrosch, David. *The Narrative Covenant*. San Francisco, 1987.

Finkelstein, J. J. "Mesopotamian Historiography." *Proceedings of the American Philosophical Society* 107:6 (1963): 461–72.

Gese, Hartmut. "The Idea of History in the Ancient Near East and the Old Testament." Trans. James F. Ross. *Journal for Theology and the Church* (1965): 49–64.

Grayson, A. K. *Babylonian Historical Literary Texts*. Toronto, 1975.

————. "Assyria and Babylonia." Or, n.s., 49 (1980): 140–94.

Hallo, W. W. "Biblical History in Its Near Eastern Setting." In *Scripture in Context*. Ed. C. D. Evans, W. W. Hallo, and J. B. White. Pittsburgh, 1980, 1–26.

Hanson, Paul D. "Jewish Apocalyptic Against Its Near Eastern Environment." RB 78 (1971): 31–58.

Hoffner, Harry. "Propaganda and Political Justification in Hittite Historiography." In *Unity and Diversity*. Ed. H. Goedicke and J. J. M. Roberts. Baltimore, 1975, 49–62.

————. "Histories and Historians of the Ancient Near East: The Hittites." Or 49 (1980): 283–332.

Lambert, W. G. "History and the Gods: A Review Article." Or, n.s., 39 (1970): 170–77.

————. "Destiny and Divine Intervention in Babylon and Israel." OTS 17 (1972): 65–72.

Maisler, B. (Mazar). "Ancient Israelite Historiography." IEJ 2 (1952): 82–88.

Malamat, A. "Doctrines of Causality in Hittite and Biblical Historiography." VT 5 (1955): 1–12.

Porter, J. R. "Old Testament Historiography." In *Tradition and Interpretation*. Ed. G. W. Anderson. Oxford, 1979, 125–62.

Roberts, J. J. M. "Myth Versus History." CBQ 38 (1976): 1–13.

Saggs, H. W. F. *The Encounter with the Divine in Mesopotamia and Israel.* London, 1978, 64–92.

Soggin, J. Alberto. "The History of Ancient Israel: A Study in Some Questions of Method." *Eretz-Israel* 14 (1978): 44–5l.

Speiser E. A. "Ancient Mesopotamia." In *The Idea of History in the Ancient Near East.* Ed. R. C. Dentan. New Haven, 1955, 37–76.

————. "The Biblical Idea of History in Its Common Near Eastern Setting." IEJ 7 (1957).

Tadmor, Hayim, and Moshe Weinfeld, eds. *History, Historiography and Interpretation.* Jerusalem, 1984.

Trompf, G. W. "Notions of Historical Recurrence in Classical Hebrew Historiography." VT Supp. 30 (1979): 213–29.

Van Seters, John. *In Search of History.* New Haven, 1983.

Williams, Ronald J. "Literature as a Medium of Political Propaganda in Ancient Egypt." In *The Seed of Wisdom*, ed. W. S. McCullough. Toronto, 1964, 14–30.

Wright, G. Ernest. *The God Who Acts.* London, 1952.

Chapter 6

HYMNS, PRAYERS, AND INCANTATIONS

There are scores of compositions from all parts of the ancient world that fall into the category of address to deity. Sumerian, Akkadian, and Egyptian literature all have numerous representatives.[1] Here we will call specific attention to only the most significant examples in each category.[2] Most of the extant hymns from the ancient Near East are from Mesopotamia (Sumeria and Babylonia) and Egypt. Even though the Ugaritic material has provided much information for understanding Hebrew poetry, that information comes largely from its mythology. Hymns per se are not attested in that literature with a few minor exceptions.[3]

In examining the various sorts of address to deity, we will look at both

---

[1] For one annotated listing that gives publication data for all of the Mesopotamian pieces known in 1953, see A. Falkenstein and W. von Soden, *Sumerische und Akkadische Hymnen und Gebete* (Zurich, 1953), 361ff. More recently, see M-J. Seux, *Hymnes et Prières aux Dieux de Babylonie et d'Assyrie* (Paris, 1976). Also in 1976 and with cross-references to Seux's work see the complete listing of W. Mayer, *Untersuchungen zur Formensprache der babylonischen "Gebetsbeschworungen"* (Rome, 1976).

[2] We are excluding from our study the Royal Hymns (Hymns to Kings) and the Temple Hymns (Hymns to Temples) because though they are well-established Sumerian genres, they have relatively little parallel in biblical literature. See the brief discussion by W. W. Hallo, "Individual Prayer in Sumerian," JAOS 88 (1968): 74.

[3] Adrian Curtis, *Ugarit* (Grand Rapids, 1985), 99. There also has now been published a ritual text that includes a prayer to Baal (RS 24.266 = KTU 1.119). Transliteration, translation, and comments can be found in P. D. Miller, "Prayer and Sacrifice in Ugarit and Israel," in *Text and Context*, ed. W. Claassen (Sheffield, 1988), 139–55. It should also be noted that there are numerous magical texts (incantations) in Hittite and a corpus of prayers as well, but these will not be treated here.

form and content. In the process I would like to see whether a particular theology of prayer is discernible from the literature at our disposal.

MATERIALS

I. Hymns and Prayers

A. Sumerian

1. Hymn to Enlil

Approximate Date of Composition
    Old Babylonian

Manuscript Data
  More than twenty fragments classified by A. Falkenstein, most found at Nippur. Other unpublished fragments are known to be at the University Museum, University of Pennsylvania, and in Istanbul. Few lacunae remain in the approximately 170 lines of text.

Publication Data
  A. Falkenstein, *Sumerische Götterlieder* (Heidelberg, 1959), 1:5–79. Translated in ANET, 573–76.

Content
    The first sixty-four lines focus on the city of Nippur, its temple, the Ekur, and the priesthood. Lines 65–90 address Enlil's role as the builder of the Ekur, while the remainder of the piece is an extended glorification of Enlil for his maintenance of all life and civilization.[4]

2. Hymn of Enheduanna to Inanna

Approximate Date of Composition
    Sargonic period

Manuscript Data
  More than fifty tablets and fragments make the text virtually complete. Comprehensive listing may be found in W. W. Hallo and A. J. A. Van Dijk, *The Exaltation of Inanna* (New Haven, 1968), 36–43.

Publication Data
  W. W. Hallo and A. J. A. van Dijk, *The Exaltation of Inanna* (New Haven, 1968); translated in ANET, 579–82.

Content
    This hymn is offered to Inanna by Enheduanna, known as the daughter of Sargon the Great and high priestess of the moon god Nanna in Ur. The hymn opens with eight lines praising Inanna for her control of the *ME* (which define and maintain civilization). Lines 9–57 note all of the cruel and merciless aspects of Inanna. Eight more lines in praise of Inanna's wisdom are followed by a lengthy description of the suffering of Enheduanna

---

[4]For a summary of the Sumerian literature see S. N. Kramer, "Sumerian Literature," in *The Bible and the Ancient Near East*, ed. G. Ernest Wright (Winona Lake, Ind., 1961), 255–57.

(66–108). This lament is followed by a brief petition. There is then a recitation of Inanna's powers and a request for mercy. The hymn ends with a note of Inanna's acceptance of the petition.

B. Akkadian

1. Prayer to Ishtar

Approximate Date of Composition
This text and the one that it was copied from are from the Neo-Babylonian period. It is tentatively dated to the middle of the second millennium.[5]

Manuscript Data
Three primary texts, one late Babylonian and two from Boghaz-Koi (one in Akkadian, one in Hittite).

Publication Data
Text:
E. Reiner and H. Güterbock, JCS 21 (1967): 257–62.
L. W. King, *The Seven Tablets of Creation* (London, 1902), vol. 2, pls. 75–84.
Translation:
ANET, 383–85.

2. Hymn to Shamash

Approximate Date of Composition
Thought to have taken its final form toward the end of the second millennium B.C.[6]

Manuscript Data
There are four major known copies. Three are late Assyrian copies from the library of Ashurbanipal; the other is a late Babylonian text from Sippar. Three other fragments from Ashurbanipal's library contain only a few lines each, and two exercise tablets contain portions of the hymn. Full documentation of the manuscripts may be found in W. G. Lambert, BWL, 125.

Publication Data
Text:
BWL, pls. 33–36. On p. 124 Lambert gives a list of previous publications.
Translation:
BWL, 126–38.
ANET, 387–89.

3. Hymn to Marduk

Approximate Date of Composition
Date cannot be determined. Extant copies are from the mid-first millennium, but the existence of interlinear copies with Sumerian (Emesal dialect) and Akkadian suggest that it is much older.

---

[5] Erica Reiner and H. Güterbock, "The Great Prayer to Ishtar and Its Two Versions from Boğazköy," JCS 21 (1967): 255–57, 263–66.
[6] See a thorough discussion of date in W. G. Lambert, BWL, 122–23.

Manuscript Data
Most complete text was found at Babylon with fragments found at Nineveh.

Publication Data
Text:
  F. H. Weissbach, *Babylonische Miscellen* (Leipzig, 1903), pl. 13.
Translation:
  ANET, 390.

C. Egyptian

1. Hymn to the Aten

Approximate Date of Composition
Second quarter of fourteenth century B.C. by Akhenaten.

Manuscript Data
Thirteen columns inscribed on the wall of the tomb of Ay.

Publication Data
Text:
  M. Sandman, *Texts from the Time of Akhenaten* (Brussels, 1938), 93–96.
Translation:
  AEL, 2:96–99.
  ANET, 369–71.
  Also, see a recent translation by V. A. Tobin in his article, "Amarna and Biblical Religion,"
    in *Pharaonic Egypt, the Bible and Christianity*, ed. Sarah Israelit-Groll (Jerusalem, 1985).

II. Incantations

A. Eršemma (Wail of the "Shem-drum")[7]

The Old Babylonian *eršemmas* tend to be narratives based on mythologi-cal motifs, while the later *eršemmas* are psalms intended to appease an angry deity. The Old Babylonian examples do not contain sections appeasing the heart of the deity, whereas the later *eršemmas* do.[8] These were composed in the Sumerian Emesal dialect (a dialect used primarily in literary texts) and were recited by temple personnel (the *gala* priest) in connection with the *balag*-lamentation. Published by M. Cohen, *Sumerian Hymnology: The Eršemma* (HUCA Supp. 2, Cincinnati, 1981). Cohen gives a catalog of 194 *eršemma* incipits and the pertinent publication data.[9] His own work gives transliteration, translation, and commentary on twenty-six selected examples.

B. Eršahunga (Lament to Calm the Heart)

These are the individual laments that generally address situations of sorrow or calamity (not usually sickness) caused by deity (as opposed to enemies). There are twenty-six examples in Sumerian Emesal, often with interlinear Akkadian. A listing of publications may be found in E. R. Dalglish, *Psalm Fifty-One in the Light of Ancient Near Eastern Patternism* (Leiden, 1962), 22, n. 21. W. W. Hallo believes that this genre "perpetuate[s]

---

[7]M. Cohen, *Sumerian Hymnology: The Eršemma*, 18.
[8]Ibid., 21–22.
[9]Ibid., 7–17.

the tradition of the neo-Sumerian letter-prayers."[10] Alternatively, Jacob Klein contends that examples of individual complaint precede the Old Babylonian period. His example is the lament of supplication (*er-ša-ne-ša*) imbedded in the Sumerian composition, "Man and His God."[11]

C. Šuilla (Raising of the Hand)

There are both Sumerian and Akkadian types of the *Šuilla*. The Sumerian *šuillas*, of which some forty-seven examples are extant, are never called incantations and do not even contain lament proper sections. They are composed in Emesal and date to the Kassite period.

The Akkadian *Šuillas* are extant in some 150 examples (many duplicates are fragmentary) and are prayers of incantation. Seventy-four of these are published by E. Ebeling, *Die Akkadische Gebetsserie "Handerhebung"* (Berlin, 1953); the genre has been thoroughly analyzed by W. G. Kunstmann, *Die babylonische Gebetsbeschworung* (Leipzig, 1931). Further bibliography on this genre may be found in Dalglish, *Psalm Fifty-One*, 43, n. 115. For an example see ANET, 386. A thorough treatment of a single *šuilla* to Marduk may be found in T. Abusch, "The Form and Meaning of a Babylonian Prayer to Marduk" in *Studies in Literature from the Ancient Near East*, ed. J. Sasson (New Haven, 1984), 3–15.

D. Ki-ᵈUTU-kam (Incantation of Utu/Shamash)

Sumerian incantation directed to the rising sun that had the purpose of purifying from sin, uncleanness, or illness. Publication data for the five examples of this genre are listed in Dalglish, *Psalm Fifty-One*, 40, n. 105.

E. Dingir.ša.dib.ba (Incantation for Appeasing an Angry God)

These are very much like the *šuilla* and the *eršahunga* texts and may just be a particular category of other genres. Dalglish, *Psalm Fifty-One*, 52, identifies seven examples of the genre and gives publication data. W. G. Lambert identifies several more examples from late Assyrian and late Babylonian libraries and publishes text, translation, and notes in Lambert, "*Dingir.ša.dib.ba* Incantations," JNES 33 (1974): 267–322.

F. Šurpu ("Burning")[12]

This is a series of prayers and incantations that were accompanied by magical rites. It consists of seven tablets. The prayers are addressed primarily to Marduk. The burning is a rite of purification. The series is used when the individual does not know what offense he has committed.

There are several other groups of texts that contain prayers to the gods in connection with incantations or rituals, including the *namburbi* texts (rituals for averting portended evil) and the *bit rimki* series (rites of

---

[10] W. W. Hallo, "Individual Prayer in Sumerian: The Continuity of a Tradition," JAOS 88 (1968): 81. For consideration of that, see also M. Cohen, *Sumerian Hymnology: The Eršemma*, 35.

[11] J. Klein, "'Personal God' and Individual Prayer in Sumerian Religion," AfO Beiheft 19 (=RAI 28) (1982): 295–306.

[12] Erica Reiner, *Šurpu: A Collection of Sumerian and Akkadian Incantations*, AfO Beiheft 11 (1958).

purification by means of ritual bath), but these are further removed from psalmic literature.

DISCUSSION

I. Form

A. Israelite

Israelite psalms can be divided generally into three major categories of form.[13] The work of identifying the psalm types was pioneered by Hermann Gunkel[14] and popularized by Claus Westermann.[15] The three categories are delineated as follows:

1. Praise

This type of psalm (e.g., Pss. 9, 134–36) focuses on either the attributes of God (descriptive praise) or the past acts of God (declarative praise). Descriptive praise is most frequently congregational in scope, and the psalms that contain it are generally labeled "hymns." Declarative praise is generally focused on specific acts of God on behalf of an individual and emphasize thanksgiving.

2. Lament

The lament psalms (e.g., Pss. 3–7) typically have the purpose of issuing a complaint to God because of some critical situation currently being encountered. A petition generally results. In this category we also find examples that are individual as well as congregational prayers. Penitential psalms form a subcategory of this type.

3. Wisdom

The wisdom psalms (e.g., Ps., 37) have few formal characteristics to distinguish them but generally offer instruction and address certain standard themes. These will not be considered for comparison in this discussion because they represent the genre of wisdom literature that is considered later. Since the Egyptians and Babylonians do not have collections of their hymns the way the Israelites do, we do not have to deal with pieces of wisdom literature that they may have included with their hymns.

This summary is quite general and is only meant to highlight key distinctions between the major types. Claus Westermann has successfully identified particular structures that are typical of each of the types and subtypes and analyzed the style of each in detail.[16]

---

[13]Many subcategories are used, and rightfully so, but the most productive level for initial discussion is the most basic level of form distinction.

[14]Hermann Gunkel, *The Psalms: A Form Critical Introduction* (Philadelphia, 1967), an English translation from the original 1933 publication.

[15]Claus Westermann, *Praise of God in Psalms* (Atlanta, 1965).

[16]Ibid.

B. Mesopotamian

One of the immediate observations to be made concerning the Sumerian and Babylonian hymns to deity is that they are not easily recognized as falling into distinct categories.[17] The earliest hymnic literature does use technical terms to differentiate praise and lament;[18] but the lament psalms almost always begin with a praise section. So while there are Babylonian hymns that include only praise (e.g., the Hymn to Shamash), it is rare to include only lament.[19] In some the praise section is extensive, while in others it is very brief. The praise sections with which Babylonian hymns precede their lament are typically descriptive. All of this makes them distinct from the Old Testament laments that do not introduce laments with sections of praise.[20] Finally, Babylonian hymns also lack the call to praise that is characteristic of the Israelite hymns.[21]

Despite a more prevalent homogeneity, the consistent classification system used by the ancients themselves warns against treating all of the hymnic literature in the same category. Since the categories are already established in those texts, it is best to follow the genre differentiation found there.

When comparing the Israelite hymnic literature to the Sumerian and Akkadian literature, one must decide how to treat the massive amount of incantation literature from Mesopotamia. Several Akkadian and Sumerian laments are incantation genres (e.g., the Akkadian *šuilla* and the *dingir.ša.dib.ba*). Though the Israelite literature does not feature incantations, there are literary parallels observable between the incantation genres of Mesopotamia and the laments, particularly the penitential psalms, of Israel.[22] Therefore we cannot leave the incantation genres out of our discussion, for though the incantation section of the works has no parallel in Israel, the hymnic sections do.

Aside from the classification of the hymnic literature into various categories, it is also possible to conduct an investigation into the poetic structures used throughout the ancient Near East. However, though there have been studies of the poetic structure of various ancient Near Eastern hymns,[23] I am not aware of any scholarship comparing the poetic structures

---

[17]This is acknowledged even by G. Widengren in his study on the Akkadian Laments, *The Accadian and Hebrew Psalms of Lamentation as Religious Documents* (Uppsala, 1936), 41.

[18]In Sumerian, praise is *za.mi.* (= Akk. *tanittum*) and hymns are designated by a number of different categories. See S. N. Kramer, *The Sumerians* (Chicago, 1963), 207. Lament is designated by the categories *šu-illa, eršemma, eršahunga, ki-ᵈUTU-kam, šigu,* and *dingir ša-dibba*. See T. Jacobsen, *The Treasures of Darkness* (New Haven, 1976), 15; Widengren, *Accadian and Hebrew Psalms,* 16; and E. R. Dalglish, *Psalm Fifty-One in Light of Ancient Near Eastern Patternism* (Leiden, 1962).

[19]For exceptions see Dalglish, *Psalm Fifty-One* p. 260, n. 58. Also, for instance, none of the *dingir.ša.dib.ba* or *eršahunga* selections published by Lambert, JNES 33 (1974): 275ff., begin with praise.

[20]Claus Westermann, *Praise and Lament in the Psalms* (Atlanta, 1981), 37.

[21]Ibid.

[22]Dalglish, *Psalm Fifty-One.*

[23]E.g., A. Falkenstein, *Sumerische Götterlieder* (Heidelberg, 1959); and W. W. Hallo and A. J. A. Van Dijk, *The Exaltation of Inanna* (New Haven, 1968), 44–47.

of Israelite hymnic literature with Babylonian in any detail.[24] Therefore, fruitful as that study may be, it will not be treated here.

C. Egyptian

There are very few hymns and prayers from the Old Kingdom or Middle Kingdom periods. The hymns that are preserved from the late period largely date to the Greek or Roman periods, so they are outside the scope of this study. The material that we are comparing, then, is from the New Kingdom, mostly from the 18th and 19th dynasties.[25] The hymns from the 19th Dynasty exhibit a distinctly different flavor from their predecessors of the 18th Dynasty, so we will deal with them separately in this summary of form.

18th Dynasty. These hymns are characterized only by grandiose descriptive praise. There is no space given to lament or petition. They describe the appearance, the attributes, and the accomplishments of the deity, often at great length. The hymns abound in confidence and optimism. In form these are much more like the Babylonian hymns of praise that omit lament than they are like the Israelite hymns.

19th Dynasty. From the 19th Dynasty there are prayers extant that display a humility that never could have been imagined from the 18th-Dynasty texts. There are still hymns of praise of the same sort that were found in the 18th Dynasty, but the texts from Deir el-Medina and those prayers found on Papyrus Anastasi II in particular contain an element of petition that is not previously observable. While it is possible that this new perspective in the 19th Dynasty is merely a reflection of the coincidence of the extant literature, some have concluded that it is the expression of an actual shift in philosophy.

> To the scholars who first studied these hymns they seemed to offer so great a contrast to the usual complacency of Egyptian religiosity that they saw in them either the emergence of a new type of religious feeling in the Ramesside period ("personal piety," Breasted), or the particular religious attitude of poor people ("the religion of the poor," Gunn). Both terms describe valid insights, but they require some modification; for at the present time we see these hymns not as something quite new but rather as the end product of a long evolution.
>
> What comes to fruition in the New Kingdom is the self-awareness of the individual person, an awareness that makes itself felt on many levels. The proliferation of Book of the Dead copies is as much a part of it as are the personal prayers from Deir el-Medina. Moreover, many personal prayers are found among the short compositions written on papyrus

---

[24] Adele Berlin, *Enmerkar and Ensuḫkešdanna* (Philadelphia, 1979), 9–31, provides a chapter on poetic structure and technique of Sumerian poetry that does demonstrate that common Israelite features such as parallelism are not unique creations of the poets of Israel. For Ugaritic poetry, see S. Segert, "Parallelism in Ugaritic Poetry," in J. Sasson, ed., *Studies in Literature of the Ancient Near East* (New Haven, 1984), 295–306; and Simon B. Parker, *The Pre-biblical Narrative Tradition* (Atlanta: 1989).

[25] While the dates of the manuscripts that preserve these hymns date to the New Kingdom period, it is certainly possible, and in some cases, demonstrable that the original composition dates to an earlier period (e.g., The Hymn to Amon-Re. See the discussion in the introduction to that work in ANET, 365).

which were used as model texts in the training of scribes [Papyrus Anastasi II]. Yet another aspect of conscious individualism is found in the love poems preserved on papyri of the Ramesside age. Thus the personal piety of the prayers from Deir el-Medina stems from the evolved individualism of the New Kingdom.[26]

Even though this represents a definite shift from what is found in the 18th Dynasty, these 19th-Dynasty prayers are still not very much like what is found in the laments of Israel. Even when petition is present or when a crisis is alluded to, the prayers begin with praise.[27] There is nothing to compare to the lament proper that is found in the individual laments of the Old Testament. Perhaps more comparable would be the declarative praise psalms found in Israel that praise God for delivering from a past crisis.[28] Even in this situation, however, the similarity is one of content rather than of form.[29]

II. Content

A. Similarities

Before proceeding to this area, it is worth repeating a caution that has been voiced by Helmer Ringgren:

> The same expression, when used in different religious literatures, does not always mean the same thing. Thus two similar phrases do not necessarily convey identical ideas. It is sufficient to recall the differing connotations of such words as "peace," "freedom," and "democracy" in the Western world and in Communist countries. Attention must therefore be paid to the whole religious and cultural environment in which an expression or a religious practice occurs.[30]

The primary similarities in content will be evident in the attributes for which deity is praised. Even though the concept of deity on the larger scale was quite different (theoretically) in Israel than in Mesopotamia or Egypt, there is nevertheless substantial overlap of certain characteristics and activities of their respective gods. Despite the fact that the ancient Near Eastern polytheistic system by definition denied total sovereignty to any individual deity, the higher level deities were often praised as if they were totally sovereign.

Activities in the realm of nature are often described in similar fashion. Various deities in the ancient Near East are praised for the smooth operation of their respective areas of control. So Shamash, as the Babylonian sun god, is seen as a protector of humankind:

> You suspend from the heavens the circle of the lands.
> You care for all the peoples of the lands,
> And everything that Ea, king of Counsellors, had created is entrusted to you.[31]

---

[26]M. Lichtheim, AEL, 2:104.

[27]Westermann, *Praise and Lament*, 46.

[28]Ibid., 44.

[29]Dalglish, *Psalm Fifty-One*, 14–17, nevertheless feels that this development within Egyptian psalms is the result of Semitic influence.

[30]H. Ringgren, *The Faith of the Psalmists* (Philadelphia, 1963), 115–16.

[31]W. G. Lambert, BWL, 127:22–24.

In any of the ancient Near Eastern societies, the gods were considered responsible for maintaining justice and were concerned about justice in the human realm. This is frequently the subject of praise and the basis for petition. So again, Shamash (also called the god of justice because he was the sun god who shines on all) is praised for maintaining justice among the people.

> You give the unscrupulous judge experience of fetters.
> Him who accepts a present and yet lets justice miscarry you make bear
>   his punishment.
> As for him who declines a present, but nevertheless takes the part of the
>   weak,
> It is pleasing to Šamaš, and he will prolong his life.[32]

Laments, whether by Israelites or Babylonians, often emphasize similar problems: sickness, oppression by enemies, abandonment by deity, confessions of sinfulness, desertion by friends, and ordeals of various sorts.[33]

This has been only the briefest of samplings. Sigmund Mowinckel provides a suitable summary statement:

> If we consider the overwhelming number of similarities in composition, metaphors, phrases and expressions, style forms, many basic ideas, we can entertain not a shadow of doubt that there are many and deep historical connexions between the religious poetry of all these oriental countries. Here as in many other domains we may as justly speak of a common oriental psalmography, as of a Babylonian one, an Egyptian one, etc. Who has influenced whom, it is often impossible to decide in any particular case. What matters is that we have here a great community of culture, which also embraces the style forms, the modes of expression, and the cultic framework and situations to which this poetry belongs.[34]

In the end, then, the similarities of subject matter, while unquestionably present, demonstrate only that people everywhere tend to approach their gods with the same sorts of problems and to praise them for many of the same sorts of activities. This reflects the common nature of humanity, not literary dependence.[35]

---

[32]Lambert, BWL, 133:97–100.

[33]See the discussion of S. Mowinckel, *The Psalms in Israel's Worship* (Nashville, 1962), 182–83. W. W. Hallo identifies some of these same elements of petition in the Neo-Sumerian letter-prayers from the Ur III period in Hallo, "Individual Prayer in Sumerian," JAOS 88 (1968): 78. For a detailed comparison of many categories supported by parallel line citations from Babylonian and Israelite psalms, see Widengren, *Accadian and Hebrew Psalms*, 94ff. K. van der Toorn, *Sin and Sanction in Israel and Mesopotamia* (Assen, 1986), 62–67, suggests that miseries that are the subject of complaint in laments both in Israel and Mesopotamia fall into four major categories: physical suffering, social adversity, divine disapproval, and mental discomfort.

[34]S. Mowinckel, *Psalms*, 177–78. See similar statements by K. R. Veenhof in his review of Dalglish in *L'Orient Syrien* 9 (1964): 144–45.

[35]See the similar conclusions of G. R. Driver, "The Psalms in Light of Babylonian Research," in *The Psalmists*, ed. D. C. Simpson (Oxford, 1926), 172–75.

B. Differences

While there is an overall similarity in the broad strokes between the hymnic literature of the ancient Near East and Israel, there are numerous points of distinction that can be observed in the details. I have identified six areas that will highlight and delineate the differences.

1. Declarative praise

The category of declarative praise is unique to Israel. We do not find Babylonians or Egyptians praising their gods for specific, individual acts of deity done on behalf of the individual. This does not mean that no such praise ever took place or that they did not think of their gods as working in that way. Alternatively, it may be that praise of a declarative nature would have been more a part of worship on the personal level and therefore is not reflected in the official corporate praise preserved in the extant literature.

2. Type of descriptive praise

Though the hymnology of the ancient Near East typically exhibits the general category of descriptive praise as a common characteristic, there is some variation in the type of descriptive praise that occurs. Here we can only identify certain tendencies. It cannot be denied that numerous similarities also exist.

Concerning the Babylonian descriptive praise, one of the distinctive elements would be the tendency to use titles to briefly enumerate the various attributes of the deity.

> In the Babylonian Hymns the main part likewise consists of a reference to the titles of honour and the great deeds of the god, in the same short enumerative style in appositional attributes or relative clauses or a few co-ordinate principal propositions. The bare enumeration is much more prominent than in Israel; frequently the hymn is but an enumeration of the names and titles of the god and other glorifying predicates of a general character, like "strong hero," "mighty lord," "lord without equal" and the like. We also find rhetorical questions such as "who is like you" or a negative sentence "nobody is like you" and other ascriptions of praise.[36]

On the other hand, Claus Westermann identifies in the Egyptian hymns a descriptive praise that focuses on depicting praise in progress. Even when the worshiper is called to praise, he is often asked to contemplate the beauty and the physical aspects of deity.

> The elevated meaning and wide distribution of the depictions of praise is characteristic of the Egyptian psalms. In the Babylonian psalms it is also encountered, but not so often and not so widespread, and it is usually strictly an effect of the epiphany. The contrast to the Psalms of the O.T. is much sharper here. In them the depiction of praise is encountered only seldom, and only in late Psalms. While the vocabulary of praise in the Egyptian psalms is overwhelmingly indicative, and thus depicts, that of the O.T. in all its fullness is almost only imperative. In the Egyptian psalms the laud and praise of the gods is constantly described as occurring in a contemplative attitude. In the Psalms of the O.T. we have

---

[36]Mowinckel, *Psalms*, 179.

almost always calls to praise. There it is a fact, but here a demand; there it is something given to God, but here something owed to God; there God is the one who receives and has received praise, while in Israel God is the one whose deeds are an ever new call to praise.[37]

While it may be that these different tendencies reflect some of the differences with regard to concept of deity in each of the cultures, the material is neither extensive nor homogeneous enough to draw firm conclusions. At this juncture it will suffice to observe that definite differences do exist and reflect to some degree each individual culture's own signature on the genre.

3. Nature of petition

We now move from the category of praise to the category of lament. Here we want to examine the nature of petitions in the psalms of the various cultures. Within the Mesopotamian materials, the most data is provided by the *eršahunga* and the Akkadian *šuilla* genres. Both of these contain primarily petitions directed toward reconciliation with the deity and requests for general well-being.[38] In Mesopotamia, laments arise, as would be expected, when the individual feels that something is awry in his relationship with deity. More often than not, this need for reconciliation was felt when there was some sort of sickness or suffering on the part of the individual. Requests for forgiveness and mercy are therefore intertwined with requests for healing or relief from affliction.[39]

Concerning such petitions for divine mercy and forgiveness, E. R. Dalglish compares the statements in the *šuilla* laments with these in Psalm 51:3–4 and concludes:

> The proximity of the foregoing *schu'illa* parallels to their counterparts in the Hebrew psalms of lamentation in general and to Psalm li.3,4 in particular is so striking that any explanation that regards the relationship as purely accidental or such as exists commonly as the predicate of world literature must be considered totally inadequate. One senses a deeper community of relationship as we progress to the *schu'illa* type with the penitential psalms. Apparent differences do exist, however, and these may be readily seen in the polytheistic orientation, in the repetitious series occasionally present, and in the magical allusions of the Accadian *schu'illa*, all of which present glaring contrasts to the Hebrew monotheism, the facile movement, and the relative absence of magical allusions in the Psalter.[40]

In this type of petition then, there are differences in the larger orientation, but the actual content of the petitions shows great similarity.

Another major category of petition in Israel is imprecatory in nature—found in those frequently discussed psalms that request in graphic terms God's punishment of the psalmists' enemies. While, to be sure, there is no shortage of cursing oaths in Mesopotamian literature,[41] imprecations in the

---

[37]Westermann, *Praise of God in Psalms*, 50–51.
[38]Dalglish, *Psalm Fifty-One*, 29, 46–47.
[39]Cf., e.g., The Prayer to Ishtar, ANET, 384:42–50.
[40]Dalglish, *Psalm Fifty-One*, 102.
[41]Curses are especially evident in the *Maqlu* texts and in *kudurru* (boundary stone)

psalmic literature of Mesopotamia are vague and not frequent.[42] There are references to affliction at the hands of enemies and requests that enemies be subdued, trampled, or destroyed.[43] It is also not unusual to find a request that the evil schemes of an enemy fall on the enemy instead of the intended victim.[44] But these all fall short of the imprecations found in Israelite psalms such as 35 and 109.

It is intriguing that these imprecations, often considered the most pagan and unreformed characteristic of the Israelite psalms, are the primary element of petition without parallel in extrabiblical psalmic material. There is, however, I believe, a ready explanation for this that greatly helps us to comprehend the imprecatory psalms.

In the monotheism of Israel, the suffering of the righteous constituted a much more serious problem than it did in the polytheistic system of Mesopotamia.[45] If YHWH was just and the retribution principle was true (both firmly believed by the pious Israelite), then the punishment of the wicked in proportion to their wickedness was a theological necessity. While it is impossible to claim that there was no personal vindictiveness motivating the psalmist to his imprecations, at least we can see that there are other important motivations for these curses. God's reputation as a just God is at stake if personal disasters such as those listed in the imprecatory psalms do not overtake the enemies of the psalmist.

The absence of such requests in the Mesopotamian laments certainly reflects the greater complexity of polytheistic theology. It may also reflect less confidence on the part of Babylonians regarding what the gods were obliged to do to protect their reputations.

Related to the imprecatory petitions are the Israelite psalmist's requests for vindication. Though the Babylonian and Sumerian laments request relief from enemies, the petitions are not framed in terms of being vindicated. This may be a reflection of uncertainty with regard to what offenses may have

---

inscriptions. See also the imprecations against the deceased's murderer in a Sumerian elegy (Kramer, *The Sumerians*, 208–13).

[42]It is in cases such as this that Widengren's failure to distinguish between genres in his comparative work is most lamentable. He gives over a dozen pages worth of examples of Akkadian curse formulas but draws them all from genres not related to the biblical psalms (*Accadian and Hebrew Psalms*, 292–306), particularly the *Maqlu* texts. According to E. Reiner (*Surpu*, 1958), "Maqlu is intended to counteract the evil machinations of people through black magic. Wax or wooden figurines of the sorceror or—more often—the sorceress who bewitched the supplicant are melted or burnt in the fire, and the conjurations that compose Maqlu address, with very few exceptions, either these sorcerors—in effigy—or the fire-god who is to destroy them" (pp. 2–3). After his lengthy treatment, Widengren still must admit that the curse formulas found in the Babylonian psalms are much more restrained than those found in the biblical psalms (p. 307). Another treatment of parallels to the imprecatory psalms by F. X. Steinmetzer deals primarily with the curse formulas found in the boundary stones (*kudurrus*), "Babylonische Parallelen zu den Fluchpsalmen," *Biblische Zeitschrift* 10 (1912): 133–42.

[43]E.g., Prayer to Ishtar, ANET, 384:56–58; 385:97–98. Cf. Widengren, *Accadian and Hebrew Psalms*, 106–9; 268–70. See also, Mayer, *Untersuchungen*, 369.

[44]Mayer, *Untersuchungen*, 274.

[45]See the discussion of this in the chapter on wisdom literature.

brought about divine disfavor. The typical approach in the Mesopotamian literature is to attempt to appease the deity, not vindicate the worshiper.[46]

Another area of difference between Israelite and Mesopotamian petitions is in the Israelite concern to be taught God's ways and be led in truth.[47] Even though this is not a common Mesopotamian request,[48] it does have parallels in Egyptian concerns.[49]

Other Israelite petitions for items such as protection, health, long life, deliverance, etc., are very similar in content to Mesopotamian counterparts.

4. Basis for petition

An important area of difference between the biblical psalms and those found in Mesopotamia is found in those expressions of why the worshiper thinks that the deity should heed his petition. Similarly we can often see the means by which the worshiper seeks to persuade the deity to be attentive and act on his behalf.

In the Akkadian *šuillas* there is a transition section that lies between the lament and the petition. A standard part of this transitional formula is a reference to the sacrifice accompanying the prayer. Since the Mesopotamian laments generally sought to appease a supposedly angry deity, rather than to request intervention on behalf of an individual, an appeasing sacrifice would be presented to try to constrain the god to forego his anger.

The fact that a large percentage of Sumerian and Akkadian laments belong to incantation genres constitutes one of the major differences between the use of laments in Israel and Mesopotamia. The basis for the petition in Mesopotamian practice was the performance of the ritual that accompanied the lamentation. Potency was found in the incantation and the ritual surrounding it.

In cases where ritual incantation is not so closely associated, other means are used to try to convince or cajole the deity to act. Some of these are observed by W. W. Hallo in the Neo-Sumerian letter-prayers:

> In addition to the complaint and the petition, the body of the letter-prayer is usually reinforced by protestations of past merits and present deserts on the part of the suppliant. He argues his moral innocence or ignorance, his cultic piety, his unswerving loyalty to the god, or simply his high political or social status.[50]

Hallo also observes:

> To persuade the deity to act on his behalf, however, the penitent does not rely solely on his own past merits and present status. Rather, in time-honored fashion, he seeks to persuade the deity . . . to act, as it were,

---

[46]The rare request for the god to judge (*dânu*) the Mesopotamian worshiper does not necessarily carry the implication that the worshiper considers himself innocent and seeking vindication. There are just a few instances where the individual may be seeking vindication; see Mayer, *Untersuchungen*, 215.

[47]E.g., Psalms 25:4–6; 86:11; 143:8–10.

[48]Though there is admission that the ways of the god are a mystery or are unknown to the worshiper.

[49]Dalglish, *Psalm Fifty-One*, 132–33.

[50]Hallo, "Individual Prayer in Sumerian," 79.

"for the sake of thy name," as well as to sway him by promise of future benefits.[51]

Certainly there are some of these elements that are also present in the Israelite laments. In Psalm 26, for instance, the psalmist contends that he has walked in integrity and that he has trusted without wavering. He challenges God to examine him for any moral or ritual defect. This psalm also contains a vow of praise that is a characteristic of both Israelite and Mesopotamian laments. Among motivation clauses in the biblical psalms are also found reminders to YHWH of the wickedness of the psalmist's enemies and requests based solely on the *ḥesed* (covenant loyalty) of the Lord.

5. Role of incantation

Incantations are a part of the magical rituals used to ward off the demons believed to be the cause of all sorts of illness and calamity in the ancient Near East. Vulnerability to the power of demons occurred when, for some reason, the protection of deity was removed. So it is that prayers of complaint attempting to appease an angry deity become closely connected with incantations and accompanying rituals to neutralize the power of the demon.[52]

That incantation rituals accompanied Mesopotamian laments is no surprise and not a matter of controversy. Based on wording found in the Israelite psalms of lament that is similar to that found in Mesopotamia, however, some have come to the conclusion that the Israelite laments, likewise ought to be viewed "almost exclusively as cultic poetry, not as expressions of individual piety or as documents of the religious experience of particular writers."[53] It is suggested by scholars such as G. Fohrer that incantations played just as significant a role in Israelite society as they did in the surrounding societies:

> The people were probably more devoted to magic than is usually assumed. Men feared the perpetual threat of demons and the magical powers of their neighbors. They therefore performed magical actions to protect themselves and injure their foes. In many Psalms we can still catch echoes of the notion that the disaster afflicting man is due to a spell that must be broken by a counterspell.[54]

The question remains, however, whether such conclusions can legitimately be drawn from the evidence that exists. H. W. F. Saggs, for one, implies that our methods of comparative study need a little more sophistication before decisions can be arrived at.

> It is no difficult task . . . to find phraseology and conceptions in Old Testament psalms similar to those in Babylonian hymns; from parallels of this kind the conclusion is then very easily drawn that the Old Testament psalms were used in rituals which, although we have no independent

---

[51] Ibid.

[52] For a brief introduction to incantations, see H. Ringgren, *Religions of the Ancient Near East* (Philadelphia, 1973), 89–93; or in more detail, H. W. F. Saggs, *The Greatness That Was Babylon* (New York, 1962), 290–307.

[53] H. Ringgren, *Israelite Religion* (Philadelphia, 1966), 179.

[54] G. Fohrer, *History of Israelite Religion* (Nashville, 1972), 155–56.

evidence of their existence, must have been similar to those in which the (apparently) corresponding Babylonian hymns were employed. If, however, the Babylonian hymns concerned were Semitic compositions superimposed upon an ancient and specifically Sumerian ritual, the parallel in literary form between the Babylonian and Hebrew would not necessarily imply a parallel in usage.[55]

Furthermore, the theology presented in the Old Testament stands in clear opposition to the worldview from which incantations arise. Sigmund Mowinckel rightly notes in this regard:

> But on this point we also find an important difference between Babylonian and Israelite psalms, rising out of the strong emphasis on Yahweh as the only effective God. This had the result that in Israel even disasters and illness are much more firmly traced back to Yahweh himself: "shall there be evil in a city, and the Lord hath not done it?" says Amos (3:6). Good and evil both come from Yahweh; evil is the punishment resulting from his wrath. We can trace the influence of this on the psalms of lamentation. In Babylonia illness and disasters are generally attributed to demons, sorcerers, and witchcraft.[56]

While it is certainly probable that popular belief and practice during certain periods of Israelite history reflected Canaanite theology more than it reflected the official position represented in the Old Testament, this should not confuse the issue. The main point is that Israelite lament psalms show no indication of reflecting a close connection with incantation ritual, while many of the types of Mesopotamian laments are designed to operate in conjunction with incantations. This does not help us to determine whether the Israelite psalms reflect personal piety or corporate liturgy; in either case, they are clearly distinguished from the function of the literature evident in Mesopotamia.

Part of the ritual in Mesopotamia was the offering of a sacrifice to appease the angered deity. In contrast, the Israelite psalms mention on occasion a thank offering that is to be offered in gratitude for the Lord's intervention; however, they contain no indication that sacrifices of appeasement accompanied a ritual uttering of the lament.[57] Psalm 51 specifically rejects the sacrifice of appeasement as a ritual course of action, even though, in this case, the identity of the sin is known.[58] This clearly distinguishes the Israelite worldview, which placed an ethical value on sacrifice, from the pagan worldview, which invested sacrifice with magical power.[59]

---

[55]Saggs, *The Greatness That Was Babylon,* 290.

[56]Mowinckel, *Psalms,* 185.

[57]This difference is reiterated in K. R. Veenhof's review of Dalglish. It is a difference that Veenhof feels Dalglish has not sufficiently noted; see K. Veenhof, *L'Orient Syrien* 9 (164): 146.

[58]In the lament psalms both in Israel and Mesopotamia the sin is often unknown. The presence of offense is surmised in Mesopotamia because of the way the worshiper is being treated. In Israel it is often asserted that there is no offense, so the psalmist seeks vindication.

[59]There is certainly not a consensus on this matter. It is not uncommon to find statements like that of John Hayes: "We should therefore think of laments to God as prayers used in conjunction with sacrificial rituals during times of illness" (*Under-*

E. R. Dalglish notes the general lack of "ethicizing" of sacrifice outside of Israel, agreeing that the ritual in Mesopotamia was usually considered effective in and of itself.

> In only three [of the potential Mesopotamian examples identified by Dalglish] . . . is there a genuine ethicizing of sacrifice, wherein the morality of the worshipper is recognized as an indispensable factor in acceptable sacrifice. Generally speaking, the other citations presuppose sacramental effectiveness *ex opere operato*. Although there are not lacking ethical overtones in the *schu'illa* texts, the adjunct rituals clearly demonstrate their dominant cultic intent. There is no true parallel to Psalm li.18,19, where sacrifice is rejected as morally irrelevant. The Near Eastern psalms and rituals clearly endorse a sacramental (or magical) view of sacrifice, but occasionally, here and there, an ethicizing of the cult is inculcated and demanded.[60]

In general, then, the Mesopotamian laments were intended to be used in ritual settings with accompanying incantations and sacrifices of appeasement. This was the function that the laments performed in society. The function of the Israelite laments in society is much less clear, though since Hermann Gunkel, the *sitz im leben* has been identified broadly as the cult.[61] Recently E. Gerstenberger has offered an analysis that understands the laments as closely connected to healing rites within the clan rather than belonging to the cult.[62] It should be noted, however, that his affirmation of the role of ritual in Israelite practice appears largely built from the model of the Mesopotamian texts, rather than inductively arrived at through the biblical material. There is little to even suggest that incantations would have had a role in the use of the biblical laments. If such a role did exist, it was contrary to the legitimate worship of YHWH as depicted in the canonical Old Testament.

6. Confession of offense

Our concern in this section is to examine the nature of offense and confession evidenced in the laments of the Bible and the ancient Near East. There were several options available to the ancients as they dealt with any perceived offense. We can identify them by asking the following questions:

a. Does the individual consider himself innocent or guilty of offense?
b. Is the offense known to the individual, unknown, or unknowable?
c. What are the areas known to the individual where offense could have occurred?
d. Is the punishment considered well deserved or too harsh?
e. If the individual considers himself guilty, is the request for

---

standing the Psalms [Valley Forge, 1976], 65). It should be noted, however, the only psalm he presents in support of such a view is Ecclesiasticus 38:9–12.

[60] Dalglish, *Psalm Fifty-One*, 199–200.

[61] For a helpful summary of the development of this concept, see J. H. Eaton, "The Psalms in Israelite Worship," in *Tradition and Interpretation*, ed. G. W. Anderson (Oxford, 1979), 255ff.

[62] Erhard Gerstenberger, *Der bittende Mensch* (Neukirchen, 1980). See also his discussion in *Old Testament Form Criticism*, ed. John H. Hayes (San Antonio, 1974), 203.

termination of punishment predicated on the mercy of deity, ignorance in the commission of offense, or the universality of human sinfulness?

I will examine each of these questions in relation to the Israelite and Mesopotamian material. The Egyptian material does not provide sufficient data for such an analysis, for there is little inclination to seek divine mercy or forgiveness. In Egyptian hymns, individual faults are generally described as the result of ignorance rather than sin.[63]

a. Innocent or guilty.

Certainly in the Israelite material one can find situations where the psalmist considers himself guilty of sin (25:7; 32; 38:3–4; 40:12; 41:4; 51:2–3;), but oddly enough, these do not occur in the psalms of lament. They typically occur in either the subcategory of penitential psalms (e.g., 51) or in psalms where the Lord is being praised for having had mercy. Even the rare occurrence of confession of guilt in a psalm of lament is of a different sort. In 25:7 the psalmist implores the Lord not to remember the "sins of his youth." Here he is concerned that past sins might be the ones he is being punished for, which implies that he considers himself innocent of current offense. In the lament psalms the psalmist consistently requests deliverance from oppression, affliction, or illness but does not acknowledge sin as the cause of those problems. Rather he affirms his trust in God and seeks vindication and the exercise of the covenant loyalty (ḥesed) of the Lord.

The situation is quite different in Babylonian literature. Here the assumption of guilt is much more frequently encountered and would be considered the norm. Sigmund Mowinckel observes:

> The person praying confesses himself guilty both of the sins he knows and the sins he does not know, and humbles himself before the god. But it may also happen that he finds no sin in himself, and pleads his innocence and his righteousness. In Babylonia the motive of penitence is much more frequent than in Israel, where the suppliant as a rule pleads his innocence. But that is a consequence of the conception of sin being much more arbitrary in Babylonia and less ethically oriented. Behind it lies the idea that the deity is arbitrary: what is right in the eyes of man may be evil in the eyes of the god and vice versa: man can never know what may have outraged the god—or some god—and why he is so angry. That is why he confesses his sinfulness without any attempt at particularization.[64]

There is reason to disagree with some of Mowinckel's analysis, which will be discussed later. To summarize this section, we could conclude that protestations of innocence and acknowledgments of guilt are evident in both Israelite and Mesopotamian psalms. The difference is that the Israelite is more inclined to assume himself innocent, while the Mesopotamian is more likely to consider himself guilty. We must be cautious, however, about inferring too much from this observation. Since the lament literature from Mesopota-

---

[63]Dalglish, *Psalm Fifty-One*, 95; Henri Frankfort, *Ancient Egyptian Religion* (San Francisco, 1948), 79.

[64]Mowinckel, *Psalms*, 183.

mia is comprised of incantations used with appeasing sacrifices, we would expect admissions of guilt. The Israelite lament psalms give no indication that they should be identified with the liturgy that accompanied the *kipper* offerings of Israel such as the *ḥaṭṭat* or the *'asham*. Therefore, even though there may be some reason to compare the genres from a literary standpoint, the function of the Israelite lament psalms differs from the function of the Akkadian incantation laments.

b. Offense known, unknown, or unknowable.

In Israelite psalms there are cases where the psalmist affirms knowledge of his sin (32:5 and 51:3 are perhaps the only examples). There are also a few occasions that may imply that the sin is unknown. Psalm 39:8 has the very general statement, "Deliver me from all my transgressions" (NASB), while Psalm 69:5 affirms, "My wrongs are not hidden from Thee" (NASB). In these cases, since there is an acknowledgment of guilt yet no affirmation that the psalmist knows the nature of his sin, one might infer that the sin is assumed but not specifically known by the psalmist. Psalm 19:12 also assumes that unknown sins exist. This is, of course, only one option. There are no statements in the psalms that imply that the individual's sin is unknowable.

In Babylonian literature there are clear affirmations that known offenses exist. On the other hand, there is rarely expressed any confidence that the individual has knowledge of what act has caused the deity to take offense. G. Widengren explains this lack of confidence.

> [Man] is unable fully to comprehend God's nature, and thus cannot be fully cognizant of God's will and intentions. There are consequently occasions when, in spite of his good intentions, he sins against the will of God. His sins may not only be unknown to himself, but it is quite possible that they must always remain unknown to any and every man because of mankind's lack of insight into the nature of God. . . . Owing to his lack of insight, man consequently cannot fully know God's will. He is not completely ignorant of the divine will, for this has been revealed. God has issued certain commandments to man. If he breaks these, he knows full well his offenses. The tendency to mention the sins committed in quite general terms corresponds to this idea of unknown sins, in which the irrational aspect of God is predominant.[65]

Numerous examples could be given to demonstrate that the norm for the Babylonian was to be ignorant of sin.[66] Many of the cultic procedures were set up so that the nature of the sin could be identified. Even in cases where specific sins are acknowledged, it is generally a situation of trial-and-error guessing. This is evident in texts in which there is first confession of specific sin followed just four lines later by the admission, "My iniquities are many: I know not what I did."[67] W. G. Lambert, commenting on the *dingir.ša.dib.ba* texts gives the following analysis:

---

[65]Widengren, *Accadian and Hebrew Psalms*, 160–61.

[66]K. van der Toorn, *Sin and Sanction in Israel and Mesopotamia* (Assen, 1986), 94–97, gives a thorough discussion on this matter.

[67]W. G. Lambert, JNES 33 (1974): 24–29.

The point of these prayers in every case is derived from the misfortune or suffering of the speaker. It is presumed that this had occurred and that the personal god (sometimes coupled with the personal goddess) was angry. This anger, then, had to be appeased. The basis for the anger is variously explained. Occasionally the sins of parents or other relatives are suggested as the cause (I 115–18). More commonly the sufferer assumes that he himself must be at the root of the trouble. Sometimes he simply confesses his many sins in the hope that confession alone will appease the angry god, as in I 121 ff. especially. This confession often invokes the excuse that man is naturally sinful and so inevitably so. A different approach is offered in II 10 ff. and elsewhere, for here the sufferer denies any consciousness of sins, though granting that they must have happened. The argument is that human conduct is something natural and inevitable, so that mankind has no consciousness of doing wrong, and therefore should be exonerated. The incantation I 71 ff. is also based on this approach but takes it further by denying that certain specific sins have been committed, though the speaker had been treated as though they had. Presumably the sins specified are intended as examples only, so the implication is that sins to merit the suffering had not taken place.[68]

The laments in both Israel and Mesopotamia are responses to various afflictions. In general, both cultures assume that affliction is a deity's response to offense. In either culture, if the offense is obvious and known, that offense would naturally be acknowledged and appeasement sought. In Mesopotamia, when the offense is not obvious, it is presumed that unknown sin is the cause, and rituals are used to identify the sin and the offended deity and to appease the deity. In Israel, when the offense is not obvious, it is typical for the individual to claim innocence. Since most examples of lament in both cultures are dealing with situations in which the sin is not obvious, the typical contrast that exists between Israelite and Mesopotamian laments is:

Israel: plea for vindication based on claim of innocence.

Mesopotamia: plea for mercy based on claim of ignorance.

c. Areas of offense.

As already mentioned, there are instances both in Mesopotamian and Israelite psalms of lament when specific offenses are enumerated. It is not unusual to see the distinction drawn that offense in Mesopotamia was viewed in ritual terms while offense in Israel was viewed in moral/ethical terms.

> Both were conscious of their deep sins, for which cognate words (Assy. *ḫiṭu* and Heb. *ḥēṭĕ'*) were used, and were ready to confess them. But their conceptions of sin were totally different; the Babylonian sought only to learn what ritual he had violated or forgotten to perform, that he might put himself right in the eyes of his god; the Hebrew prayed to be washed thoroughly from moral sin, and to have a clean heart created within him. In this lies the difference between the Hebrew's cry . . . and the Babylonian's request.[69]

---

[68]Ibid., 270.

[69]G. R. Driver, "The Psalms in Light of Babylonian Research," in *The Psalmists*, ed. D. C. Simpson (Oxford, 1926), 136.

While this is generally true, there are exceptions that should be noted. In the *dingir.ša.dib.ba* texts published by Lambert there are certainly confessions made that have ethical aspects to them, though it may be that there are explanations for each that are more ritually oriented than would be evident on first reading.

> I frivolously took a solemn oath in your name,
> I profaned your decrees, I went too far[70]
> I promised and then reneged; I gave my word but then did not pay.
> I did wrong, I spoke improper things,
> I repeated [what should not be uttered], improper things were on my
>   lips.[71]
> I spoke lies, I pardoned my own sins,
> I spoke improper things, you know them all.
> I committed offence against the god who created me,
> I did an abomination, ever doing evil.
> I coveted your abundant property,
> I desired your precious silver.
> I raised my hand and desecrated what should not be so treated.
> In a state of impurity I entered the temple.[72]

Whatever category these confessions would belong to, a reading of the biblical psalms evidences a clear difference in the nature of offenses considered. The Israelite claims himself innocent of falsehood, bloodshed, deceit (5:6), and general injustice (7:3). He claims to walk in integrity, to do righteousness and speak truth in his heart (15:2). The psalmist does not follow the paths of the violent (17:4) but has kept the ways of the Lord (18:21). He does not deal treacherously (25:3; 28:3). The list could go on and on. Though not part of the Psalms, one would notice that even Job, a non-Israelite, in making his final defense of his innocence (Job 31), asserts his integrity in ethical rather than cultic terms. Likewise, outside the psalmic literature, the *Šurpu* incantations in Mesopotamia include a wide range of offense including both ritual and ethical areas.[73]

d. Punishment well deserved or too harsh.

Since the Israelite generally considers himself relatively innocent, the "punishment" (if it can be called that) is treated as being too harsh. Even when guilty there is some concern that God looks too closely at human behavior and that human beings can only stand so much scrutiny (Ps. 139; cf. Job 7:11ff.). Rarely does the psalmist acknowledge that the punishment is well deserved (but see 51:4).

In contrast, since the Mesopotamian generally considers himself guilty, it is not at all unusual for him to admit that he deserves the punishment that he receives. He only wishes that he could discover what he is punished for so that he could start working toward appeasing the angry deity.

---

[70]Lambert, JNES 33 (1974): 24–25.

[71]Ibid., 124–26.

[72]Ibid., 137–44.

[73]H. W. F. Saggs, *Encounter with the Divine in Mesopotamia and Israel* (London, 1978), 117.

e. Termination of punishment based on mercy, ignorance, or universality.

In the Israelite psalms two of these situations may be found. The plea for mercy comes when the sin is acknowledged (25:11, 18; 51:1). The universality of human sinfulness is noted in 143:2 and 130:3. With regard to ignorance, the Israelites again claim innocence if they are not aware of any sin. They do not ask the deity to relent and excuse them because they sinned unwittingly. In the Mesopotamian literature there is generally a combination of the three used in the approach to deity. Dalglish provides us a summary of the Mesopotamian approach to confession of sin in his discussion of several characteristics of the *eršahunga* literature:

1. Restraint in the mention of definite sins.
2. Deep consciousness of sin.
3. Admission that divine retribution is justly deserved.
4. Sin was committed unwittingly, therefore ignorance of precisely which sin he is being punished for.
5. Uncertainty concerning which god is offended.
6. All mankind is tainted with sin, so his case should not be treated as unique.[74]

C. Implications

1. Theology of prayer

What does prayer accomplish and how does it accomplish its objective? These are difficult questions to answer under any circumstances, and it must be admitted that at any given time individuals within a society will give widely divergent answers. In the literature of Mesopotamia, it is not difficult to find examples where prayer and its accompanying ritual were intended to magically coerce supernatural forces. As time passed this may have yielded to an inclination toward what we would recognize as manipulation.

> The literature of praise included hymns to gods, temples, or deified human rulers, as well as myths, epics, and disputations. It activated power already present or at least near at hand. The literature of lament, on the other hand, was directed to powers lost, difficult or impossible to regain: the dead young god of fertility in the nether world, the destroyed temple, the dead king or ordinary human. In the lament the vividness of recall and longing was an actual magical reconstitution, an attempt to draw back the lost god or temple by recreating in the mind the lost happy presence. Progressively, however, under the influence of sociomorphism, the aspect of magical forcing seems to have lessened, yielding in the classical periods to petition. In its new aspect praise literature was primarily aimed at blessing the ruling powers and thereby making them favorably inclined to human petition. The laments were aimed at influencing and swaying the divine heart by reminding the god of past happiness, rather than by magically recreating that past.[75]

Many scholars, following J. Begrich and S. Mowinckel, have found no motive but flattery for the praise section that precede the petitions in Babylonian psalms.

---

[74]Dalglish, *Psalm Fifty-One*, 26–27.
[75]Jacobsen, *Treasures of Darkness*, 15.

In Babylonian and partly also in Egyptian hymns the eulogy is generally an introduction to a prayer for something one wants. The naive idea of flattering the deity by means of ascriptions of honour shows through everywhere. That is why so many of these hymns are a dull and unending enumeration of honorific titles and phrases of homage, often in endless repetition.[76]

Others have felt that such a conclusion was too facile and revealed only the author's predisposition toward the Babylonian religion.

When Begrich characterises the honorific titles and the praise of deity in the Sumero-Accadian psalms as largely in the category of flattery to cajole the petitioned deity to be favorable, he manifests a somewhat unfair bias. Could not one with equal propriety say that the Hebrew psalms of lamentation begin quite abruptly and, at times, without due orientation to the augustness of Jahweh? It seems more reasonable to believe that the multiplied names of honor and the praise of the deity found usually at the beginning of the Sumero-Accadian psalms of lamentation manifest a true sincerity and express the trust of the suppliant in the ability of the invoked god to succour him in accordance with the divine powers delineated in the praise formula.

Moreover, it is interesting to note that in the later Hebrew prayers the honorific titles and praise formulae such as in Dan. ix. 4; Nehemiah ix. 5ff.; 2 Macc. i. 24–25; and especially the Prayer of Manasseh 1–7, conform more nearly to their counterpart in the Sumero-Accadian psalms of lamentation which marshal at their beginning the honorific titles of the god/s and his praise.[77]

In the end, neither literary analysis nor exegesis can provide answers to this question, for the attitude of the individual worshiper would make all the difference. While the Mesopotamian literature seems to lend itself more to mechanical ritual usage and can be seen being used in that way, one can certainly not rule out the possibility that it could be a vehicle for true worship. The formal preference for descriptive praise prior to petition hardly seems sufficient basis to condemn the material as theologically deficient or superficial.

It is rather the ritual orientation and the general ignorance of the nature of the assumed offense that place the Mesopotamian psalms at a different level of religious experience from that observable in the Israelite psalms. The Mesopotamians approach deity with the assumption that there is an angry god (what could it be this time?) who needs to somehow be appeased. Appeasement is the objective. Ritual and manipulation are the most evident means used to reach that objective.

In contrast, it is clear above all else that the Israelite believes he prays to a sovereign and just God. The Israelite seeks to remind God of his obligations. God is obliged only through his promises (the covenant) and through his attributes. So while the Mesopotamian uses prayer to oblige God to act through coercion or cajoling, the Israelite uses prayer to remind God of the ways that he has obliged himself. While this of necessity is a

---

[76]Mowinckel, *Psalms*, 180–81. Cf. also H. Gunkel and J. Begrich, *Einleitung in die Psalmen* (Göttingen, 1933), 183.

[77]Dalglish, *Psalm Fifty-One*, 260.

generalization, I believe that it captures a difference that exists in the objectives of prayer.

2. Personal prayer and personal piety

The question remains as to what the psalms of Mesopotamia or Israel can relay to us concerning personal piety. Do we have in this literature any personal prayers that convey a spiritual sensitivity of the individual, or are these simply corporate liturgies and magical rites? This is a matter of scholarly controversy that affects both Israelite and Mesopotamian literature. For A. L. Oppenheim, the preponderance of ritual suggests that there is little of personal piety to be inferred from the prayers found in Mesopotamian literature.

> Prayers in Mesopotamian religious practice are always linked to concomitant rituals. These rituals are carefully described in a section at the end of the prayer which addresses either the praying person or the officiating priest—rather, "technician"—in order to regulate his movements and gestures as well as the nature of the sacrifice and the time and place it should be undertaken. Ritual activities and accompanying prayers are of like importance and constitute the religious act; to interpret the prayers without regard to the rituals in order to obtain insight into the religious concepts they may reflect distorts the testimony. Just as the acts and offerings of the prayer are fixed, with little variation and few departures from the small number of existing patterns, so the wording of the prayer exhibits a limited number of invocations, demands and complaints, and expressions of thanksgiving.[78]

Despite Oppenheim's categorical denials, there are some who find evidence for personal, noncultic prayer in Mesopotamia.

> Indisputable evidence of a more intimate kind of personal approach to a deity is provided by certain personal names. Some personal names are recognized as deriving from a cry of the mother during childbirth, and such a name as Ahulap-Ishtar—"How long, O Ishtar"—indicates that a woman in the anguish of labour could spontaneously cry out for the compassion and help of a deity. Here plainly is an example of the emotion charged relationship between man and the divine which Oppenheim was unable to find.[79]

H. W. F. Saggs admits, however, that the evidence is slim. Generally the issue of personal piety in Mesopotamia has been approached through the concept of a personal god.[80] At this juncture we can only say that the psalmic literature cannot provide evidence either for or against the existence of personal piety in Mesopotamia.

In contrast, it is usually the psalms of Israel that have been considered the best source for observing the personal nature of the Israelite religion.[81] This century has seen opposition to that in the writings of H. Birkeland,

---

[78]A. L. Oppenheim, *Ancient Mesopotamia* (Chicago, 1977), 175.

[79]Cf. Saggs, *Encounter with the Divine*, 172–75.

[80]See especially Jacobsen, *Treasures of Darkness*, 147–64.

[81]This was affirmed even by Hermann Gunkel; see J. H. Eaton, "The Psalms and Israelite Worship," in *Tradition and Interpretation*, ed. G. W. Anderson (Oxford, 1979), 255.

S. Mowinckel, J. H. Eaton, and others who believe that "the 'I' of the laments is the king acting in behalf of or as representative of the people in crying out for help against national enemies."[82] H. J. Kraus rejects the idea that the Israelite psalms represent simply an impersonal ritual literature, preferring, with Gerhard von Rad, to view them as containing generalized formulae.

> Oddly enough, the present-day reader finds that this converse of the individual with God in these laments yet lacks that final personal note which he expects. No doubt he constantly comes up against formulations of incomparable personal fervour and earnestness: but form-criticism long ago showed that, as far as phraseology goes, even the wholly personal prayers of lamentation move with few exceptions in an obviously completely conventionalised body of formulae. In spite of the entirely personal form of style in these prayers, the exegete will hardly ever succeed in discerning anything like an individual or biographically contoured fate behind the details given by the suppliant.[83]

Regardless of one's own opinion about the original setting of the individual laments, what is clear is that the language of the psalms may be interpreted in a number of ways. Gerstenberger has identified the difficulty that exists in trying to verify real emotional involvement on the part of the author by linguistic or literary analysis.[84] He maintains that "in order to be able to distinguish personal style from general usage we need a far more thorough knowledge of Hebrew literature than we can ever hope to attain."[85] However convinced one might be, then, of the clarity of the text, it must be acknowledged that the language admits several possible interpretations. While my own opinion is that the Israelite psalms evidence a much deeper level of personal piety than that observable in the psalmic literature of Mesopotamia, others have come to opposing conclusions.

D. Conclusions

K. R. Veenhof summarizes the problem well as he concludes his review of Dalglish's comparative study between Psalm 51 and the Akkadian lament genres.

> Cétte etude montre qu'il faut encore beaucoup de travail préparatoire sur le terrain des genres littéraires accadiens, comme exégèse des prières et des lamentations, analyse des métaphores et des motifs, recherches sur la fonction liturgique des prières et des conjurations, et surtout de nouvelles

---

[82]This summary statement is by Patrick Miller, *Interpreting the Psalms* (Philadelphia, 1986), 8; Miller's treatment of the issue as a whole is woven throughout this book and represents something close to a consensus within critical scholarship. Miller's reference is to H. Birkeland, *The Evildoers in the Book of Psalms* (Oslo, 1955); S. Mowinckel, *The Psalms in Israel's Worship* (Nashville, 1962); J. H. Eaton, *Kingship and the Psalms* (London, 1976).

[83]G. von Rad, *Old Testament Theology* (New York, 1962), 398–99. See Kraus's discussion in *Theology of the Psalms* (Philadelphia, 1986), 138ff. All of these approaches are summarized well in Eaton's contribution in *Tradition and Interpretation*, 255–60.

[84]This in Gerstenberger's contribution to *The Hebrew Bible and Its Modern Interpreters*, ed. D. A. Knight and G. M. Tucker (Chicago, 1985), 421–22.

[85]Ibid., 421.

éditions et traductions de beaucoup de textes, avant qu'on puisse vraiment les comprendre et les comparer avec les psaumes bibliques.[86]

[This study again shows the need for much preparatory work in the area of Akkadian literary genres, such as exegesis of prayers and lamentations, analysis of metaphors and motifs, research on the liturgical function of prayers and incantations, and especially for new editions and translations of many of the texts before one could really be able to understand and compare them with the biblical psalms.]

The genre question is still somewhat unresolved. While I have identified numerous differences between Israelite psalms and Mesopotamian literature in the above treatment, such differences are expected between opposing thought systems. The similarities, however, suggest that we do have literature roughly comparable to the extent that it represents address to deity. As a result, our study should at least provide some insight into some of the theological concepts and ritual practices of their respective societies, even if it is insufficient for providing a framework analyzing the parallel literary forms.

It is therefore off the mark to identify the primary differences between Israelite and Mesopotamian hymnic literature in the formal area (e.g., that Mesopotamian laments always begin with praise). The formal elements lack significance where the presence of parallel genres has not been established. Of much greater significance for understanding the respective societies and religions are the differences in content. This would include, as discussed above, the use of declarative praise by Israel and the differing nature of descriptive praise. It would also include the Israelite pleas for vindication and claim of innocence as opposed to the Babylonian desire to appease and to claim ignorance. Certainly the function of the Babylonian laments in connection with magical incantations and appeasing ritual would also constitute a key difference.

EXCURSUS: LAMENTATIONS OVER FALL OF A CITY

Sumerian literary catalogues dating to the eighteenth or nineteenth centuries B.C. identify a category of literature lamenting the destruction of Sumerian city states including Eridu, Ur, Akkad, Lagash, and Nippur. Of these, there are five examples extant in more than just minor fragments:
- Lamentation over the destruction of Ur
- Lamentation over the destruction of Sumer and Ur[87]
- Nippur Lament
- Eridu Lament
- Uruk Lament[88]

---

[86]Veenhof, review of Dalglish, *L'Orient Syrien* 9 (1964): 147.

[87]This includes those formerly referred to as the Second Lamentation of Ur, the Ibbi-Sin Lamentation, and the Lamentation over the destruction of Sumer and Akkad, all of which have have been shown to join into a single composition.

[88]Kramer, "Sumerian Literature, A General Survey," in *The Bible and the Ancient Near East* (Winona Lake, Ind., 1979), 257 (originally published in 1961). See also Thomas McDaniel, "The Alleged Sumerian Influence Upon Lamentations," VT 18 (1968), 198. McDaniel gives a listing of publication data. The two lamentations over

These laments all date to the twentieth century B.C.[89]

Many interpreters of the biblical Lamentations do not hesitate to suggest that the biblical author has borrowed heavily from the Sumerian genre, though a defense of such a position has never been fully developed.[90] Recently, however, W. C. Gwaltney has undertaken to offer such a defense.[91] Gwaltney is responding to a 1968 article by Thomas McDaniel in which the relationship between Lamentations and Sumerian literature was largely discounted.[92] After analyzing fourteen points that suggested significant similarities between the biblical book and the Sumerian exemplars, McDaniel concluded,

> All of the motifs cited from Lamentations are either attested otherwise in biblical literature or have a prototype in the literary motifs current in Syria-Palestine. Second, certain dominant themes of the Sumerian lamentations find no parallel at all in this Hebrew lament. For example, one would expect to find the motif of the "evil storm" somewhere in the biblical lamentation if there were any real literary dependency.[93]

After discussion of the chronological place and geographical dispersion of the Sumerian laments, McDaniel further concluded,

> Thus without any evidence that the Sumerian literary works survived in Syria-Palestine, or that this particular lamentation genre was known in the West, it is highly improbable that one can construct a reasonable chain of literary transmission. Even if this lamentation genre had been known during the Amarna period, there is no reason to assume that the tradition was kept alive. Residents of Syria-Palestine were more apt to rejoice than lament over the destruction of Mesopotamian cities. If the Hebrew poets of the sixth century had knowledge of this Sumerian literary tradition, it is difficult to see how they could have learned of it in Palestine.
>
> Since the suggested parallel motifs discussed above have at best only general—and quite natural—similarities, and in light of the difficulties encountered in accounting for the transmission of this literary genre down to mid-sixth century Palestine, it seems best to abandon any claim of literary dependence or influence of the Sumerian lamentations on the biblical Lamentations. At most the indebtedness would be the *idea* of a lamentation over a beloved city. But since there is such a natural corollary to individual and collective lamentations or funeral laments, indebtedness may be properly discarded.[94]

---

the Destruction of Ur are translated in ANET, 455–63; 611–19. The most up-to-date publication data can be found in W. C. Gwaltney, "The Biblical Book of Lamentations in the Context of Near Eastern Lament Literature" in *Scripture in Context II*, ed. W. W. Hallo, J. C. Moyer, and L. G. Perdue (Winona Lake, Ind., 1983), 195.

[89]See the discussion by W. C. Gwaltney, "The Biblical Book," 195–96.

[90]Most seem to take the word of Kramer, who mentions in passing that there can be little doubt that a close connection exists. Kramer, "Sumerian Literature and the Bible," AnBib 12 (*Studia Biblical et Orientalia* 3, 1959), 201, n. 1; "Lamentation Over the Destruction of Nippur: A Preliminary Report," *Eretz Israel* 9 (1969): 90.

[91]Gwaltney, "The Biblical Book," 191–211.

[92]Thomas F. McDaniel, "The Alleged Sumerian Influence Upon Lamentations," VT 18 (1968): 198–209.

[93]Ibid., 207.

[94]Ibid., 209.

Gwaltney does not feel that McDaniel's arguments concerning time and geography can be maintained. Though the lamentations over the destruction of cities are limited to the twentieth century B.C. in Sumerian literature, Gwaltney suggests that the genre referred to as *balag* lamentations is a literary outgrowth of the city laments. The *balag* laments survive down into the Seleucid period (third–second centuries B.C.) and enjoy a much wider distribution.[95] So while Gwaltney admits to dissimilarities, he nevertheless concludes that the biblical authors were dependent upon the Mesopotamian literature on the basis of what he identifies as "strong analogies" between Mesopotamian lament typologies and the book of Lamentations.

> Because of the polytheistic theology underlying the Mesopotamian laments and their ritual observance, they could not be taken over without thorough modification in theology and language. Still the biblical book of Lamentations was more closely associated with the Near Eastern lament genre than simply borrowing the "idea" of a lament over the destruction of a city as McDaniel conceded.[96]

In insisting on only "strong analogies," Gwaltney appears to have yielded to McDaniel's data concerning the phrases that had previously been alleged to demonstrate dependence. We certainly expect to find typical lamenting terminology. Some of the similarities that most would agree on include:

1. A focus on the power of the deity who caused the destruction.
2. Deity is seen as the cause of the destruction.
3. The protector deity is viewed as abandoning the city.[97]
4. God is pictured as a mighty warrior.
5. The wrath of God is depicted.
6. The divine word brought about the destruction.
7. Deity is called upon to view the destruction.
8. Stylistically there is an interchange of speakers (first-, second-, and third-person usage).
9. Cries of woe throughout.

Key differences observable in the biblical book of Lamentations would include:

1. The righteousness of YHWH is seen as creating a necessity for the destruction, whereas in Mesopotamia the gods are simply carrying out what the fates decreed.
2. In the Bible, the destruction is the sign of abandonment by the destroying deity, YHWH. In Mesopotamia, the city's patron deity leaves while Enlil carries out the destruction.

---

[95] Gwaltney, "The Biblical Book," 197–200. See also Mark Cohen, *Balag-compositions: Sumerian Lamentation Liturgies of the Second and First Millennium* B.C. (Malibu, 1974). Balag-Laments are differentiated from the city laments primarily in that the former, though they are national in scope, do not deal with a specific historical event as the latter do (Cohen, *Balag-compositions*, 11). For more recent discussions on *Balag* compositions, see J. A. Black, "The Sumerian *Balag* Compositions," BO 44 (1987): 36–79. Includes lists of incipits and a catalogue of texts with museum numbers.

[96] Gwaltney, "The Biblical Book," 211.

[97] For a full discussion of the divine abandonment motif, see D. I. Block, *The Gods of the Nations* (Jackson, Miss., 1988), 125–61.

3. Instead of the goddess or consort viewing the destruction, Jerusalem is personified and views the destruction.
4. Key elements missing from the biblical material include:
   a. YHWH not aroused from sleep.
   b. No pacification of YHWH's liver.
   c. No call for the deity to return to his city.
   d. No plea for intercession to lesser gods.
   e. No extensive lists so characteristic of Mesopotamia.
   f. No known cultic use (but see Zech. 7).
5. Generally much more attention is paid to the human plight.[98]
6. Lamentations in the Bible serves as a major piece of theology that is intrinsically connected to the covenant.

Though we hear of human misdeeds calling forth divine punishment on a national scale and about national gods temporarily angry with their people and leaving them—we find little talk of nationwide repentance and self-abasement as a means of regaining divine favor. As far as we can see, it is only Israel that decisively extended the attitude of personal religion from the personal to the national realm.[99]

The theological significance of Lamentations surfaces as we come to understand the book as the Israelite response to the destruction of the city. In contrast, T. Jacobsen has contended that the Sumerian city laments were composed at the time of the reconstruction of the city, rather than as a response to its destruction.[100]

In conclusion, there are sufficient similarities between the Sumerian genre (and its relatives) and the biblical genre to prevent one from denying any possible relationship. Even on a superficial level, the biblical genre functions like the Sumerian. However, the theological function that is served by the book of Lamentations has no parallel in Mesopotamian literature.

CASES OF ALLEGED BORROWING

I. Psalm 104

A. Relationship to Egyptian Literature

Since early in the twentieth century, from James Breasted onward, it has been fashionable to identify Akhenaten's Hymn to the Aten as a source of Psalm 104 or at least to suggest a close relationship between the two.[101] The basis for this alleged relationship is found in a series of suggested parallels in wording between the hymn to the Aten and Psalm 104. The parallels are not so strong that someone would claim that the Hebrews simply translated portions of the hymn to the Aten. Rather, they entail

---

[98] These are gleaned from the list in Gwaltney, "The Biblical Book," 208.

[99] Jacobsen, *Treasures of Darkness*, 164.

[100] Jacobsen, AJSL 58 (1951), cited in W. W. Hallo, "The Cultic Setting of Sumerian Poetry," RAI 17 (1969): 119.

[101] For a good survey of some of the history of this position see Peter Craigie, "The Comparison of Hebrew Poetry: Psalm 104 in the Light of Egyptian and Ugaritic Poetry," *Semitics* 4 (1974): 10–21.

similar motifs, analogies, and subject matter—some of which are also present in other Egyptian sun hymns.

Certainly, however, there have been some, even since the time of Breasted, who have not been convinced of a close relationship. As early as 1926, G. R. Driver had concluded the relationship was not on the literary level.

> Even indeed when Psalms civ. and the Egyptian hymn of Amenophis IV handle the same themes–the creation of the world, the blessing of the water, night, day, the maintenance of life–they surely prove their independence by following a different order, although the theme appears to be one where the natural order would be adopted by both writers; nor can it be forgotten that such a subject is likely to have, and indeed has, occurred independently to poets all over the world.[102]

More recently, Miriam Lichtheim has also favored the view that the similarity is generic. "The resemblances are . . . more likely to be the result of the generic similarity between Egyptian hymns and biblical psalms. A specific literary interdependence is not probable."[103]
Peter Craigie offers the following resolution:

> There is a general similarity at many points between Psalm 104, the Aten Hymn, other Egyptian sun-hymns and the Shamash hymn. The similarity is not such as to suggest a direct relationship between any of the texts, but may be the result of certain themes common to all the texts. It is suggested that the principal common theme in the texts under consideration is not the sun but creation. Furthermore, the similarity in terms of creation is that of general cosmological thought, not that of specific cosmogonic thought. That is to say, it is not the means of creation that are similar, but the concentration on the parts of the created order and their relationship to the creator. Given this kind of interpretation, the fact that the closest similarity is to be found between Psalm 104 and the Aten hymn finds a different significance. Of all the Egyptian texts, the basic theological characteristics of the Aten hymn are the closest to those of the Israelite religion; I do not think that this suggests a relationship between Atenism and Israelite religion, but it does suggest a reason for the parallels. Given a common subject-matter, those traditions with more basic theological similarities have produced the most similar hymns.[104]

There are reasons why a direct relationship would be unlikely:
1. The pieces are separated in time by at least four hundred years.
2. The pieces are composed in languages that are not even from the same language group.
3. The Aten hymn was inscribed on the wall of a sealed tomb in the area of Amarna which was deserted soon after the death of Akhenaten. While there are reasonable possibilities for the circulation of the piece, evidence is lacking.[105]

---

[102]G. R. Driver, "The Psalms in the Light of Babylonian Research," in *The Psalmists*, ed. D. C. Simpson (Oxford, 1926), 122.

[103]M. Lichtheim, AEL, 2:100, n. 3.

[104]Craigie, *Semitics* 4 (1974): 14.

[105]Ibid., 12–13.

B. Relationship to Ugaritic Literature

Craigie has also discussed the parallels that exist between Psalm 104 and the Ugaritic Baal cycle, particularly the segment that concerns the building of a house for Baal.[106] Included in the common material would be the description of riding in the clouds, references to fire, the thundering voice of the deity, the deity bringing rain from his abode, mention of the cedars of Lebanon, and a possible parallel to Psalm 104:3, where the beams of the upper chambers are laid on the waters.[107]

The presence of such parallels is not taken by Craigie to indicate a direct relationship between the two texts. Rather, it is the parallel that leads him to a hypothesis concerning the original setting of the psalm. His suggestion is that the psalm was originally associated with the dedication of Solomon's temple. In this connection the similarities to the sun-hymns of Egypt are reasonable in the role of apologetic for the transcendence of YHWH. The temple symbolically would represent the cosmos. YHWH is worshiped as creator and king. Craigie summarizes his conclusions:

> While the psalm is thoroughly Hebrew in its present form, it employs language reminiscent of both Egyptian and Ugaritic poetry; the Near Eastern parallels, however, have been adapted to fit their new context, but serve both to give cosmic significance to the context of the psalm's initial use, and perhaps also they have apologetic value vis-a-vis other Near Eastern religions. Thus although the Hebrew temple had many similarities to other Near Eastern temples and had been constructed with the help of Phoenician craftsmen, it was nevertheless made to become a distinctively Hebrew temple. And the psalm, which also contains many similarities to other Near Eastern poetry, was nevertheless distinctively Hebrew in the substance of its praise of Yahweh.[108]

II. Psalm 29

As early as 1936, just a few years after the decipherment of the Ugaritic tablets, H. L. Ginsberg had proposed that Psalm 29 was in actuality a piece of Ugaritic poetry, and others have added to the case for and against this as years have gone by.[109] The basis for concluding that Psalm 29 is Canaanite includes issues of meter,[110] word pairs,[111] morphology,[112] type of parallel-

---

[106]Ibid.

[107]Ibid., 16–17.

[108]Ibid., 21.

[109]H. L. Ginsberg, *Kitbe Ugarit* (Jerusalem, 1936); T. H. Gaster, "Psalm 29," JQR 37 (1946–47): 55ff.; F. M. Cross, "Notes on a Canaanite Psalm in the Old Testament," BASOR 117 (1950): 19–21; F. C. Fensham, "Psalm 29 and Ugarit," *Studies on the Psalms* (Potchefstroom, 1963): 84–99; B. Margulis, "The Canaanite Origin of Psalm 29 Reconsidered," Biblica 51 (1970): 332–48; P. C. Craigie, "Parallel Word Pairs in Ugaritic Poetry: A Critical Evaluation of their Relevance for Psalm 29," UF 39 (1985): 332–38. Certainly the most thorough treatment is Carola Kloos, *Yhwh's Combat with the Sea* (Leiden, 1986), where the conclusion is reached that the psalm depicts YHWH as Baal.

[110]Cross, "Notes on a Canaanite Psalm," 19–21.

[111]Craigie, "Parallel Word Pairs in Ugaritic Poetry," 332–38.

[112]Fensham, "Psalm 29 and Ugarit," 85.

ism,[113] verb syntax,[114] and vocabulary.[115] In each of these areas there are questions concerning the degree to which the observed linguistic phenomenon can be identified strictly as Canaanite. Examination of other Hebrew literature is often able to turn up other examples of the so-called Canaanite characteristics of Psalm 29.[116] As a result, much of the alleged evidence becomes ambiguous at best.

> The evidence for the position that, but for the recensional substitution of Yahweh for Baal-Hadad, Ps. 29 is a veritable Canaanite hymn has never been decisive. The case has rested heavily on such prima facie data as the undeniable Baal-*like* (note emphasis!) imagery, canons and characteristics of Canaanite prosody, and especially the alleged N. Syrian setting provided by the references to Lebanon, Anti-Lebanon (Sirion/Hermon), and the assumed identification of *midbar Qadeš* with the Great Syrian Desert.

> That the author of Ps 29 has gone to school with the Canaanite bards— and this in a relatively early period . . .—is undeniable, and is further strengthened by the comparative material newly available. But the references to the Sinai/Red Sea area, to which *midbar Qadeš* may now be added in good conscience, leaves no room for doubting that the original subject of the poem was *Yahweh*, not Baal, and that its author was accordingly a Yahwist.[117]

As we have found in many of the genres that have been studied, the substantial evidence that would be necessary to build a case of literary dependence simply does not exist. Geographical, chronological, and genre difficulties do not make such dependence impossible, but they do confine the suggestion of dependence to the realm of hypothesis.[118] It is not necessarily that there is no clear proof of literary dependence; rather the evidence gathered to support literary dependence is not sufficient to establish the fact.

The similarities that exist between Psalm 29 and the poetry of Ugaritic mythology certainly help us to see and appreciate some of the common motifs and poetic techniques of the ancient Near East. To the extent that the use of well-known motifs and techniques may reflect a polemic effort on the part of the Hebrew poets, we may also appreciate the stark theological contrasts that existed between Israel and her neighbors.

---

[113]H. L. Ginsberg, "The Rebellion and Death of Ba'lu," Or 2 (1936): 180.

[114]Fensham, "Psalm 29 and Ugarit," 85–86.

[115]Ibid., 86–93.

[116]See e.g., Craigie, "Psalm XXIX in the Hebrew Poetic Tradition," 143–51.

[117]Margulis, "The Canaanite Origin of Psalm 29 Reconsidered," 346.

[118]See the discussion of P. C. Craigie, "The Poetry of Ugarit and Israel," TB 22 (1971): 15–19.

FOR FURTHER READING

Assmann, Jan. *Aegyptische Hymnen und Gebete*. Zurich, 1975.

Blackman, A. M. "The Psalms in the Light of Egyptian Research." In *The Psalmists*. Ed. D. C. Simpson. Oxford, 1926, 177–97.

Craigie, Peter. "The Poetry of Ugarit and Israel." TB 22 (1971): 3–31.

_____. "Psalm XXIX in the Hebrew Poetic Tradition." VT 22 (1972): 143–51.

_____. "The Comparison of Hebrew Poetry: Psalm 104 in the Light of Egyptian and Ugaritic Poetry." *Semitics* 4 (1974): 10–21.

_____. "Parallel Word Pairs in Ugaritic Poetry: a Critical Evaluation of Their Relevance for Psalm 29." UF 11 (1979): 135–40.

Cross, Frank M. "Notes on a Canaanite Psalm in the Old Testament." BASOR 117 (1950): 19–21.

Dalglish, E. R. *Psalm Fifty-One in the Light of Ancient Near Eastern Patternism*. Leiden, 1962.

Driver, G. R. "The Psalms in the Light of Babylonian Research." In *The Psalmists*. Ed. D. C. Simpson. Oxford, 1926, 109–73.

Farber, W. et. al. *Texte aus der Umwelt des Alten Testaments*. 2.2. Rituale und Beschworungen, 1987.

Green, Margaret Whitney. *Eridu in Sumerian Literature*. Unpublished dissertation, University of Chicago, 1975. Pages 277–325 contain technical discussion of the genre of "Lament Over Destroyed Cities." Pages 326–65 contain publication of text, transliteration, translation, and commentary of the Eridu laments.

Gwaltney, W. C. "The Biblical Book of Lamentations In the Context of Near Eastern Lament Literature." In *Scripture in Context II*. Ed. W. W. Hallo, J. C. Moyer, and L. G. Perdue. Winona Lake, 1983, 191–211.

Hallo, W. W. "Individual Prayer in Sumerian." JAOS 88 (1968): 71–89.

Kloos, Carola. *Yhwh's Combat with the Sea: A Canaanite Tradition in the Religion of Ancient Israel*. Leiden, 1986.

McDaniel, Thomas F. "The Alleged Sumerian Influence Upon Lamentations." VT 18 (1968): 198–209.

Mayer, Werner. *Untersuchungen zur Formensprache der babylonischen "Gebetsbeschworungen."* Rome, 1976.

Mowinckel, Sigmund. *The Psalms in Israel's Worship*. Nashville, 1962, 2:176–92, 266–67.

Ringgren, Helmer. *The Faith of the Psalmists*. Philadelphia, 1963.

Seux, Marie-Joseph. *Hymnes et Prières aux Dieux de Babylonie et d'Assyrie*. Paris, 1976. This contains French translations of nearly all of the hymnic material, including incantations.

van der Toorn, K. *Sin and Sanction in Israel and Mesopotamia*. Assen, 1986. Offers about a dozen *šigu* prayers in transliteration and translation.

Veenhof, K. R. Review of E. R. Dalglish. *Psalm Fifty-One in the Light of Ancient Near Eastern Patternism*. In *L'Orient Syrien* 9 (1964): 138–47.

Westermann, Claus. *Praise and Lament in the Psalms*. Atlanta, 1981.

Widengren, George. *The Accadian and Hebrew Songs of Lamentation as Religious Documents*. Uppsala, 1936.

Williams, R. J. "A People Come Out of Egypt." VT Supp. 28 (1974): 239–52.

Chapter 7

WISDOM LITERATURE

$\mathbf{T}$he Egyptian wisdom literature provides more parallels with Israelite literature than any other Egyptian genre. Since many different types of wisdom literature are represented, we will classify the material into categories and then deal with the major compositions.[1] Besides dealing with the issue of borrowing, we will discuss the nature of wisdom and what we can learn from the wisdom literature concerning how the ancients viewed their world—particularly in their view of retribution.

---

[1]A comprehensive listing of all of the extant pieces of instructional literature (widely defined) may be found in Kenneth Kitchen, "Proverbs and Wisdom Books of the Ancient Near East: The Factual History of a Literary Form," TB 28 (1977): 111–14. A comprehensive survey of all of the most recent finds and publications of Egyptian Wisdom Literature is given in R. J. Williams, "The Sages of Ancient Egypt in the Light of Recent Scholarship," JAOS 101 (1981): 2–4. For Sumerian and Akkadian wisdom literature, see E. I. Gordon, "A New Look at the Wisdom of Sumer and Akkad," BO 17 (1960): 122–52. He categorizes all of the literature into eleven genres: Proverbs, Fables and Parables, Folk-Tales, Miniature Essays, Riddles, *Edubba* Compositions, Wisdom Disputations, Satirical Dialogues, Practical Instructions, Precepts, and Righteous Sufferer Poems. Proverbs are further divided into Precepts, Maxims, Truisms, Adages, Paradoxes, Bywords, Taunts, Compliments, Wishes, and *Blason Populaire*. In each of his major categories, he gives detailed manuscript data and discusses the pieces that exist in that particular category.

MATERIALS

I. Mesopotamia

A. Categories of Wisdom Literature

1. Dialogues/monologues

2. Admonitions/instructions

3. Fables/contest literature

4. Sayings/proverbs

B. Major Compositions in the Dialogue/Monologue Category

1. Man and his God

Approximate Date of Composition
    About 2000 B.C., during the Ur III dynasty.[2]

Manuscript Data
Six Sumerian fragments from Nippur (four in the University Museum in Philadelphia, two in the Museum of the Ancient Orient in Istanbul) represent a copy from about 1700 B.C. CBS 13394, CBS 8321, CBS 15205, Ni 4137, Ni 4587.

Publication Data
Text, transliteration, translation, and commentary of five of the fragments are all published by S. N. Kramer in VT Supp. 3, *Wisdom in Israel and in the Ancient Near East*, ed. Martin Noth and D. Winton Thomas (Leiden, 1955), 170–82. Translation also in ANET, 589–91. The sixth fragment was published by E. I. Gordon, BO, 17:149ff.

Content
    This is a first-person complaint to God concerning suffering that was considered undeserved. Called by Kramer the "Sumerian Job," the writer details the nature of his suffering and claims to have been neglected by the deity. He requests a hearing and relief. In the end, the nature of his transgression is revealed to him so that it can be dealt with.

2. Ludlul Bel Nemeqi (I Will Praise the Lord of Wisdom)

Approximate Date of Composition
    Kassite Period (fourteenth–twelfth centuries B.C.).

Manuscript Data
Twenty-five manuscripts and fragments—most complete K3291 found in Ashurbanipal's library. Recent addition ND5485 (see Wiseman in next section) has virtually completed the recovery.

Publication Data
Given in detail in BWL, 27–28; ANET, 434–37, 596–601.

---

[2]Samuel Kramer, "Man and His God," VT Supp. 3, 170. An unrelated Old Babylonian text likewise called "Man and His God" has recently been republished by Lambert, "A Further Attempt at the Babylonian 'Man and His God'" in *Language, Literature and History*, ed. Francesca Rochberg-Halton (New Haven, 1987), 187–202. Though this text has some similarities to the righteous sufferer motif, Lambert considers it closer to a psalm of lament.

Additional Pieces: E. Leichty, "Literary Notes," in *Essays on the Ancient Near East* (Finkelstein festschrift), ed. M. deJong Ellis (Hamden, Conn., 1977), 145.
D. J. Wiseman, *Anatolian Studies* 30 (1980): 102–7.

Content
    This is a monologue of an individual (Šubši-mešrê-Šakkan) about how he suffered disaster of every sort and was eventually restored to his high status by Marduk. It has been called "the Babylonian Job." It is comprised of four tablets, most of which have been preserved. The outline could be presented as follows:

  I. Introduction (not preserved)

  II. Deserted by Gods

  III. Forsaken by Friends and Associates

  IV. Attempts to Appease Gods, Yet Suffering Increases

  V. Three Dreams Portend Deliverance

  VI. Restoration to Health and Prosperity

3. Babylonian Theodicy

Approximate Date of Composition
    1000 B.C.[3]

Manuscript Data
    About fifteen manuscripts and fragments. Earliest and most complete from Ashurbanipal's library (K8463, K8491, K3452, K9290, K9297—British Museum).

Publication Data
    Given in detail in BWL, 68–69; ANET, 438–40, 601–4.

Content
    An acrostic dialogue, twenty-seven stanzas of eleven lines each, between a sufferer and his friend. The friend seeks to defend current views of the universe and society against the sufferer's complaints. The acrostic spells out the sentence: "I Saggil-kinam-ubbib, the incantation priest, am adorant of the god and the king."[4]

4. Dialogue of pessimism

Approximate Date of Composition
    Uncertain. Lambert refers to it only as "comparatively late."[5] The earliest possible date is thought to be late in the second millennium.

Manuscript Data
    Six manuscripts and fragments, the most complete being VAT 9933.

---

[3] BWL, 63, 67.
[4] Ibid., 63.
[5] Ibid., 141.

Publication Data
  Given in detail in BWL, 142; ANET, 437–38.

Content
  Dialogue between a master and his slave in which the master states his intention to embark on various different enterprises. Each suggestion is greeted with the slave's affirmation of the positive things to be gained from the course of action. In each case, however, after the slave's affirmation, the master changes his mind and decides not to carry out his plans. The slave then replies with an affirmation of this decision as well, citing all the disadvantages the action would have incurred. The topics include going to the palace, eating, hunting, settling down with a family, leading a revolution, loving a woman, offering sacrifice, setting up a creditor business, and serving public charity. The piece ends as the master finally asks the slave about a suggested course of action. He responds, "To have my neck and your neck broken and to be thrown into the river is good."[6]

II. Egypt

A. Categories of Wisdom Literature

1. Instructions (generally father to son)

2. Admonitions (defending public good)

3. Dialogues (debate form)[7]

B. Major Compositions in the Instruction Category

1. Instruction of Ptahhotep

Approximate Date of Composition
  Old Kingdom, perhaps Sixth Dynasty, late third millennium.[8]

Manuscript Data
  Four copies, none prior to Middle Kingdom; most complete, *Papyrus Prisse*, pp. 183–94 (Bibliothique Nationale). Recently also three ostraca have been found, designated O.IFAO 1232–1234.

Publication Data
  Text:
    E. Devaud, *Les Maximes de Ptahhotep* (Fribourg, 1916).
    G. Jequier, *Le Papyrus Prisse et Ses Variantes* (Paris, 1911).
    Z. Zába, *Les Maximes de Ptahhotep* (Prague, 1956).
  Translation:
    AEL, 1:61–80.
    ANET, 412–14.
    For complete data see AEL, 1:62

Content
  Prologue, epilogue, and thirty-seven maxims given by Ptahhotep, who is presented as vizier of King Isesi (Fifth Dynasty). These are given to his son for instruction in human relations.

---

[6]Ibid., 149, lines 81–82.
[7]M. Lichtheim, AEL, 1:134.
[8]Ibid., 6–7.

2. Instruction of Merikare

Approximate Date of Composition
Nineth–Tenth Dynasties—late third millennium

Manuscript Data
Three papyrus fragments dating from the Eighteenth Dynasty (mid-second millennium).
Leningrad 1116 A (most complete)
Moscow 4658
Carlsberg 6

Publication Data
Text:
W. Golenischeff, *Les Papyrus Hieratiques de L'Ermitage Imperial à St. Petersbourg* (St. Petersburg, 1913), pls. 9–14.
W. Helck, *Die Lehre für König Merikare* (Wiesbaden, 1977).
A. Volten, "Zwei altägyptische politische Schriften," *Analecta Aegyptiaca* 4 (Copenhagen, 1945);
See AEL, 1:98, for further data.
Translation:
AEL, 1:99–109.
ANET, 414–18.

Content
Instruction given from elderly King Khety (Nebkaure?) to his son and successor, Merikare, primarily concerning aspects of kingship. It gives advice about rebellion, dealing with subjects, raising troops, and carrying out religious obligations. The conclusion is a hymn to the creator-god.

3. Instruction of Any

Approximate Date of Composition
Most likely a product of the Eighteenth Dynasty (mid-second millennium).

Manuscript Data
Cairo Museum Papyrus Boulaq 4 (copy from the Twenty-first or Twenty-second Dynasty) was long the only manuscript. Now added to that are Berlin Museum tablet 8934, three papyrus fragments, Papyrus Chester Beatty V in the British Museum, and four ostraca from Deir el-Medina. Several other papyri and ostraca have recently been found, see R. J. Williams, JAOS 101:2.

Publication Data
Text:
E. Suys, *La Sagesse d'Ani: Texte traduction et commentaire, Analecta Orientalia*, 2 (Rome, 1935).
Translation:
AEL, 2:135–46.
ANET, 420–21.
A. Volten, *Studien zum Weisheitsbuch des Anii* (Copenhagen, 1937–38).

Content
These are instructions from a lower official in the temple of Neferteri, the queen of Ahmose, given to his son, who, judging from the epilogue, is not inclined to follow the advice. Most of the advice concerns living a cautious, courteous, and conservative lifestyle.

4. Instruction of Amenemope

Approximate Date of Composition
Highly disputed in the past, most now agree, based on the new fragments that have been found, that the date of composition ought to be set ca. 1200 B.C. (Ramesside Era, R. J. Williams, Lichtheim, established as a result of Ruffle's unpublished thesis) rather than in the middle of the first millennium as previously thought (Wilson, Erman).

Manuscript Data
B. M. papyrus, 10474 complete. Five other fragments (see Williams, JAOS 101:2.; or Ruffle, TB 28:33–34).

Publication Data
E. W. Budge, *Facsimiles of Egyptian Hieratic Papyri in the British Museum* (London, 1923), 9–18, 41–51, pls. 1–14.
A. H. Gardiner, *Ancient Egyptian Onomastica*, I–III (1947).
I. Grumach, *Untersuchungen zur Lebenslehre des Amenemope*, Munchner Ägyptologische Studien, Heft 23 (Munich, 1972).
Translation:
AEL, 2:148–63.
ANET, 421–24.

Content
A prologue and thirty chapters giving "instructions for well-being" (1:2).

III. Aramaic

A. Major Composition

1. The Words of Ahiqar

Approximate Date of Composition
Sixth–fifth centuries B.C.

Manuscript Data
Elephantine Papyri (Imperial Aramaic).

Publication Data
James M. Lindenberger, *The Aramaic Proverbs of Ahiqar* (Baltimore, 1983).
A. Cowley, *Aramaic Papyri of the 5th Century B.C.* (Oxford, 1923), 204–48.
E. Sachau, *Aramäische Papyrus und Ostraka aus einer judischen Militar-Kolonie zu Elephantine* (Leipzig, 1911), pls. 40–50.
Translation:
ANET, 427–30.

Content
Eleven sheets, fourteen columns, including both the story and sayings of Ahiqar, who is presented as a high official in the Assyrian court during the reigns of Sennacherib and Esarhaddon. An adopted nephew accuses Ahiqar of treason, and the official is condemned to death. He is spared by an executioner who had been spared by him years before. The king is told that Ahiqar is dead while he remains in hiding. When a situation arises in which

the king wishes he had his advisor, Ahiqar resurfaces, saves the day, and is restored to favor.

DISCUSSION

Since our primary interest is to examine those categories of literature having similarities between Israelite and ancient Near Eastern pieces, our discussion here will be limited to the primary areas of correspondence. The instructional literature, primarily from Egypt, will be examined first as it correlates to the book of Proverbs. Second, the dialogue/monologue category, primarily seen in Mesopotamia, will be examined as it correlates to the books of Job and Ecclesiastes. Third, even though it is not technically part of the wisdom genre, I will include here a comparison of the Song of Solomon with the love poetry of the ancient Near East. In conclusion I will consider specifically the case of the alleged borrowing of sections of the Instruction of Amenemope in the book of Proverbs.

I. Instruction

In the materials section, I presented in detail three of the major pieces of Egyptian instruction literature. Here, for reference, is a more extensive listing (still not entirely comprehensive):

MAJOR EGYPTIAN INSTRUCTION LITERATURE

Old Kingdom: (2700–2200)	Instruction of Hardjedef Instruction for Kagemni Instruction of Ptahhotep
First Intermediate Period: (2200-2040)	Instruction for Merikare
Middle Kingdom: (2134–1786)	Instruction of Amenemhet Satire on the Trades Instruction of Sehetepibre Instruction of a Man for his Son
New Kingdom: (1550–1069)	Instruction of Any Instruction of Amenemope Instruction of Amennakhte
Demotic Period: (Late first millennium)	Instruction of Onkhsheshonqy Papyrus Insinger

Michael Fox has clearly stated the modern consensus of those who have studied the wisdom literature.

> The similarities in form and content between Israelite and Egyptian didactic wisdom literature have been so well established that there can be no doubt that Israelite wisdom is part of an international genre (which includes Mesopotamian wisdom) and cannot be properly studied in isolation.[9]

---

[9] Michael Fox, "Two Decades of Research in Egyptian Wisdom Literature," ZÄS 107 (1980): 120. This has been confirmed through many avenues of research. See N. Shupak, "The 'Sitz in Leben' of the Book of Proverbs in the Light of a Comparison of

These similarities, as well as the differences, will be the object of our study.

A. Form

The formal characteristics of instruction literature have been examined in detail by Kenneth Kitchen.[10] It is not my purpose here to do the form-critical analysis. What follows is Kitchen's summary of his findings.

(a) *Entire Compositions.* (i) EML [Egypt, Mesopotamia, Levant]. Two basic types: A, title and main text; B, title, prologue, main text; subtitles, etc., optional. (ii) Prov. Solomon II [25–29], Agur [30], Lemuel [31] are all of Type A; Solomon I (1–24, entire) is of Type B, as one unit.

(b) *Titles.* (i) EML. All regions and periods show one basic form: the author is named in the 3rd person, usually with titles/epithets; formulation may be substantival (Egypt; W. Semitic) or verbal (Mesopotamia). Short, medium, long titles occur in all periods and regions; no unilinear development. (ii) Prov. Therefore the modestly long title of Solomon I cannot be treated as needfully any later than the shorter titles of Solomon II, Agur or Lemuel. Elsewhere, far longer titles amply precede it in time.

(c) *Subtitles.* (i) EML. "Occasional" subtitles and titular interjections (all lengths) occur at all periods, but are optional. "Recurrent", numbered cross-headings crop up in early 2nd, late 2nd, and later 1st millennia B.C. (ii) Prov. Subtitles occur only in Solomon I, and only in simplest form, showing clearly their role as subheadings and not as main titles.

(d) *Direct Personal Address.* (I) To sons in titles. (i) EML. In Egypt overwhelmingly, and in Mesopotamia mainly, authors address a son (often named) in their title lines. (ii) Prov. The four works of Proverbs never do this. (II) To sons in the text. (i) EML. In Egypt, this never occurs; In Mesopotamia and the Levant, it is quite frequent. (ii) Prov. Solomon II, Agur and Lemuel stand closer to Egypt, but Solomon I closer to W. Asia. Solomon I also stands midway between Mesopotamian works of the 2nd millennium and Ahiqar of the mid-1st millennium. (III) Concerning calls to heed. (i) EML. Calls to pay heed are frequent in the prologues (esp. with "my son", W. Asia only), but not in main texts. "My son(s)" occurs in main texts in *non*-hearkening contexts only. (ii) Prov. Closely similar usage obtains.

(e) *Prologues.* (i) EML. All periods and areas. Short and medium prologues occur side-by-side in 3rd and 2nd millennia (no development), while long ones probably begin in late 2nd millennium (Aniy?) and characterize the 1st millennium—possible development here. On content, biographical material occurs early and late; during 2nd millennium, exhortation to pay heed is the main emphasis in prologues. (ii) Prov. Solomon I stands on its own, midway between 2nd and 1st millennia: by length, with 1st, on content (calls to heed), with 2nd—it is transitional.

Biblical and Egyptian Wisdom Literature" RB 94 (1987): 98–119. Of fourteen Hebrew terms and expressions that are characteristic of biblical wisdom literature and found only in the wisdom literature, Shupak finds that eight "show an affinity with forms of speech and expressions found in the Egyptian literature" (p. 101).

[10]Kitchen, "Proverbs and Wisdom Books," 69–114. See also his article, "The Basic Literary Forms and Formulations of Ancient Instructional Writings in Egypt and Western Asia," in *Studien zu altägyptischen Lebenslehren*, ed. E. Hornung and O. Keel (Freiburg/Göttingen, 1979), 235–82.

(f) *Main Texts*. (I) Overall. (i) EML. Undifferentiated texts are in a clear majority (two to one) over all types of segmented text; but all types occur in all periods and regions. (ii) Prov. Solomon II and Agur belong with the undifferentiated majority. Solomon I and Lemuel are 2/3 sectioned texts, former with, latter without subtitles, etc. (II) Detailed formulation. (i) EML. All lengths of basic unit—from 1-line to 7-line and more—occur in all periods and places, no development. The 2-line couplet dominates, in itself or as a basis of many 4-line and 6-line units. In later 1st millennium, Egypt sees decline in use of poetic parallelism, couplets, etc. (ii) Prov. In all four works, the couplet dominates, in line with earlier usage as opposed to later usage (such as Ahiqar's miniature paragraphing, or Egyptian reiteration).

(g) *Authors*. (i) EML. All works are assigned to human authors, almost always named (never to deities, etc.). Earliest Mesopotamian ones, shadowy; later, Ahiqar to be taken seriously. In Egypt, most attributions to the named authors should be treated seriously, i.e., at face value. (ii) Prov. Position here potentially is like Egypt—historical figures, to whom the attributions given in text are reasonable in themselves on literary grounds.[11]

Kitchen's study not only demonstrates the unity and the likely Solomonic date of the section he designates Solomon I (chs. 1–24); it also demonstrates that a great amount of formal similarity exists between the Instruction of the ancient Near East and the book of Proverbs. This is not a surprising conclusion given that Scripture does not hesitate to compare Solomon's wisdom to the wisdom of the "sons of the East" and the "wisdom of Egypt" (1 Kings 4:30). As each of the genres of literature have been studied, we have consistently found formal similarities between the Bible and the ancient Near East, and this is no exception.[12]

However, there is a prominent dissimilarity that ought to be mentioned at this point. Israelite wisdom literature (as well as psalmic literature) makes abundant use of an antithetical mode of expression, whether between the wise man and the fool or between the righteous and the wicked. K. van der Toorn posits this as a "distinctive feature of the sapiential literature of the Old Testament, largely absent from Mesopotamian as well as Ugaritic literature."[13]

---

[11] Kitchen, "Proverbs and Wisdom Books," 96–97, quoted by permission.

[12] For a detailed analysis of the structure and genre of the Ugaritic material relative to the Bible, see Duane Smith, "Wisdom Genres in RS 22.439" in *Ras Shamra Parallels* 2 (1975): 217–47. Kitchen has included this material in his summary, so I will not discuss it in further detail here.

[13] K. van der Toorn, *Sin and Sanction in Israel and Mesopotamia* (Assen, 1986), 101. Van der Toorn agrees that while it is distinctive in Israelite literature, it is not unique. Though it is largely absent from Mesopotamian wisdom, there are some reflections of it in Egyptian literature and Greek classical literature. For its absence in Ugaritic poetry, see S. Segert, "Parallelism in Ugaritic Poetry," in *Studies in Literature from the Ancient Near East*, ed. J. Sasson (New Haven, 1984), 300. Akkadian examples do occur, particularly in the Dialogue of Pessimism. For a complete treatment of antithetic parallelism see J. Krašovec, *Antithetic Structure in Biblical Hebrew Poetry* (VT Supp 35) (Leiden, 1984).

B. Content

One of the basic elements in comparing the content of the Instructional literature of Israel and Egypt is to identify as closely as possible a definition of wisdom in each culture. In Egypt, there is no term used that is parallel to the Hebrew term *ḥokmah* ("wisdom"). The term used to define the genre is *sboyet* ("instruction"). While this term does not place any emphasis on reverence for deity as *ḥokmah* does, it would be incorrect to say that it carried no religious implications. Religious and secular elements contribute to what can be considered the central focus of Egyptian wisdom—*ma'at*.

> The fundamental concept which underlies these Instructions is *ma'at*, which may be translated as justice, order, truth. No distinction exists between secular and religious truth for this literature. God's will can be read from the natural order, social relations and political events. Life in accordance with that principle of order paid off in tangible blessings, just as conduct at variance with *ma'at* brought adversity.[14]

Some of the characteristics of the wise individual are good manners, eloquent speech, discretion, and the ability to be silent and listen.

In general, what is most noticeable about the content is what I might call the orientation. The Egyptian literature, while certainly not ignoring religious aspects of life, has a social orientation. Proverbs, on the other hand, while not unconcerned about social graces, has an orientation toward deity, YHWH. This Israelite orientation is not unexpected and is merely an elaboration of the stated conviction of the author that "The fear of YHWH is the beginning of wisdom" (Prov. 9:10; see also 1:7). The statements concerning the gods in the Egyptian literature seem to be an outgrowth from one's social behavior or the result of that behavior. In the Israelite literature, the statements concerning one's social conduct appear to be built out of one's relationship to YHWH.[15]

Likewise, the existence of many similarities in content cannot be denied, but John Ruffle puts this in proper perspective.

> If we have to be cautious about differences of form and content we can be more affirmative about the similarities of thought and expression where the subject matter does coincide. . . . The folk wisdom enshrined in these collections of precepts is the distillation of the accumulated experience of related peoples with cognate languages living in similar circumstances and meeting comparable situations. It is not surprising that they have much in common; it would be noteworthy indeed if their reactions were particularly disparate. In fact, much of this wisdom relates to the community of experience shared not only by the inhabitants of the ancient Near East but by all men everywhere. It is, in short, good sense.[16]

---

[14]Crenshaw, *Old Testament Wisdom* (Atlanta, 1981), 214. For a discussion of *ma'at* and its related concepts, *ḥu* ("authority") and *sia* ("perception"), see L. Kalugila, *The Wise King* (Uppsala, 1980), 21–37.

[15]Cf. R. N. Whybray, *Wisdom in Proverbs* (Naperville, ILL., 1965), 53–71.

[16]John Ruffle, "The Teaching of Amenemope and Its Connection with the Book of Proverbs," TB 28 (1977): 37.

II. Dialogue

In this category, it is primarily the Mesopotamian literature that provides parallels to the material found in the Bible, particularly to the book of Job. As in Egypt, there is no term in Mesopotamia that corresponds to the Hebrew *ḥokmah* (wisdom). The most frequent Akkadian term, *nēmequ*, is more properly applied to the field of divination. So W. G. Lambert comments:

> "Wisdom" is strictly a misnomer as applied to Babylonian literature. As used for a literary genre the term belongs to Hebraic studies and is applied to Job, Proverbs and Ecclesiastes. Here "Wisdom" is a common topic and is extolled as the greatest virtue. While it embraces intellectual ability the emphasis is more on pious living: the wise man fears the Lord. This piety, however, is completely detached from law and ritual, which gives it a distinctive place in the Hebrew Bible. Babylonian has a term, "wisdom" (*nemequ*), and several adjectives for "wise" . . . but only rarely are they used with a moral content. Generally "wisdom" refers to skill in cult and magic lore, and the wise man is the initiate.[17]

However, despite the terminological differences, which are not without significance, there are several literary pieces from Mesopotamia that show certain affinities in form and content to the books of Job and Ecclesiastes from the class of Israelite wisdom literature. My major focus will be the book of Job, and I will bring Ecclesiastes into the discussion later where appropriate.

A. Form

The dialogue/monologue category features either discussion between protagonists (at times including deity) or a soliloquy. The book of Job includes dialogue between Job and his friends, soliloquies directed toward Deity, and dialogue with Deity. This combination, along with its inclusion of prologue and epilogue, sets it apart from the Mesopotamian examples of the dialogue category. The only similarity then is the dialogue structure and the nature of the topic under discussion.

B. Content

The problem under discussion that ties all of these works together is theodicy—the justice of God/the gods. At times, as in Job, this is framed in the context of a righteous sufferer, but that is not always the case. The third element in tension with the justice of God and human suffering is the retribution principle.[18] The retribution principle can be best expressed in the following series of conditional propositional statements:

PROPOSITION:	If a man is righteous, then he will prosper.
INVERSE:	If a man is not righteous (wicked), then he will not prosper (suffer).
CONVERSE:	If a man prospers, then he is righteous.

---

[17]BWL, 1. For a more detailed survey of Akkadian terminology, see Kalugila, *Wise King*, 38–39.

[18]See M. Tsevat, *The Meaning of the Book of Job and Other Biblical Studies* (New York, 1980), 36.

CONTRAPOSITIVE: If a man does not prosper (suffers), then he is not righteous (wicked).

C. The Retribution Principle

Belief in the retribution principle brings the justice of God and righteous suffering into tension. If a righteous person is suffering, and the retribution principle is accepted, then God must not be just. While these three elements are the ones creating the tension, W. von Soden has shown that other elements must also be present for the tension to be maintained or to be a problem.[19]

1. There must be a clear enough sense of right and wrong so that the sufferer could reasonably claim that his suffering was unmerited.

2. The individual must be considered sufficiently significant that personal suffering required justification.

3. There must be a minimalization of the competition within the godhead that might cause one deity to punish a human for his loyalty to another deity.

4. There must be a limited view of judgment to come in the afterlife so that divine justice is seen as necessary in this temporal context.

If any of these four elements is not present, the tension can be easily relieved, because any one of them has the power to negate or qualify the retribution principle. When the retribution principle is qualified, the question of theodicy may not be totally resolved, but in the end, God is "let off the hook" because the accusations of injustice cannot be made as stridently. It is the qualification of the retribution principle, either agnostically or philosophically by rationalization, that provides the solution in most of the ancient literature that deals with the subject.

First of all, however, I would like to examine von Soden's four points relevant to each of our subject civilizations, so that the extent of the problem for each civilization may be grasped.

Sense of Right and Wrong. In Mesopotamia, one could say that this element was present to some degree in the ritualistic requirements,[20] even though the concept of moral right and wrong in any absolute sense was absent. However, even in the performance of the ritual, there was not great confidence, and this proved to be one of the more vulnerable areas in the Mesopotamian discussions of theodicy.[21] The Mesopotamian sufferers could not always claim with confidence that their suffering was unmerited. Rather, they speak of all of their unsuccessful attempts to identify what they might have done wrong. The incantations reveal nothing and the gods do not communicate any wrongdoing.[22] The claim to "righteousness" then becomes a claim that the individual has done all that he knew to do and that the gods have not communicated any failings in his observance.

In Egypt, to do right was to conform to *ma'at*. While the knowledge of

---

[19]W. von Soden, "Das Fragen Nach der Gerichtigkeit Gottes im Alten Orient," MDOG 96 (1965): 41–59.

[20]*Ludlul bel Nemeqi,* II.12–32; *Babylonian Theodicy,* 45–55, 219–20.

[21]Cf. *Ludlul bel Nemeqi,* II.23–38; *Prayer to Every God.*

[22]*Ludlul bel Nemeqi,* I.52; II.4–9.

ma'at could never be exhausted and conformance could never be complete, this was their guide for right and wrong. In the Instruction of Merikare, there is frequent reference to right and wrong doing and admonitions to do justice and righteousness and *ma'at*.[23]

In Israel, righteousness was defined by adherence to the Torah of YHWH. In the book of Job, of course, the Torah is mentioned only in passing, nontechnical senses, for Job is not an Israelite. Nevertheless, he demonstrates an awareness of a revealed law of God which he firmly believes he has not violated. Chapter 31 contains Job's final speech in which he highlights the more significant areas of potential wrongdoing. It is immediately evident that none of these are in the area of the performance of the cult. They are all of a societal or ethical nature.

Significance of the Individual. Each of the three societies had this in sufficient amounts to sustain the retribution principle. However, the distance between national religion and personal religion in Mesopotamia does create a different level of concern for individual suffering.

> In Mesopotamia the suffering individual did not disturb the conscience of the community. Since national religion and personal religion followed two separate tracks, the contradictions experienced in the latter did not seriously affect the former. The individual distress of a righteous man could be discarded by those around him on the assumption that this was a private matter between a man and his god. The ideological structure fostered a religious individualism, counterpoised by a religious nationalism. This social fragmentation had its parallel in the fragmentation of experience. Many factors could be responsible for each individual misfortune, and human understanding fell irredeemably short of penetrating the designs of the gods. One could always be plagued on account of an unknown sin. With so many possibilities and such a multiplicity of reference points every misfortune, however grave, was always beset with ambiguity.[24]

Conflict of Divine Wills. While in Israel this is, of course, no difficulty, it proves to be the most complex of these four points in the polytheistic settings of Egypt and Mesopotamia. Regardless of the significance given to the conflict of divine wills concerning individual destinies in Egypt and Mesopotamia, neither wisdom literature considers it as a potential factor in the cases of unmerited suffering. Whether this was due to a virtual monotheism on the practical level of worship, as maintained by von Soden,[25] or whether other factors were involved is difficult to say. While the mythology of Mesopotamia is replete with divine conflict, it is rare to find a human individual who is a victim of that conflict, although it is more common when speaking of groups (i.e., cities, countries, tribes, etc.). Divine protection guarded against attacks from the demonic realm rather than from competing deities. Whatever the reasons, then, conflict of divine wills was not seen as providing an explanation for unmerited suffering.

Judgment in the Afterlife. This is the category that effectively removed the

---

[23]See Morenz, *Egyptian Religion*, 130–33.

[24]K. van der Toorn, *Sin and Sanction in Israel and Mesopotamia* (Assen, 1986), 114.

[25]W. von Soden refers to this as "monotheotetism" (46), agreeing with B. Landsberger.

issue of theodicy from Egyptian discussion. If there is a firm belief that all individuals will be judged after death, then it can be assumed that all scores will be settled there, and therefore, in the sphere of the living, it is never too late for God to vindicate himself. That does not mean that individuals do not question God's intentions, nor that incongruity in human destiny relative to conduct goes unnoticed. Despite these ongoing uncertainties, the theological concern for the justice of God is not an unresolved problem when the tension can be alleviated by reward and punishment being doled out in the next life. Such is the situation in Egypt.[26]

Concerning both Mesopotamia and Israel there is no doubt that there is belief in an afterlife; there is likewise no indication (through the first half of the first millennium B.C.), that the religious beliefs of those cultures included any kind of judgment in the afterlife. With regard to Babylonia and Assyria, Helmer Ringgren notes

> There are incantation texts which speak of a judgement in the under-world, and the meaning is clearly that a sick man is really in the land of the dead, and that his fate will be determined by a verdict, which by reason of the incantation is one of acquittal.[27]

These incantations would then result in the sick man's being restored to health and therefore do not suggest any theology of judgment in the afterlife that, based on an individual's conduct, would define his status in the afterlife. There are judges in the netherworld (the *Anunnaki*), but this is not their task.[28]

> Despite the mention in Babylonian literature of judges of the Underworld, and some allusions, in both Sumerian and Akkadian texts, to judgment after death, there is very little if any suggestion that a moral verdict was at any point passed on a man's course of life: references to "good" and "evil" in connection with judgment seem to relate to observances of ritual rather than moral requirements. The fate of the dead seems to have depended only upon their status in life, their manner of death, and the correctness or otherwise with which the heirs carried out the funeral ritual.[29]

Good and evil are not requited after death, and, therefore, if the justice of God is to be maintained, they must be requited in this life.

In preexilic Israel, beside the lack of any text that would confirm hope or belief in the righteous or wicked receiving the fruits of their deeds as a result of judgment after death, there are several passages that make it clear that the biblical authors expect that judgment needs to take place in the temporal sphere (Pss. 27:13; 119:84; Prov. 11:31). This is also supported by

---

[26]Cf. R. J. Williams, "Theodicy in the Ancient Near East," in *Theodicy in the Old Testament*, ed. J. Crenshaw (Philadelphia, 1983), 47–48.

[27]Helmer Ringgren, *Religions of the Ancient Near East* (Philadelphia, 1973), 123. Note that this has much similarity to the more highly developed concepts in Egypt. Cf. Morenz, *Egyptian Religion*, 130–31.

[28]One of their primary tasks was decreeing death or life: "He who fears the *Anunnaki* extends [his days]," BWL, 105:147.

[29]H. W. F. Saggs, "Some Ancient Semitic Concepts of the Afterlife," *Faith and Thought* 90 (1958): 168.

the expectation that the righteous and the wicked will each witness the day when things are set right (Pss. 23:5; 37:34; 59:10; 91:8).

Von Soden's four points explain the tensions surrounding theodicy that existed in Mesopotamia and Israel but did not exist in Egypt. In Egypt, the retribution principle could not provide a point from which deity could be accused of injustice, because justice could be carried out in the final judgment. In Mesopotamia and Israel, however, the retribution principle seems to have been at least generally acknowledged, thus creating an expectation concerning individual destinies that in turn cast God's justice in a very poor light.

If the retribution principle is maintained, the tension needs to be resolved (if it is resolved at all) in one of the other two areas that create the tension: the justice of God or the righteousness of the sufferer. The justice of God could provide resolution if it was decided that God was not just after all, or at least not in the same way that humans understand justice. Another possibility is that justice could be seen not as an inherent obligation of deity and the right of all human beings, but rather as a favor to be bestowed by the gods, as was the case in Egypt.[30] With regard to the righteousness of the sufferer, resolution could be reached if it were determined that no one was really righteous (so that no one could claim that suffering was unmerited), or that unconscious sins of omission were somehow a cause of the suffering. These are the options that existed for these ancient philosophers, and we will now examine which options were promoted in which situations.

1. Mesopotamian Solutions

a. Sumerian: Man and his God.

In this work the writer complains of what he perceives as unmerited suffering. He has had a turn of fortunes and does not know why. He views the suffering as having been sent by his god and begs for an opportunity to let his mourning be heard by his god. This is where the similarity ends. This sufferer does not question the justice of his god; he merely complains about his ignorance concerning what might have brought about the sudden change. The solution is reached when the individual is shown his sin. This is not a righteous sufferer, but an ignorant one. He accepts the word of the sages: "Never has a sinless child been born to its mother." Here, then, the problem is really not pursued to the degree that it is in Job. There is no unmerited suffering, for all are guilty of sin.

b. Ludlul Bel Nemeqi.

Here the question is plainly, "Why does Marduk allow his servant to suffer?" This "why" is not a shout of accusation but a groan of searching. The closest the speaker comes to questioning the justice of Marduk occurs when he briefly considers the possibility that the "justice" of the gods is not to be understood in the same way as humans think of justice[31] —that the gods are inscrutable. This is not pursued any further. Not unlike the Sumerian composition, in the end there are sins that are carried away,

---

[30]This is another reason why Egypt did not struggle with this problem as the rest of the ancient Near East did. Cf. Williams, "Theodicy," p. 47.

[31]Ludlul bel Nemeqi, II.34–38.

though we are not told what those sins were.[32] So again, the accusations against deity are not clear, and in the end it is determined that the suffering was not unmerited after all—rather, the sufferer was unaware of what could have caused his suffering.

c. Babylonian theodicy.

This work has an additional similarity to Job in that it takes the dialogue form. Just as Job's friends help him explore the possible resolution to the theological tension, accepting some elements as unquestionable and suggesting other areas where solution could be found, this work presents a dialogue in which the friend seeks to defend certain popular views while the sufferer points out their inadequacies. The justice of God is more directly attacked here, but the sufferer questions divine justice more because of the prosperity of the wicked than because of any feeling that his suffering is unmerited. While he does not feel that he should be classed with the wicked, neither has he departed from the standard Babylonian doctrine that humanity is intrinsically sinful. The friend's repeated affirmations of the retribution principle are met by the sufferer with claims that he is aware of no act of transgression on his part and that the system does not seem to work as the retribution principle would suggest. The friend not only affirms the retribution principle, but we also find him affirming such doctrines as the inscrutability of the gods (VIII, XXIV) and the eventual balancing of the scales of justice (XXII). In the end, however, the friend's logic fails and he is forced to admit that the system is not easily explained. W. G. Lambert summarizes the conclusion as follows:

> Both sufferer and friend began by assuming that the gods were responsible for maintaining justice among men. They end by admitting that these very gods made men prone to injustice. In a sense the real problem has been shelved. The view that the wicked ultimately receive their due was stated, and the practical experience that evil men prosper was set against it. Apparently the author could not resolve the conflict between the deep-seated conviction and actual life, so his way out was to assert a thesis which seemed to him logically irrefutable, and in some way related to the problem. Whatever evil men do, he argues, is done because the gods made them that way.[33]

The Mesopotamian solutions can be summarized with ease, for there was some unanimity among their thinkers. The retribution principle was largely affirmed, but when there was dissenting thought, it centered on the conviction that the righteous man did not exist. The justice of God was not often questioned. The only option seriously considered was that the gods were inscrutable. Generally, resolution to the problem reverted to the sufferer himself.

> Basic to Sumerian Theology was the notion that man's misfortunes result from sin which taints all. The problem of justice is not so acute in such a view, since any human suffering could be regarded as merited. When evil

---

[32] Ibid., III.57–60.
[33] BWL, 65.

befalls a man, there is no recourse but to admit one's guilt and praise one's god and plead for mercy.[34]

Whether the cause was unknown sin, intrinsic sin, or unknowable sin, the suffering could never be assumed to be unmerited, only the cause unknown. Despite the existence of the *Šurpu* incantation list that detailed sins of every sort so that they could be named and exorcised, there was no confidence that a comprehensive understanding of what constituted offense against the gods could be determined.

> Even if a man kept within the guidelines provided by *Šurpu*, he could still have no assurance of avoiding sin. The consequence of such views was clearly that everyone merited punishment. Therefore divine punishment of an apparently good man did not call in question the justice of the gods.[35]

This situation certainly created a sense of despair. The justice of the gods becomes inscrutable when one is not told or is not aware of the standards by which justice is administered. The result is an anonymous guilt with no real sense of wrongdoing.

> It is true that the Mesopotamians lived under a divine imperative and knew themselves to fall short of what was asked of them. But they did not have "The Law." The will of God had not been revealed to them once and for all, nor were they sustained by the consciousness of being a "chosen people." They were not singled out by divine love, and the divine wrath lacked the resentment caused by ingratitude. The Mesopotamians, while they knew themselves to be subject to the decrees of the gods, had no reason to believe that these decrees were necessarily just. Hence their penitential psalms abound in confessions of guilt but ignore the sense of sin; they are vibrant with despair but not with contrition—with regret but not with repentance. The Mesopotamian recognized guilt by its consequences: when he suffered, he assumed that he had transgressed a divine decree. He confessed, in such a case, to be guilty, although he declared: "I do not know the offense against the god, I do not know the transgression against the goddess."[36]

2. Solutions in Job

Like the Babylonian theodicy, the book of Job uses the dialogue form to explore the various potential solutions to the problem at hand. More than the ancient Near Eastern literature, this book goes out of its way to establish Job as a righteous sufferer. This is accomplished not primarily by Job's own claims but by the description of the narrator and the testimony of the deity. This sets the problem in much sharper relief than any other ancient work, for the uncertainty concerning ignorant sin is removed as an easy resolution.

---

[34]Marvin Pope, *Job* (Garden City, 1965), 60.

[35]H. W. F. Saggs, *Encounter with the Divine in Sumeria and Mesopotamia* (London, 1978), 117.

[36]H. Frankfort, *Kingship and the Gods* (Chicago, 1948), 278–79. M. Weinfeld, "Job and Its Mesopotamian Parallels," in *Text and Context*, ed. W. Claassen (Sheffield, 1988), has rightly shown that "the basic elements of the 'Job literature' in Mesopotamia have then more affinities with the individual complaint in the Psalmodic literature than with the Job story," 221–22.

The setting is also much more poignant in that this does not long remain a gentlemen's quarrel. Even midway through the book, positions have become entrenched and points are made with clear antagonism.

The solution offered in the cycles of speeches by Job's friends is basically common in the ancient Near East and one we have seen in Mesopotamian literature. The retribution principle is affirmed (Job 4:7; 8:4, 20; 36:6–7), and the justice of God is defended (8:3–6; 34:10–12). We find affirmation of the intrinsic sinfulness of man (4:17, if this is not Job speaking) and the inscrutability of deity (11:7). The major thrust of their argument is the logical extension from the inverse (if you are wicked you will suffer) to the contrapositive (if you suffer, you must be wicked). Job and his presumed righteousness is assailed at every point. While this solution seems obvious to Job's friends, Job is unwilling to grant that sin of any sort is the cause of his suffering.

Job's solutions are somewhat more difficult to determine, perhaps because of his own uncertainties. He certainly defends his own integrity (7:20; 9:20–21; and 31 present some of the clearer statements of this). Likewise, it seems that it never occurs to him to question the validity of the retribution principle except in chapter 21 where Job attempts to cast doubt on the converse in order to discredit, logically, the contrapositive. All that is left is to question the justice of God, and most of Job's groping lies in trying to figure out how the justice of God can be questioned without undoing all theology. In the end, it is the justice of God that Job sees as necessarily the weak link in the system (9:22–23; 12:13–25; 13:23–26; 30:19–23; 40:8). It is of interest to note that Job's integrity is maintained precisely in the sense that he was unwilling to follow "Mesopotamian advice"—that is, acknowledge sins though he believed himself innocent (27:3–6). "If Job had repented of some contrived sin to find relief, he would have compromised his own integrity and violated the purity of his faith in God by seeking to use God for personal gain."[37]

While this is the direction that Job's speeches take, it is not the solution finally offered by the book. The solution of the book is reached through the speeches of deity.[38] There, the justice of God is held as unquestionable (40:8–9). While the righteousness of Job is not addressed in the speech, the epilogue defends it as the prologue had done. When God speaks, the retribution principle is finally denied (38:12–15, 26–29; 40:10–12). All suffering is not caused by wickedness, and neither is all prosperity the result of righteous behavior. To use our terminology, this means that the converse and contrapositive cannot be logically deduced from the proposition and the inverse. It is not God who is inscrutable but a created system that is beyond simple understanding. The book does not give a reason for Job's suffering, for its solution is that one cannot determine the cause of suffering. God's speeches suggest that just as His wisdom is real, yet infinite and unfathomable; so is His justice real, infinite and unfathomable. The author cannot tell us what the cause of suffering is; he can only tell us what it is not. While this

---

[37] J. Hartley, *The Book of Job* (Grand Rapids, 1988), 517.

[38] Hartley (Ibid., 488, n. 5) has pointed out some formal similarity between the YHWH speeches and the Egyptian text, papyrus Anastasi I, which uses rhetorical questions composed from an encyclopedic list to refute a rival in a dispute.

is hardly a satisfying resolution from a human standpoint, it resists and rejects the easy agnosticism of Babylonian thinking. It seems designed to specifically do so, and in its depth it mocks the Babylonian philosophers. It is particularly the prose prologue and epilogue (along with the God speeches) that elevate Job into a unique category. The prologue does not question whether the retribution principle exists but rather takes it for granted because it is a "given" in human philosophy. Satan, however, implies that God may not be justified in rewarding the righteous as much as he does, for in so doing, disinterested righteousness is inhibited. This challenge is addressed when Job retains his integrity; and God defends himself, not Job, in his speeches. The epilogue also addresses this issue by reporting God's subsequent blessing of Job. God has no intention of changing his operation of the cosmos. The poetic sections of Job conclude that the retribution principle cannot provide a universal philosophy for explaining human destinites and fortunes. The prose sections defend God's decision to use the retribution principles to the extent that he does. The Mesopotamian literature never approximates Job in the way that it deals with the issue or in the sophistication of the resolution.

> The literature of the ancient Near East has not yielded another "Job." There is a considerable list of writings from this region, and a few from further afield, which remind one of Job in this way or that. But none comes close to Job when each work is examined as a whole. Each shows more differences than similarities, and not one can be considered seriously as a possible source or model for Job. The doleful Israelite in the grip of calamity did not have to read a Mesopotamian or an Egyptian work to raise the question of why God sends such experiences to men. The closest parallels are sufficiently explained by the common back-ground of Wisdom tradition, without implying direct borrowing. . . . Job stands far above its nearest competitors, in the coherence of its sustained treatment of the theme of human misery, in the scope of its many-sided examination of the problem, in the strength and clarity of its defiant moral monotheism, in the characterization of the protagonists, in the heights of its lyrical poetry, in its dramatic impact, and in the intellectual integrity with which it faces the "unintelligible burden" of human existence. In all this Job stands alone. Nothing we know before it provided a model, and nothing since, including its numerous imitations, has risen to the same heights. Comparison only serves to enhance the solitary greatness of the book of Job.[39]

3. Ecclesiastes.

The book of Ecclesiastes is a monologue in the dialogue/monologue category. It also has been related to a subcategory that has come to be identified as literature of pessimism. We have already discussed the dialogue of pessimism known from Babylonian literature; we could add to that the Egyptian works—The Harpers' Songs[40] and The Dispute Between a Man and His Ba[41] These all express a high degree of cynicism regarding the value of life, the coherence of the created system, and the role played by deity.

---

[39] F. I. Andersen, *Job* (Downers Grove, 1976), 31–32.
[40] AEL, 1:193; ANET, 467.
[41] AEL, 1:163; ANET, 405.

Again, however, we see a variety of suggested responses to this skepticism born of empirical philosophy. The issue here is not so much the *cause* of suffering (as in Job) as it is coping with suffering or perceived injustice or inequity in the world.

In The Dispute Between a Man and His Ba, the solution under consideration is death. Since a blissful afterlife was anticipated in Egyptian thinking, death would appear to be the perfect escape. In this work, however, death is presented by the man's *ba* (soul) as not being all that it is thought to be, so that the best option is to enjoy life as much as possible under the circumstances fate brings. This latter opinion is also that voiced in the Harpers' Song from the Tomb of King Intef.

> Hence rejoice in your heart!
> Forgetfulness profits you,
> Follow your heart as long as you live!
> Put myrrh on your head,
> Dress in fine linen,
> Anoint yourself with oils fit for a god.
> Heap up your joys,
> Let not your heart sink!
> Follow your heart and your happiness,
> Do your things on earth as your heart commands![42]

For Mesopotamians, death was not as easy a solution as it appeared to be for Egyptians, yet it still is presented as the most logical course to pursue, given the convoluted state of life. The Dialogue of Pessimism differs from the mortuary texts of Egypt that we just discussed. There is still considerable discussion as to whether this piece can be interpreted as serious philosophy or only satire.[43] Whatever the outcome of that discussion, if any solution is offered, it is that death is the only answer to the implied and stated problems.

In Ecclesiastes it is of great interest that, unlike what we found in the book of Job, the standard answers of the ancient Near East were not entirely rejected. While neither hedonism (2:10–11) nor death (4:2–3; 9:3–8 expresses the convictions that the dead may be happier than the living, but neither death nor life is worth seeking) are seen as acceptable solutions to the problem, the idea of enjoying life as it comes is the preacher's basic philosophy (2:24; 3:12–13, 22; 5:18–20; 8:15; 9:7–9). Of greater interest is that the solution apparently favored by the author of Ecclesiastes is in virtual harmony with the suggestions of the book of Job. The book of Job implied that nature cannot be expected to act in full accord with the attributes of its creator. In the same vein, Ecclesiastes suggests that it is not the retribution principle that is the main force to be reckoned with; rather, time and chance are more significant in the course that a life takes. As in the book of Job, the converse and contrapositive are tacitly rejected as not being legitimate deductions, while the basic proposition and inverse are left in place. Likewise, the author does not urge an agnostic attitude toward God but maintains that we must admit our inability to understand the complexity of the created system.

---

[42] AEL, 1:196–97.
[43] See the discussion in BWL, 139–41.

> When I applied my mind to know wisdom and to observe man's labor on earth—his eyes not sleeping day or night—then I saw all that God has done. No one can comprehend what goes on under the sun. Despite all his efforts to search it out, man cannot discover its meaning. Even if a wise man claims he knows, he cannot really comprehend it (8:16–17 NIV; cf. also 3:11; 11:5).

What this demonstrates is that while the philosophical answers to life's problems took a different path in Israel than they did in her neighbors, the practical results were not very much different. What difference did exist resurfaced in beliefs about God. For the author of Ecclesiastes, though ritualism and legalism are both discarded (5:1–7; 7:15–18), the fear of God is one tenet not singled out as meaningless; it is rather encouraged because of the meaninglessness of everything else (5:7). God is taken seriously. In contrast to this, the Egyptian works do not bring deity into the issue, while the Mesopotamian work includes religious practice (ritual) in its cynicism (53–61). The ancient Near Eastern advice then is "Enjoy life," while the Israelite advice is "Enjoy life and fear God." The pessimism literature in Israel was not blasphemous or set against religious practice. Religion had a very significant part to play, even if all of the pieces of how the world operates could not be put together.

EXCURSUS: LOVE POETRY

Though technically not in the category of wisdom literature, the Song of Songs is regularly classed with the wisdom books of the canon in the Bible. Because of this, it can be discussed here.

The primary parallels that have been drawn to the Song of Songs are found in The Sacred Marriage literature from Mesopotamia[44] and from a series of Egyptian Love Songs.[45]

The Egyptian Love Songs date to the New Kingdom Nineteenth and Twentieth Dynasties (1300–1150 B.C.).[46] The Sacred Marriage texts from Mesopotamia may be described as follows:

> Six songs, representing five versions of the love story of the Sumerian shepherd-king Dumuzi (= Tammuz) and his sister Inanna (Ishtar), have been discovered, as well as five texts that describe the marriage and wedding night. The texts, which date from the Neo-Sumerian period (ca. 2000 B.C.), describe in detail the lovers' desire for each other and praise

---

[44]Samuel Kramer, *The Sacred Marriage Rite* (Indiana University Press, 1969); ANET, 637–45.

[45]ANET, 467–69, translates just a few examples. For a comprehensive presentation see Michael Fox, *The Song of Songs and Ancient Egyptian Love Songs* (Madison, 1985). This excellent work includes not only translation and commentary of the Egyptian Love Songs and the Song of Songs but also a detailed comparative examination of all literary aspects of the literature from Egypt, Israel, and Mesopotamia. His analysis includes form criticism, literary criticism, and a comparison of the content of each culture. For a critical review, see C. J. Eyre, JSS 31 (1986): 252–53.

[46]Fifty-four Egyptian love songs have been identified, though Fox thinks that some of them should be seen as sections of larger unified works (*Song of Songs*, 194). The sources listed by Fox on p. 195 are: P. Harris 500, a Cairo vase, P. Turin 1966, P. Chester Beatly 1, and miscellaneous ostraca.

their sexual attractions. Although the meaning of these compositions and the details of the ceremonies are still obscure in many ways, it appears that the king (the incarnation of Dumuzi and the representative of the land) ritually married the goddess (represented by a priestess) and had intercourse with her. This ritual was intended to ensure abundance and fertility for the land.[47]

Samuel Kramer has gone to some length to attempt to establish a connection between the literature of the Sacred Marriage Rite and the Song of Songs. Similarities may be seen in certain stylistic features, uses of terminology, and occurrence of common motifs. Michael Fox acknowledges these areas of similarity but considers the differences far more significant and of such a nature as to entirely rule out the possibility that the Song of Songs was composed for or used in an Israelite rite of Sacred Marriage. Among these differences he lists:[48]

1. The absence of reference to myth or ritual in the Song, though common in the Sacred Marriage texts.
2. The Song does not seek to effect universal fertility.
3. The Song does not use resurrection as a figure of the rebirth of nature.
4. The Song does not treat the cycle of nature as requiring divine intervention but rather as a natural process.
5. The Song is not interested in woman's fertility, a primary motif of the Sacred Marriage texts. Beauty is stressed instead.
6. Sexuality in the Song is a matter of human desire, not of universal fertility.
7. The Song is characterized by a "gentle eroticism" rather than the explicit sexuality of the Mesopotamian literature.

Fox concludes by suggesting that

> Such resemblances as there are between the Song and the Sacred Marriage songs can be explained in two ways. First, since both speak of sexual love, a general human experience, some similarities in formulation and motif are inevitable. . . . Second, it is possible that miscellaneous expressions and motifs used in Mesopotamian literature—oral or written—found their way to Canaan, where they were taken into secular love poetry.[49]

The Egyptian material is considered as a more likely parallel to Song of Songs.[50] Again formal characteristics could be cited both for similarities and differences,[51] but the content, when compared, shows noticeable and

---

[47] Ibid., 240.

[48] This list is excerpted from Fox's presentation, Ibid., 242. Fox also cites a long list of thematic differences on p. 269.

[49] Ibid., 242.

[50] There are also some cultic love songs known from Ugarit, particularly text 603 published in *Ugaritica* 5, p. 556, (RS 24.245), which has been compared to Song of Songs 5:10–16. For discussion of this particular case, see Peter Craigie, "The Poetry of Ugarit and Israel," TB 22 (1971): 11–15; and Loren Fisher, *Ras Shamra Parallels*, 2:134–38. Fisher also includes discussion of other Ugaritic examples of love songs.

[51] Fox, *Song of Songs*, 253–66; G. Lloyd Carr, "The Love Poetry Genre in the Old

striking similarities. The primary area of similarity is that of literary types. The Egyptian Songs have been divided into three categories:

The Descriptive Song. Describing of lovers' characteristics, often in lengthy anatomical listings, though at times emphasizing qualities or more general appearance.

The Paraclausithyron. A song of the lover at his mistress's door.

The Day Song. A song of parting lovers at daybreak.

The descriptive song occurs in genres other than love songs. For instance, in Mesopotamia it is used in hymns describing the gods. The Hymn of Ninurta associates different parts of Ninurta's anatomy with other deities. These lists are also used in the incantation literature for healing. The descriptive songs are, however, primarily found within the genre of love songs and constitute one of the most common forms that the love songs take. Even though only two of the Egyptian love songs may be characterized totally as descriptive songs (31 and 54), description is a recurring theme in many of the other songs as well. The Song of Songs makes much more extensive use of this form. Fox identifies three different types of descriptive song (he calls them "Praise of the Beloved") that occur in the Song of Songs: (1) anatomical praise (the only sort that occurs in the Egyptian songs); (2) admiration song, referring to beauty as a whole; and (3) admiration dialogue, mutual praise, and admiration.[52]

The other literary categories also find similarities between the Egyptian literature and the Song of Songs, and Fox identifies several other motifs or themes that show similarity. Fox's conclusion of his study is that

> the similarities justify a hypothesis of at least indirect dependence, that is to say, the supposition that the Song is a late offshoot of an ancient and continuous literary tradition, one whose roots we find, in part at least, in the Egyptian love poetry.[53]

Similarities have also been seen in isolated works from Mesopotamia such as "The Message of Ludingirra to His Mother"[54] and a dialogue between a young man and woman about love.[55] It is difficult to deny that formal and content similarities do exist, as we have found in nearly every genre that we have studied.

It will be recalled that in every other genre the greatest differences have been seen when Israelite beliefs about YHWH and her monotheistic faith enter the picture. In a work like the Song of Songs, that never happens. Fox insists with good reason that this is secular literature (as opposed to the literature of the Sacred Marriage Rite that was used in cultic performances). Without the element of monotheism or the perception of deity being

---

Testament and the Ancient Near East: Another Look at Inspiration," JETS 25 (1982): 491–95.

[52]Fox, *Song of Songs*, 271.

[53]Ibid., xxiv.

[54]J. S. Cooper, "New Cuneiform Parallels to the Song of Songs," JBL 90 (1971): 157–62.

[55]This love poetry was published by Moshe Held, JCS 15 (1961): 1–26. Perhaps now attention ought also be given to J. A. Black's suggested genre of ballad. See his "Babylonian Ballads: A New Genre," in Sasson, *Studies in Literature*, 25–34.

involved, we would expect that Israelite literature would look like any other literature in the ancient Near East, and, indeed, that seems to be the case here.

This does not suggest that the Israelite literature is unoriginal or totally taken over from other cultures. There are after all literary differences that exist. For instance, the Egyptian material is composed almost entirely in the form of interior monologue in which the speaker soliloquizes. The Song of Songs, on the other hand, is comprised almost entirely of dialogue.[56] What it does indicate, however, is that there is very little in the conceptual realm that would differentiate the Song of Songs from other literature in its genre throughout the ancient Near East.[57]

CASES OF ALLEGED BORROWING

In this category I would like to present a fuller treatment of the parallels between Proverbs 22:17–24:22 and the Instruction of Amenemope. For the purposes of comparison I will reproduce here in parallel columns Proverbs 22:17–23:11, where most of the similarities occur (leaving out for the moment the four verses that are not paralleled in Amenemope, 22:19, 23, 26, 27) and the parallel sections from Amenemope rearranged into the order of Proverbs.

Proverbs	Amenemope
Pay attention and listen to the sayings of the wise; apply your heart to what I teach, for it is pleasing when you keep them in your heart and have all of them ready on your lips. Have I not written thirty sayings for you, sayings of counsel and knowledge, teaching you true and reliable words, so that you can give sound answers to him who sent you? Do not exploit the poor because they are poor and do not crush the needy in court. Do not make friends with a hot-tempered man, do not associate with one easily angered, or you may learn his ways and get yourself ensnared. Do you see a man skilled in his work? He will serve before kings; he will not serve before obscure men. When you sit to dine	Give your ears, listen to the things which are spoken; Give your mind to interpret them. It is profitable to put them in your heart; They will act as a mooring post to your tongue. See for yourself these thirty chapters. They are pleasant, they educate. To know how to rebut an accusation to the one who makes it. To return a charge to the one who made it. Guard yourself from robbing the poor, from being violent to the weak. Do not associate with the rash man nor approach him in conversation . . . when he makes a statement to snare you and you may be released by your answer. As for the scribe who is experienced in his office, He will find himself worthy of being a courtier. Do not eat food in the presence of a

---

[56]Fox, *Song of Songs*, 259, 263.

[57]This does pose a problem for some concerning the interpretation of the Song of Songs, its inspiration, and its presence in the canon of Scripture. It is outside of the purview of this book to deal with those matters here, but Fox deals with them extensively, and they are also reviewed in a preliminary way by G. L. Carr, JETS 25, who promises us a forthcoming fuller treatment of the whole genre.

with a ruler, note well what is before you, and put a knife to your throat if you are given to gluttony. Do not crave his delicacies, for that food is deceptive. Do not wear yourself out to get rich; have the wisdom to show restraint. Cast but a glance at riches, and they are gone, for they will surely sprout wings and fly off to the sky like an eagle. Do not eat the food of a stingy man, do not crave his delicacies; for he is the kind of man who is always thinking about the cost. "Eat and drink," he says to you, but his heart is not with you. You will vomit up the little you have eaten and will have wasted your compliments. Do not move an ancient boundary stone set up by your forefathers (2:28). Do not move an ancient boundary stone or encroach on the fields of the fatherless, for their Defender is strong; he will take up their case against you. (NIV)

---

diminish respect for you (yourself). Do not remove the boundary stone on the boundaries of the cultivated land nor throw down the boundary of the widow lest a dread thing carry you off.[58]

noble or cram your mouth in front of him. If you are satisfied pretend to chew. It is pleasant in your saliva. Look at the cup in front of you and let it serve your need. Do not strain to seek excess when your possessions are secure. If riches are brought to you by robbery, they will not stay the night in your possession. When the day dawns they are no longer in your house. Their place can be seen but they are no longer there. The earth opened its mouth to crush and swallow them and plunged them in Dust. They make themselves a great hole, as large as they are and sink themselves in the underworld. They make themselves wings like geese and fly to heaven. Do not covet the property of a poor man lest you hunger for his bread. As for the property of a poor man it obstructs the throat and wounds the gullet. It is like a false oath that makes something (evil) happen to him and his heart is deceitful within him. The large mouthful of bread, you have swallowed it and vomited it out (immediately) you are deprived of your advantage. Do not pour out your heart to everybody so that you

It should be understood, of course, that this comparison is very artificial, for it leaves out phrases that are not parallel and rearranges the text so th at the parallels are more evident. It is merely presented in this form for the convenience of the reader who may not be familiar with the texts.[59] There are parallels to Amenemope in other sections of Proverbs as well. It should also be mentioned that some of the parallels shared between Proverbs and Amenemope are also found in Egyptian wisdom literature that precedes Amenemope.

In considering the similarities, by far the most thorough study has been

---

[58]Translation used from Ruffle, "Teaching of Amenemope."

[59]The sections from Amenemope are the following in order: iii, 9–11, 16; xxvii, 7–8; i, 5–6; iv, 4–5; xi, 13–14, 17–18; xxvii, 16–17; xxiii, 13–18; ix, 14–x, 5; xiv, 5–10, 17–18; xxii, 11–12; vii, 12, 15; viii, 9–10.

done by Glendon Bryce.[60] After presenting the case that has been made in the past for Semitic dependence on the Egyptian and vice versa, he argues strongly for a multilevel dependence of Israel on Egyptian wisdom. According to Bryce, some Egyptian material has been adapted by Israel with very little alteration. A second level is composed of Egyptian material adapted by the Israelites and then assimilated by introducing significant theological modifications. Finally, Bryce feels that some of the Israelite composition has its origins in the Egyptian material but has been so thoroughly integrated that it is barely recognizable. In each category he gives examples and defends his conclusions. He fully acknowledges that each successive stage creates greater difficulties in recognizing and proving dependence, but he is convinced that the number of examples that can be delineated is itself sufficient to support the hypothesis. While it is not within our purpose here to analyze each of Bryce's alleged parallels, we will now identify some of the most evident similarities and differences between Amenemope and the particular section of Proverbs under consideration.

Similarities occur in almost any area that one looks, but as we have come to expect, there are differences in each of the areas as well. Structure, form, content, vocabulary, and imagery all contain some parallel features. We will look briefly at each.

I. Structure/Form

Both Amenemope and the "Words of the Wise" (I will use this title to refer to the section in Proverbs from 22:17–24:22) are introduced by an exhortation to hear and a statement about the profitability of paying attention to the instruction. This feature is not unique to these pieces but is a common structural element. More striking is the possible parallel in the division of the pieces into thirty units. Amenemope 27.7 identifies the instruction as comprised of thirty chapters. Prior to the discovery of Amenemope, Proverbs 22:20 was translated in many different ways because of one term that was used only here in Scripture. The term ($\check{s}l\check{s}wm$) was translated "previous, former" or "excellent, noble" but was considered quite obscure. When the connections with Amenemope were identified, it seemed to many scholars that the thirty chapters of Amenemope were paralleled in Proverbs by thirty sayings. "Thirty" was then suggested as the proper translation of the obscure term. The Hebrew text had preserved two variant readings (Kethib: shilshom, "previous"; and Qere: shalishim, "excellent"). The reading "thirty" would use the consonants of the Qere but would require an alternate pointing (sheloshim). This third reading is partially supported by the versions.[61]

Despite the fact that the reading "thirty" has been widely accepted (even in conservative circles, as the NIV rendering demonstrates), there are some persistent detractors, John Ruffle being one of them. There are three problems with the translation "thirty" that are brought out. First, it is difficult to identify thirty clear sections in the "Words of the Wise." Most who have done so have had to do some verse rearranging to make it at all

---

[60]Glendon Bryce, A Legacy of Wisdom (Cranbury, N.J., 1979).

[61]The Septuagint reading of "threefold" (trissos) is followed by the Syriac, Targum, and Vulgate. For discussion of the versions see Bryce, Legacy, 84–85.

convincing. Second, there is a grammatical difficulty in that the word *thirty* is awkward if not accompanied by the noun that it refers to.[62] Third, some have felt that the translation "previously" makes more sense because it can be seen as parallel to the "today" of verse 19. While these are acknowledged as problems, many feel that they are hardly insuperable, so the discussion goes on.[63] At present this could be considered a potential area of parallel, but the whole argument should not rest on this point.

Another matter of form concerns the length of the units that comprise the larger work. The "Words of the Wise" in the book of Proverbs generally has four- to six-line sections, while Amenemope is comprised of chapters that more resemble individual psalms in length. While some of the chapters may not be entirely homogeneous in subject matter, they average twelve to sixteen lines in length, thereby being substantially different from what is found in Proverbs.

II. Content

As is obvious from the parallel presentation above, the subject matter dealt with in the two works is very similar. We must exercise caution, however, if we seek to use this similarity to suggest that borrowing has taken place. That argument loses some force when it is observed that all of wisdom literature, whether ancient or modern, Near Eastern or Western, Israelite, Egyptian, or Mesopotamian shares this same basic subject matter. Nevertheless, it could be claimed that the closeness of the parallels between the "Words of the Wise" and Amenemope seems to suggest a little more than coincidental overlapping due to common human experience. Fox does not feel that Amenemope in particular has had any more influence than Egyptian wisdom literature in general.

> Some of the presumed parallels are strikingly close; others are too dissimilar to be parallels. In some cases the Hebrew proverbs parallel sayings in other Egyptian books no less closely than those in Amenemope. The relation between the similar proverbs may in fact be only that of the general debt of Israelite to Egyptian wisdom. It may be that transmission of motifs, ideas and various sayings common to several wisdom books can sufficiently explain the similarities.[64]

Ruffle is in general agreement:

> I would be prepared to accept that about half of the first part of the *Words of the Wise* can be considered to deal with the same subjects as *Amenemope* and that this could be an indication of some sort of relationship closer than coincidence.
>
> I cannot believe that there is sufficient correspondence to justify a claim that Proverbs was borrowed from *Amenemope* in the sense that that term is normally understood, and there is no justification in my view for any emendation of the Hebrew text to bring it in line with the Egyptian.[65]

---

[62]Thirty *what*? Notice that the NIV supplies "sayings" to alleviate the awkwardness.

[66]Bryce, *Legacy*, 82ff.

[64]Fox, "Two Decades of Research," 131.

[65]Ruffle, "Teaching of Amenemope," 65.

It must also be kept in mind that the comparison printed above is artificial. There is much material in each work not paralleled in the other, and the order is different. Some of the passages that have been patched together here are in strikingly different contexts in the text.

Before we leave the area of subject matter, we should take stock of the content that is religious in orientation, for that is where the largest content differences have had a tendency to appear in other genres. In the "Words of the Wise," YHWH is referred to by name five times (22:19, 23; 23:17; 24:18, 21) and by attribute in two other places (23:11; 24:12). Two of these comprise the theological *inclusio* (22:19 and 24:21), whereby the purpose and result are stated in terms of trusting and fearing YHWH. All of the other references speak only of the role of deity in maintaining the system (except 23:17, which contains the exhortation to fear YHWH).[66] Amenemope mentions "god" generically about a dozen times and two gods specifically.[67] Most of these speak of the attributes or role of deity in maintaining the system. There is one exhortation[68] and one statement about what God desires.[69] In this element then there is also similarity, with the exception of the importance placed on the fear of YHWH in the "Words of the Wise," an element not elaborated within the individual instructions. Both have a high ethical tone, so there is little to distinguish the two pieces from the perspective of their religious content.

III. Vocabulary/Imagery

One argument set forth by those suggesting Egyptian dependence mentions a number of phrases and terms in Amenemope which were not written in fluent Egyptian and seemed to have been influenced by Semitic usage.[70] However, since the appearance of a detailed rebuttal of that position by R. J. Williams, not many have chosen to retain that line of argumentation.[71]

Although the shared vocabulary and imagery cannot be used as the basis for proving dependence one way or the other, there is no question that there is much in common. Again, however, this has not been sufficient to make a strong case for direct borrowing.

In the end, it cannot be denied that Israelite wisdom shares much with the wisdom of Egypt, and there is no reason to doubt or deny that the

---

[66]For discussion of the slight textual problem here see William McKane, *Proverbs* (Philadelphia, 1970), 387.

[67]Aton mentioned in x.12; Thoth in xviii.2.

[68]"Thou shouldst make prayer to the Aton when he rises, Saying 'Give me prosperity and health.'"

[69]"God desires respect for the poor more than the honoring of the exalted," xxvi. 13–14.

[70]This was pursued in detail by both R. O. Kevin, *The Wisdom of Amen-em-apt and Its Possible Dependence upon the Hebrew Book of Proverbs* (Austria, 1931) and E. Drioton, "Sur la sagesse d'Amenemope" in *Mélanges bibliques rédiges en l'honneur de Andre Robert* (Paris, 1957) and is still presented as valid in articles such as that by A. K. Helmbold (see bibliography), and in Gleason Archer, *Survey of Old Testament Introduction* (Chicago, 1974).

[71]Ronald Williams, "The Alleged Semitic Original of the 'Wisdom of Amenemope,'" JEA 47 (1961): 100–106.

Israelites were aware of and influenced by Egyptian literature. Whatever the amount of this general indebtedness, it has not yet been demonstrated that any specific Israelite work was merely an adaptation of any specific Egyptian work. Amenemope is a fine example of Egyptian wisdom; we would therefore expect it to share certain commonalities with a work like the "Words of the Wise," a fine example of Israelite wisdom. Ruffle is of the opinion that the following scenario can explain the similarities:

> The sort of relationship that can be demonstrated can be adequately explained by the suggestion that this passage was contributed by an Egyptian scribe working at the court of Solomon based on his memories of a text that he had heard and, maybe, used in his scribal training. I believe this proposal fits all the requirements: a striking metaphor and the thirty chapter framework are remembered clearly, and the subject of much of the *Teaching* is recalled though the details and order are muddled. It seems to me that this conforms with the internal evidence of the Hebrew text and the specific note that this is part of a section based on the teaching of wise men, it conforms with our knowledge that Amenemope was used in Egyptian scribal schools, and it conforms with the known facts of the historical situation in which Proverbs was probably compiled.[72]

---

[72]Ruffle, "Teaching of Amenemope," 65–66.

FOR FURTHER READING

Albertson, R. G. "Job and Ancient Near Eastern Wisdom Literature." In *Scripture in Context II*. Ed. W. W. Hallo, J. C. Moyer, and L. G. Perdue. Winona Lake, Ind., 1983, 213–30.

Bryce, Glendon. *Legacy of Wisdom*. Cranbury, N.J., 1979.

Buccellati. Giorgio. "Wisdom and Not: The Case of Mesopotamia." JAOS 101 (1981): 35–47.

Carr, G. Lloyd. "The Love Poetry Genre in the Old Testament and the Ancient Near East: Another Look at Inspiration." JETS 25 (1982): 489–98.

Cooper, J. S. "New Cuneiform Parallels to the Song of Songs." JBL 90 (1971): 157–62.

Crenshaw. James L. *Old Testament Wisdom*. Atlanta, 1981, 212–35.

Fox, Michael. "Two Decades of Research in Egyptian Wisdom Literature." ZAS 107 (1980): 120–35.

————. *The Song of Songs and the Ancient Egyptian Love Songs*. Madison, 1985.

Gordon, Edmund I. "A New Look at the Wisdom of Sumer and Akkad." BO 17 (1960): 122–52.

Gray, John. "The Book of Job in the Context of Near Eastern Literature." ZAW 82 (1970): 251–69.

Helmbold, Andrew K. "The Relationship of Proverbs and Amenemope." In *The Law and the Prophets*. Ed. John Skilton. Philadelphia, 1974, 348–59.

Kidner, Derek. *The Wisdom of Proverbs, Job and Ecclesiastes*. Downers Grove, 1985, 125–41.

Kitchen, Kenneth. "Proverbs and Wisdom Books of the Ancient Near East: The Factual History of a Literary Form." TB 28 (1977): 69–114.

————. "The Basic Literary Forms and Formulations of Ancient Instructional Writings in Egypt and Western Asia." In *Studien zu altägyptischen Lebenslehren*. Ed. E. Hornung and O. Keel (*Orbis Biblicus et Orientalis 28*). Göttingen, 1979, 235–82.

Kramer, Samuel N. *The Sacred Marriage Rite*. Indiana University Press, 1969.

Lambert, W. G. *Babylonian Wisdom Literature*. Oxford, 1960.

McKane, William. *Proverbs*. Philadelphia, 1970, 51–208.

Noth, Martin; and D. Winton Thomas, eds. *Wisdom in Israel and in the Ancient Near East*. VT Supp. 3. Leiden, 1955.

Pope, Marvin. *Job*. Garden City, 1965, lvi–lxxi.

———. *Song of Songs*, 69–85. Garden City, 1977.

von Rad, Gerhard. "Job XXXVIII and Ancient Egyptian Wisdom." Reprinted in *The Problem of the Hexateuch and Other Essays*.London, 1984, 281–91.

Ruffle, John. "The Teaching of Amenemope and its Connection with the Book of Proverbs." TB 28 (1977): 29–68.

Saggs, H. W. F. *The Encounter With the Divine in Mesopotamia and Israel*. London, 1978, 114–24.

Sasson, Jack. "A Further Cuneiform Parallel to the Song of Songs." ZAW 85 (1973): 359–60.

Scott, R. B. Y. *The Way of Wisdom in the Old Testament*. New York, 1971, 23–47.

von Soden, W. "Das Fragen nach der Gerichtigkeit Gottes im Alten Orient." MDOG 96 (1965): 41–59. Note: An English summary of some of the significant suggestions of von Soden is found in Saggs, *Encounter*, 115–17.

Smith, Duane E. "Wisdom Genres in RS 22.439." In *Ras Shamra Parallels* 2 (1975): 217–47. In the same volume, John Khanjian gives a detailed list of parallel words and phrases from the Hebrew, Ugaritic, and Akkadian wisdom texts, 373–400.

Waltke, Bruce. "The Book of Proverbs and Ancient Wisdom Literature." *BibSac* 136 (1979): 221–38.

Weinfeld, Moshe. "Job and Its Mesopotamian Parallels." In *Text and Context*. Ed. W. Claassen. JSOT Supp. 48. Sheffield, 1988, 217–26.

Williams, Ronald J. "Theodicy in the Ancient Near East." Reprinted in *Theodicy in the Old Testament*. Ed. James Crenshaw. Philadelphia, 1983, 42–56

———. "Egypt and Israel." In *The Legacy of Egypt*. Ed. J. R. Harris. 2d ed. Oxford, 1971, 275–85.

———. "A People Come Out of Egypt." VT Supp. 28 (1974): 239–52.

———. "The Sages of Ancient Egypt in the Light of Recent Scholarship." JAOS 101 (1981): 1–19.

———. "Wisdom in the Ancient Near East." IDB Supplement. Nashville, 1976.

Wiseman, D. J. "Israel's Literary Neighbours in the 13th Century B.C." *Journal of Northwest Semitic Languages* 5 (1977): 77–91.

Chapter 8

PROPHETIC LITERATURE

$\mathbf{P}$rophecy is a form of divination that was practiced legally by the Israelites. In classical Greece and Rome, divination was divided into "technical divination," in which knowledge and training were used in the observation of omens and the like, and "natural divination," which required direct inspiration by the deity.[1] It was only in this second category that Israelite personnel were permitted to be involved. Prophecy belongs to this category and was practiced throughout the ancient world.

Texts that speak of prophets and present the messages of prophets are scattered throughout ancient Near Eastern literature. In Egypt there are also extant entire prophetic works written by the author-prophet. Our interest in this chapter will focus on the nature of the prophetic message and the function of the prophet in society.

MATERIALS

I. Mesopotamian

A. Mari

Approximate Date of Composition
    Eighteenth century B.C.

Manuscript Data
  Mari documents from Tell Hariri, excavated by André Parrot, 1933–38.

---

[1]D. Aune, *Prophecy in Early Christianity* (Grand Rapids, 1983), 23–24.

Publication Data

Many prophecy sections are published in Archives Royales de Mari (ARM) as follows:
ARM II: 90.

III: 40.

III: 78.

VI: 45.

X: 4, 6–10, 50, 5l, 53, 80, 8l, 94, 100, 117.

> (ARM X texts are transliterated and translated (and annotated) in W. Moran, *Biblica* 50:29–56.

XIII: 23, 112–14.

Other texts:

A.15 G. Dossin, "Une révélation du dieu Dagan à Terqa," RA 42 (1948): 125–34; ANET, 623a.

A.1121 G. Dossin, A. Lods, *Studies in Old Testament Prophecy* (Robinson festschrift), ed. H. H. Rowley (Edinburgh: T. & T. Clark, 1950), 103–7.

A.222 G. Dossin, "Le songe d'Ayala," RA 69 (1975): 28–30.

Translation:

> Most of the ARM X texts and several unpublished texts (A. 455,273l [sometimes incorrectly 2925], 4260) are translated by G. Dossin, "Sur le Prophétisme à Mari," *La Divination en Mesopotamie Ancienne, Rencontre Assyriologigue Internationale* 14 (1966): 78–86; ANET, 623–25, 629–32.

See also:

A. Malamat, "A Forerunner of Biblical Prophecy: The Mari Documents," in *Ancient Israelite Religion*, ed. P. D. Miller, P. D. Hanson, and S. D. McBride (Philadelphia, 1987), only A 222.

H. B. Huffmon, "Prophecy in the Mari Letters" (Garden City, 1970), 199–224; *Biblical Archaeologist Reader*, vol. 3, ed. E. Campbell and D. N. Freedman (Garden City, 1970).

A. Malamat, "Prophetic Revelations in New Documents from Mari and the Bible," VT Supp. 15 (1965): 207–27.

Content

B. Neo-Assyrian (Esarhaddon and Ashurbanipal)

Approximate Date of Composition
Seventh century B.C.

Publication Data

K883: S. A. Strong, "On Some Oracles to Esarhaddon and Asurbanipal," *Beitrage zur Assyriologie II* (1891–94), 633–35, 645.

> J. A. Craig, *Assyrian and Babylonian Religious Texts* (Leipzig, 1895, 1897), 1:26–27. ANET, 450–5l.

K6259: S. H. Langdon, *Tammuz and Ishtar* (Oxford, 1914), pl. 4.

K2401: Strong, 627–33, 637–43.

K4310: H. C. Rawlinson, *The Cuneiform Inscriptions of Western Asia*, 2d ed. (London, 1891): 4:6l.

> ANET, 605.

> E. J. Banks, "Eight Oracular Responses to Esarhaddon," AJSL 14 (1897–98): 267–77.

K12033: Unpublished.

K2647 + Rm 2.99: A. W. A. Leeper, CT 35:13–15.

> T. Bauer, *Das Inscriftwerk Assurbanipals* (1933), 2:79–81.

K6064: CT 35:26–27.

> Bauer, 2:82.

A few additional texts are noted as well as some transliteration and translation of sections of a number of these texts in Manfred Weippert, "Assyrische Prophetien der Zeit Asarhaddons und Assurbanipals," in *Assyrian Royal Inscriptions: New Horizons*, ed. F. M. Fales (Rome, 1981), 71–115.

Additional references to prophets and their messages occur in the letters and annals of Esarhaddon and Ashurbanipal.[2]

Content
These are collections of oracles coming mostly from the goddess Ishtar of Arbela. They proclaim victory and prosperity for the king.

II. Egyptian
It is debatable whether any Egyptian literature should be classed in the same genre with biblical prophecy. The works given this label do indeed include prediction and rebuke on society and the king, but a very key element is missing—none of them purport to bring a message from deity. We will, nevertheless, include them in the discussion here for the sake of contrast and because of certain similarities.

A. The Admonitions of Ipuwer
Approximate Date of Composition
Controversial. A. Gardiner: Twelfth Dynasty. M. Lichtheim: Late Middle Kingdom.

Manuscript Data
1, heavily damaged.
Papyrus Leiden 344 (Nineteenth Dynasty), seventeen pages.

Publication Data
Alan Gardiner, *The Admonitions of an Egyptian Sage* (Leipzig, 1909; reprint, Hildesheim, 1969).
Translation:
AEL, 1:149–63.
ANET, 441–44.

Content
Ipuwer, a wise man, addresses the king concerning the bad social and economic conditions in Egypt.

B. The Prophecies of Neferti
Approximate Date of Composition
Reign of Amenemhet I, Twelfth Dynasty (1991–1962 B.C.).

Manuscript Data
Papyrus Leningrad 1116B (Eighteenth Dynasty).

Publication Data
W. Helck, *Die Prophezeiung des Nfr tj* (Wiesbaden, 1970).
W. Golenischeff, *Les papyrus hieratiques nos. 1115, 1116A et 1116B de l'Ermitage imperial a St. Petersbourg* (St. Petersburg, 1916), pls. 23–25
Translation:
H. Goedicke, *The Protocol of Neferyt* (Baltimore, 1977).
AEL, 1:139–45.

---

[2] See Robert R. Wilson, in *Prophecy and Society in Ancient Israel* (Philadelphia, 1980), 111–15.

Text	Translation	Deity	Prophet's Name	Title
ARM II 90	ANET, 624g*	Dagan	————	none
ARM III 40	ANET, 624e*	Dagan	————	muḫḫu
ARM III 78	ANET, 624f*	————	————	muḫḫu
ARM VI 45	Huffmon 212–13	————	————	muḫḫu
ARM X 4	ANET, 629k	Dagan, Adad Itur-mer Belet-Ekallim	————	none
ARM X 6	ANET, 630l*	Annunitum	Ili-Khasnaya	assinnu
ARM X 7	ANET, 630m*	Annunitum	Shelebum	assinnu
ARM X 8	ANET, 630n*	Annunitum	Akhatum	none
ARM X 9	ANET, 632u*	Diritum	Qishti-Diritim	apilu
ARM X 10	ANET, 630o*	Itur-mer	Kakkalidi	none
ARM X 50	ANET, 631p*	Annunitum	————	muḫḫu
ARM X 51	ANET, 631q*	Belet-biri	Iddin-ili	šangu
ARM X 53	ANET, 632v*	Khishametum	Isi-akhu	apilu
ARM X 80	ANET, 632x*	Dagan	Qamutum	none
ARM X 81	ANET, 632w*	Annunitum ?	Innibana	apilu
ARM X 94	ANET, 631r	————	————	none
ARM X 100	ANET, 631s	Dagan	————	none
ARM X 117	ANET, 631t	————	Timlu	none
ARM XIII 23	ANET, 625i*	Dagan	————	apilu
ARM XIII 112	ANET, 623b*	Dagan Ikrub-el	————	none
ARM XIII 113	ANET, 624c*	Dagan Ikrub-el	————	none
ARM XIII 114	ANET, 624d*	Dagan	————	none
A 15	ANET, 623a*	Dagan	Malik-Dagan	none
A 222	Malamat (AIR)46	————	Ayala	none
A 455	Huffmon 211–12	Dagan	————	muḫḫu
A 1121	ANET, 625h*	Adad	————	apilu
A 2731(2925)	Huffmon 205–6	Adad	————	apilu
A 4260	Huffmon 206–7	Shamash	————	apilu

*Published also in Huffmon

Recipient	King	Message
Kibri-Dagan	Zimri-Lim	Offer sacrifice for the dead
Kibri-Dagan	Zimri-Lim	Offer mortuary sacrifices to Yahdun-Lim
Kibri-Dagan	Zimri-Lim	Warned to begin building gate
Bahdi-Lim	Zimri-Lim	Not given
Shibtu (daughter of Yarim-Lim)	Zimri-Lim	Success against Assyrian king, Ishme-Dagan
Shibtu	Zimri-Lim	Defeat of an enemy
Shibtu	Zimri-Lim	Beware of Revolt
Shibtu	Zimri-Lim	Rebellion will be unsuccessful
Shibtu	Zimri-Lim	Obscure; seems to concern Mari's security
Shibtu	Zimri-Lim	Declaration of king's sovereignty
Addu-Duri	Zimri-Lim	Warning not to go on expedition
Addu-Duri	Zimri-Lim	Warning to guard himself
Addu-Duri	Zimri-Lim	Enemies defeated
Inibshina	Zimri-Lim	Eshnunna to be defeated
Inibshina	Zimri-Lim	Unclear; concerns battle at Sharrakiya
Shibatum	Zimri-Lim	Directed to summon specific girl
_____	Zimri-Lim	Release of slave girl directed
Addu-Duri	Zimri-Lim	Unclear
Mukannishum	Zimri-Lim	Babylon to be given over to Mari
Kibri-Dagan	Zimri-Lim	Do not rebuild the temple
Kibri-Dagan	Zimri-Lim	Unclear
Kibri-Dagan	Zimri-Lim	Reassurance concerning Hammurabi
Itur-asdu	Zimri-Lim	Instructions for defeating Yaminites
_____	_____	Quarrel among rival high priestesses
Lanasum	Zimri-Lim	Pure water libation requested
Nur-Sin	Zimri-Lim	Conditional granting of royal requests
Nur-Sin	Zimri-Lim	Exhortation to just rule
_____	Zimri-Lim	Reminder of things owed; defeat of Hammurabi

ANET, 444–46.
A. Gardiner, JEA 1 (1914): 100–106.

Content

Snefru, a pharaoh of the Fourth Dynasty, is addressed by Neferti, the priest, concerning the future of Egypt. He foretells destruction and chaos followed by a restoration brought by a king named Ameny.

III. Canaanite

A. The Stela of Zakkur

Approximate Date of Composition
Eighth century B.C.

Manuscript Data
Inscription found at Afis (south of Aleppo) in 1904.

Publication Data
J. C. L. Gibson, *Textbook of Syrian Semitic Inscriptions,* vol. 2 (Oxford, 1971).
Donner and Rollig, *Kanaanäische und aramäische Inschriften* (Wiesbaden, 1964ff.), 202.
Translation:
ANET, 665–66.
See also:
J. F. Ross, "Prophecy in Hamath, Israel, and Mari," HTR 63 (1970): 1–28.
J. C. Greenfield, "The Zakir Inscription and the Danklied," *Proceedings of the Fifth World Congress of Jewish Studies* (Jerusalem, 1969), 175–76.

Content

In the midst of military crisis, Zakkur, king of Hamath and Lu'ash, asked help of Baal-Shemayn. Through prophets he was told that the enemy would be destroyed.

DISCUSSION

I. The Nature of the Prophetic Message

A. Ancient Near East

The first element for comparison between Israel and the ancient Near East concerns the nature of the prophetic message. The first observation that should be made concerning ancient Near Eastern prophecy is that it is always directed toward the king. Whether the messages concern the private actions of the king or public policy, they are of national significance. These messages generally address ritual activity, military matters, or building projects. At times they encourage the king; in other cases they may be quite negative and serve as a warning. Following are two examples, the first from Mari and the second from the Neo-Assyrian period.

> Speak to my lord: Thus Shibtu your maidservant. In the temple of Annunitum in the city, Akhatum, the servant of Dagan-malik, went into a trance and spoke as follows saying: "O Zimri-Lim, even though you have spurned me, I for my part shall embrace you. I shall deliver your enemies into your hand, and the men of Sharrakiya I shall seize and gather them to the destruction of Belet-ekallim." On the following day Akhum the

priest brought me this report together with the hair and fringe, and I have written to my lord, sealed the hair and fringe, and sent them to my lord.[3]

The goddess Ninlil is highly regarded as a sibyl. This is the word of Ninlil herself to the king, "Fear not, O Ashurbanipal! Now, as I have spoken, it will come to pass: I shall grant it to you. Over the people of the four languages and over the armament of the princes you will exercise sovereignty. . . . The kings of the countries confer together saying, 'Come, let us rise against Ashurbanipal. . . . The fate of our fathers and our grandfathers [the Assyrians] have fixed: [let not his might] cause divisions among us.' " Ninlil answered saying, "[The kings] of the lands [I shall over]throw, place under the yoke, bind their feet in [strong fetters]. For the second time I proclaim to you that as with the land of Elam and the Cimmerians [I shall proceed]. I shall arise, break the thorns, open up widely my way through the briers. With blood I shall turn the land into a rain shower, fill it with lamentation and wailing. You ask, 'What lamentation and wailing?' Lamentation enters Egypt, wailing comes out from there." Ninlil is his mother. Fear not! The mistress of Arbela bore him. Fear not! As she that cares for her child, so I care for you. I have placed you like an amulet on my breast. At night I place a spread over you. In the early morning heed your supplication, heed your conduct. Fear not my son whom I have raised.[4]

B. Israel

Before we are able to draw a comparison to the prophetic message in Israel, we must classify Israelite prophecy into several categories.

1. Premonarchic

This includes the prophets before the institution of kingship who, because of their prophetic function, served as leaders of the people. Moses, Deborah, and Samuel (before the crowning of Saul) belong in this category. The premonarchic prophet provided national guidance as the mouthpiece of God. The prophetic messages given by these individuals concerned military matters and the maintenance of justice.

2. Preclassical

This period begins with Samuel after the anointing of Saul and extends until the beginning of the writing prophets in the middle of the eighth century B.C.[5] These prophets—Nathan, Elijah, Elisha, Micaiah, etc.—primarily address the king. They serve as advisors (officially or unofficially) to the king. As in the last category, the message can be either military advice or pronouncement of rebuke or blessing on the king. The people as a whole are not addressed.

---

[3] ANET, 623n. An updated translation in German can be found in Manfred Weippert, "Assyrische Prophetien der Zeit Asarhaddons und Assurbanipals," in *Assyrian Royal Inscriptions: New Horizons*, ed. F. M. Fales (Rome, 1981), 71–115.

[4] Ibid., 451. An updated translation in German can be found in Weippert, "Assyrische Prophetien."

[5] Cf. J. Holladay, "Assyrian Statecraft and the Prophets of Israel," HTR 63 (1970): 29–51.

3. Classical

This category includes the writing prophets and reflects a major shift in the prophetic movement. Here we find the prophet addressing the people as a social/spiritual commentator. The message is similar in that it includes the pronouncement of rebuke or blessing, but this is now directed toward society as a whole, which gives it quite a different flavor. The prophetic rebuke concerns the current condition of society and includes what will result from unacceptable behavior. As a result we now see warnings concerning captivity, destruction, and exile that are new to this period. A subcategory in this class is the apocalyptic prophecies that shift their focus to a time when the pronounced judgment has taken place and encouragement is needed. This subcategory will be treated in a separate chapter.

It will be immediately recognized that prophecy in Mesopotamia is most comparable to the preclassical category of prophecy in Israel. These similarities are well summarized by H. W. F. Saggs.

> The Mesopotamian counterparts of Israelite prophecies were bounded in the same sense that the pre-canonical [=pre-classical] Israelite oracles were; that is, they had their points of application contained within certain restricted limits of time, subject-matter, and personalia. In terms of time, the application was always to events in the near future, not eschatological time. Like the messages of pre-classical Old Testament prophecy, the Mesopotamian oracles always related wholly or predominantly to royal affairs. Above all, the subject-matter, even at its least trite, concerned only the will or intention of the god for a particular person in particular circumstances.[6]

C. Comparison of Prophetic Literature

We can now identify several areas for comparison and deal with them individually as follows:

1. Mode of revelation

The mode of revelation may be immediately divided into two main ancient Near Eastern categories. In one category revelation came by means of a dream. This was normally the case when the prophet was not a cultic official. In the cases where the prophet was a cultic official, the means by which the revelation came is not given. In the latter case, there are also a couple of different possibilities. In some instances, the prophet enters a trance, while in others no such indication is present, and the prophet appears to retain his identity as the prophecy is given.[7]

Neither dreams/visions or trances are unknown in the history of Israelite prophecy, but more frequently the mode of revelation is unknown. Still, in all, the fact that the Mari prophecies can be classed as intuitive prophecy, as opposed to prophecy that utilizes omens or other mantic techniques of the ancient Near East, places it in contrast with the norm in Mesopotamia and nearer to the biblical mode.

---

[6]H. W. F. Saggs, *The Encounter with the Divine in Mesopotamia and Israel* (London, 1978), 150.

[7]Cf. W. Moran, "New Evidence from Mari on the History of Prophecy," *Biblica* 50:27; John Craghan, "Mari and its Prophets," *Biblical Theology Bulletin* 5:37–39.

2. Target audience

As was already mentioned, the target audience of the prophets of the ancient Near East was the king, and in this aspect the closest parallel in Israel can be seen in the preclassical period. In the other periods of prophecy in Israel, it was the people, or Israelite society, that was the recipient of the prophetic message. It should be recognized, however, as urged by Abraham Malamat, that the data may distort our view on this matter.

> At Mari, nearly all the "prophetic" documents were discovered in the royal-diplomatic archive of the palace (room 115), and this would explain their tendency to concentrate on the king. Prophecies directed toward other people presumably existed, but on account of their nature they were not preserved. In comparison, had only the historiographic books of the Bible—Samuel, Kings and Chronicles—survived, we would be faced with a picture resembling that at Mari, in which Israelite prophecy as well was oriented primarily toward the king and his political and military enterprises.[8]

3. Subject matter

It is in this category that many see the most drastic differences between the prophecy in Israel and that in the ancient Near East. A good example may be found in John Craghan's statement:

> By far the most patent line of demarcation is the content of the revelations. The earlier Mari texts looked to cultic needs and the king as the patron of the temples. The more recent texts stress the personal safety of the king. Hosea's attack on the Canaanite fertility rite, Amos' battle for justice for the underprivileged, Isaiah's insistence on faith, and Ezekiel's homilies on the fall of the nation as the condition for the rise of the people could not even be envisioned in Mari.[9]

While we would generally be in agreement with these observations, it must also be recognized that there are noticeable similarities in the subject matter, however general the similarities may be. These similarities are visible in the general categories into which the subject matter may be divided. For instance, "military matters" could be a category that would include prophecies concerning future victory or defeat for the king (Mari), prophecies of defeat of a king found in the preclassical period in Israel (e.g., 1 Kings 22), and prophecies of the coming exile in the classical prophets. "Cultic matters" would cover the multitude of cultic directions given by prophets in the ancient Near East to their kings and would likewise include the rebuke for incorrect worship or wrong priorities in worship found in the prophetic messages of Israel. This general sort of similarity is observable in the subjects the prophet would address. What the prophet had to say about those concerns, however, would still be vastly different.

---

[8] Malamat, "A Forerunner of Biblical Prophecy: The Mari Documents," in *Ancient Israelite Religion*, ed. P. D. Miller, P. D. Hanson, and S. D. McBride (Philadelphia, 1987), 36.

[9] Craghan, "Mari and Its Prophets," *Biblical Theology Bulletin* 5:51.

4. Range

H. W. F. Saggs rightly pointed out that the eschatological focus of some of the classical prophets' messages characterizes them as unique in the ancient world. This difference results from distinctions discussed in our earlier chapter on history. The only reason that the Israelites can have an eschatology is that they believe in a God who is sovereign over time and history, who does not intervene arbitrarily or just respond to the status quo, but who has a plan in history and is intervening to carry out the details of that plan. The prophetic message is often a comment on that plan, which in turn is largely understood in light of the covenant of YHWH with Israel. This covenant is also a unique aspect of Israelite belief, so again, we are not surprised that the eschatological aspect of Israelite prophecy is not paralleled in the ancient Near East.

Another aspect of range is addressed by H. W. F. Saggs:

> Never in any circumstances did the message of the Mesopotamian ecstatic break through these bounds to give a message not to a man but to Man, not merely about the behavior demanded from a particular man in a particular situation but about the behavior demanded from mankind, not about the intentions of the gods for the immediate circumstance but about God's very nature.[10]

In this sense also, the range of Israelite prophecy far exceeds what is currently known from the ancient Near East. These differences, as we have come to expect, are firmly rooted in the different way Israel perceived God and represent at their root a theological difference that goes back to the very nature of Deity.

5. Response to prophecy

There is always the possibility of false prophets, and therefore the question of how a prophetic word may be verified always arises. In Israel, it is not infrequent that a sign of some sort is given so that the one who hears the prophet might have his legitimacy confirmed. At times we might also see a short-term prophecy whose accuracy is intended to confirm the accuracy of a more significant long-range prophecy.

In Mesopotamia there is generally a different approach to confirmation, though the methods already mentioned are not unknown. William Moran has pointed out that in Mari several of the texts witness to the practice of verifying the prophetic message by divination. He concludes:

> It [the system of controls on the prophetic message] integrates the accepted sources of revelation within a hierarchy and gives primacy to the "science" of the technician. In this system dreams and prophecies can never demand unqualified acceptance or reveal absolute imperatives. They can merely "propose"—it is the haruspex who "disposes."[11]

Thus the prophetic word will normally be verified by omens in the ancient Near East. At times the texts mention that a lock of hair or a piece of the

---

[10]H. W. F. Saggs, *The Encounter With the Divine in Mesopotamia and Israel* (London, 1978), 151–52.

[11]Moran, "New Evidence From Mari," *Biblica* 50:23.

fringe of the garment of the prophet is being supplied. This is thought to have been used in the divination process.[12] In A 222, both verification by omen and the sending of hair and hem are listed: "By the Hurru-bird I have examined this matter and she saw (the dream well). Now her hair and the hem of the garment I am sending along. May my lord investigate the matter."[13] Since the use of omens was forbidden to the Israelites, a distinct difference exists here.

II. The Function of the Prophet

One of the primary indicators for the function of the prophet is the terminology of titles attributed to the prophets, or, according to recent convention, the "oracular speakers."[14] In the Mari materials, some of the oracular speakers have titles while others do not. The most frequent titles used are *āpilu, muḫḫu* and *assinnu*.[15]

A. Āpilu

The noun would appear to be related to the verb, *āpalu*, to answer. From the usage in the texts, however, it is clear that the *āpilu* was not limited to responding when oracles were requested. Their oracles were at times spontaneous and unsolicited. Robert Wilson provides us with several observations concerning the *āpilu*.

> 1. Often appear representing local deities outside of Mari.
> 2. Messages often relate to the concerns of their local region rather than to the cult or politics of Mari.
> 3. The message of the *āpilu* was often ignored by the king.
> 4. There seems to have been some negligence in reporting to the king the messages given by the *āpilu*.[16]

Wilson's conclusions are that the role of the *āpilu* was peripheral within Mari society.

B. Muḫḫu

This noun is related to the verb *maḫû*, "to go into a trance."[17] We would therefore expect this to refer to ecstatics—that assumption is supported by the texts. The *muḫḫu* frequently, but not always, has a cultic function. Various deities are represented by *muḫḫus*, from the central deity, Ishtar, to various deities from outlying areas. Robert Wilson observes, "Muḫḫus in Mari were somewhat concerned for the safety of the king and the stability of the government, [while] the *muḫḫus* outside of the capital were concerned with the well-being of their cults and deities."[18]

The message of the *muḫḫu* was likewise frequently checked by

---

[12] Wilson, *Prophecy and Society*, 102.

[13] Translation by Malamat, "A Forerunner of Biblical Prophecy: The Mari Documents," p. 46. Other examples of Mari prophecies indicating omen verification are also listed by Malamat, p. 47 (ARM X 6; X 94; X 81; X 80).

[14] Cf. Ibid., 99, n. 27.

[15] I will be using the masculine forms, though the first two refer also to females.

[16] Taken from Wilson, *Prophecy and Society*, 101–2.

[17] AHw, 582b.

[18] Wilson, *Prophecy and Society*, 105.

divination. Unlike the *āpilu*, the *muḫḫu* is also known from the Neo-Assyrian texts and is held in high regard by Esarhaddon and Ashurbanipal.

C. Assinnu

The *assinnu* is known, not only from three Mari texts, but also from other cuneiform literature, where they are among Ishtar's cultic personnel.[19] Their cultic function in major festivals makes their role in society clearer than that of the *āpilu* and *muḫḫu*. Again, we find that the oracles of the *assinnu*, like those of the other oracular speakers, were confirmed by divination.

D. Raggimu

While not known from the Mari texts, the *raggimu* is the most frequently attested title in the Neo-Assyrian prophetic literature. The noun derives from the verb *ragāmu*, "to call or shout." No observable common denominator marks the nature of the message or its presentation.

From the above survey we can see that the oracular speakers in the ancient Near East were often professionals. It must also be recognized that there are many oracles given by untitled individuals. This is not unlike the situation in the Old Testament, where individuals such as Nathan or Isaiah have official court positions, others seem to be professional prophets (e.g., Elisha), while still others are laypeople who become burdened with a message from God (e.g., Amos). Whatever the prophet's background and professional standing, the common functional denominator is that a message from God must be presented. As a mouthpiece or herald of God, the prophet of Israel or of the ancient Near East is obligated to deliver the message entrusted to him. The methods by which the message was received, the form in which the message was passed on by the oracular speaker, and the general reaction of society toward the prophet do not show much variation when Israel and the ancient Near East are compared.

III. Prophecies from Canaan and Egypt

Most of the above discussion has focused on the materials from Mesopotamia, because that is the source of a large majority of our information. A brief examination of the Zakkur Stela and the Egyptian materials is now in order.

A. Canaanite Prophecies: The Zakkur Stela

In this inscription, the king of Lu'ash and Hamath, Zakkur, is the one to whom the oracle was given. It was presented to him upon request by the seers (*hzyn*) and messengers (*'ddn*). The former of these terms is known in Hebrew (e.g., 2 Sam. 24:11). The latter is possibly reflected in the Hebrew verbal root, *'od*.[20] The content of the message concerns military matters and so follows the well-known pattern from Mari, Assyria, and preclassical Israel. Little information is provided concerning the function of these oracular speakers within the society of that time. As a result, the Zakkur

---

[19]See Wilson, *Prophecy and Society*, 106.

[20]In the Hiphil, to warn; cf. J. F. Ross, "Prophecy in Hamath, Israel and Mari," *HTR* 63 (1970): 5–7.

Stela merely joins the Assyrian data in providing a basis for comparative studies.

B. Egyptian Prophecies

The so-called Egyptian prophecies fall into quite a different category from those found in Mesopotamia, yet they still have some points of resemblance to prophecy in Israel. Given that these prophecies do *not* purport to be oracles from a deity,[21] their classification as prophecy could be questioned. The reason for considering them here is that they are comprised of observations concerning the chaotic state of society and warnings of judgment coming or of the restoration of order. In general terms, this shows some similarity to the message of the classical prophets in Israel. It should be recognized, of course, that the similarity ends there. In Israel it is the covenant that governs both the rebuke and the predicted outcomes. In Egypt it is an inherent order in society, *ma'at*, that is being violated. A reader could also wonder if the chaotic state described in the Egyptian texts accurately reflects reality. In the opinion of some modern interpreters, it does not.[22] These works appear to be of the wisdom genre, and their descriptions of society are exaggerated to make a point. They appear to serve a propagandistic function. This also then creates great difficulties in attempting to compare them with Israelite prophecy.

Despite some similarity in the nature of the message, there is no observable prophetic institution in Egypt like that found in the rest of the ancient Near East. The most obvious reason for this difference is that in Egypt alone, deity was incarnate in the person of the pharaoh. There was therefore not the need of a mouthpiece speaking for deity—deity was in their midst. This fact does not preclude the practice of divination or the asking of oracles from various Egyptian deities. These were part of the priestly office. But prophetic guidance in military or cultic matters was unnecessary, given the presence of pharaoh.

IV. Conclusions

The major differences between prophecy in Israel and in the ancient Near East lie in the content of the message that was presented by the oracular speaker. The Israelite variation from the norm stems from the differences in the God who gives the message. In the ancient Near East the message is frequently cultic, because the primary demands of deity in that polytheistic setting were cultic. In Israel, the demands seem at times anticultic.[23] The problem the prophets identified in Israel was its tendency to think of God's demands as being cultic and to ignore his demands on its lifestyle.

In the ancient Near East there is much prophecy that is military/political in focus. It would be wrong to suggest that even classical prophecy lacks a political focus. But the political element has a far different connection in the

---

[21]Cf. S. Herrmann, "Prophetie in Israel und Ägypten: Recht und Grenze eines Vergleichs," VT Supp. 9 (Leiden, 1963): 47–65.

[22]Cf. AEL, 1:139; 149–50.

[23]1 Samuel 15:22; Isaiah 1:10–17; 66:3; Jeremiah 6:20; 7:21–23; Hosea 6:6; Amos 5:21–27; Micah 6:6–8.

oracles of Israel's prophets. Instead of oracles that suggest that this battle or that battle will be won or lost, we discover messages concerning the long-range political destiny, not only of Israel, but of many nations of the ancient Near East as well. These messages reflect belief in a God who is totally sovereign and carrying out a plan in history rather than belief in the ancient Near Eastern gods who intervene arbitrarily.

A third difference observable in the content of the message is the result in the audience to whom it is addressed. When the classical prophets of Israel begin to bring their messages to the people rather than the king, they depart from anything known from the ancient Near East context. John Holladay has suggested that this element of classical prophecy is patterned after an observable shift in the function of the king's herald in the Neo-Assyrian period.[24] I am not inclined to see a cause and effect process at work here (i.e., a conscious borrowing on the part of Israelite prophets from the Assyrian model) but rather two distinct reflections of complex changes taking place within society as a whole. It must be observed that prophecy in Assyria itself did not reflect a shift of audience.[25]

As in the other instances, this difference is explained by the nature of the God who gives the message. The messages that warn the people of exile and destruction, that rebuke them concerning the injustice in society, that hold them responsible for good maintenance of the covenant that was made with YHWH—all are unique in the ancient world, largely because they are all integrally related to the covenant between YHWH and Israel—which was also unique in the ancient world.

As in many of the other genres, then, we can conclude that prophecy in Israel had much in common with the phenomenon at large in the ancient Near East. The occurrence of unique features is directly related to the beliefs Israel had about its God, YHWH.[26]

---

[24]Holladay, "Assyrian Statecraft and the Prophets of Israel," 43–44.

[25]Note that the earliest of the classical prophets, Amos and Hosea, precede the changes incorporated by Tiglath-Pileser III.

[26]A text that should not be overlooked is the Poem of Erra (English translation, L. Cagni, *The Poem of Erra* [Malibu, 1977]). Tablet 5, lines 25–44, contains instructions that Kabti-Ilani-Marduk claims to have received from deity and which he recorded word for word. While the section is still far removed from classical prophecy, it does address restoration after the destruction of Erra. D. Bodi has identified a number of points of contact and common motifs between Erra and Ezekiel in *The Book of Ezekiel and the Poem of Erra* (Freiburg, 1989).

FOR FURTHER READING

Craghan, John. "Mari and Its Prophets." *Biblical Theology Bulletin* 5 (1975): 32–54.

Dietrich, M., et al. *Texte aus der Umwelt des Alten Testaments,* 2.1: Deutungen der Zukunft in Briefen, Orakeln und Omina. Gütersloher, 1986. Contains bibliography and German translations.

Hayes, John H. "Prophetism at Mari and Old Testament Parallels." *Anglican Theological Review* 49 (1967): 397–409.

Herrmann, Siegfried. "Prophetie in Israel und Ägypten: Recht und Grenze eines Vergleichs." VT Supp. 9 (Leiden, 1963): 47–65.

Holladay, John. "Assyrian Statecraft and the Prophets of Israel." HTR 63 (1970): 29–51.

Huffmon, Herbert B. "The Origins of Prophecy." In *Magnalia Dei: The Mighty Acts of God*, ed. F. M. Cross, W. E. Lemke, and P. D. Miller. Garden City, 1976, 171–86.

————. "Prophecy in the Ancient Near East." IDB Supp., 697–700. Nashville, 1976.

————. "Prophecy in the Mari Letters." *Biblical Archaeologist Reader*, 3, ed. E. Campbell and D. N. Freedman. Garden City, 1970, 199–224.

McFaddon, W. Robert. "Micah and the Problem of Continuities and Discontinuities in Prophecy." *Scripture in Context*, II, ed. W. W. Hallo, J. C. Moyer, and L. G. Perdue. Winona Lake, Ind., 1983, 127–46.

Malamat, Abraham. "Prophetic Revelations in the New Documents from Mari and the Bible." VT Supp. 15. Leiden, 1965, 207–27.

————. "A Forerunner of Biblical Prophecy: The Mari Documents." In *Ancient Israelite Religion*. Ed. P. D. Miller, P. D. Hanson, S. D. McBride. Philadelphia, 1987, 33–52.

Moran, William L. "New Evidence from Mari on the History of Prophecy." *Biblica* 50 (1969): 15–56.

Rabe, Virgil W. "Origins of Prophecy." In *Essays in Honor of George Ernest Wright*. Ed. E. Campbell and R. Boling. Chicago, 1976, 125–28.

Ross, James F. "Prophecy in Hamath, Israel and Mari." HTR 63 (1970): 1–28.

Ringgren, Helmer. "Prophecy in the Ancient Near East." In *Israel's Prophetic Tradition*. Ed. R. Coggins, A. Phillips, and M. Knibb. Cambridge, 1982, 1–11.

Saggs, H. W. F. *The Encounter with the Divine in Mesopotamia and Israel.* London, 1978, 139–52.

Smith, Gary V. "Prophet." In *International Standard Bible Encyclopedia* (rev.) 3:986–1004. Grand Rapids, 1986.

Weinfeld, Moshe. "Ancient Near Eastern Patterns in Prophetic Literature." VT 27 (1977): 178–95.

Wilson, Robert R. *Prophecy and Society in Ancient Israel.* Philadelphia, 1980, 90–134.

Chapter 9

APOCALYPTIC LITERATURE

The genre known as apocalyptic is difficult to define. It is not within the scope of this book to consider all suggestions and decide among them. Rather, I will examine the five Akkadian pieces that are designated prophecies or apocalypses and see what they have in common with the Old Testament literature that is frequently classified as apocalyptic. This is not to insist that either the Akkadian literature or the Old Testament literature in question actually *is* pure apocalyptic. We simply want to observe what similarities and differences exist between the Akkadian apocalypses and Old Testament apocalyptic, especially Daniel 11. Where the differences may well be genre related, we will attempt to identify them as such.

MATERIALS[1]

I. Text A

Approximate Date of Composition

---

[1] Text B is no longer included in this genre, though it had initially been discussed along with the others in the seminal article by A. K. Grayson and W. G. Lambert in 1964. Further examination, particularly by Robert Biggs suggested that this text was simply a collection of omens featuring astrological protases followed by a long list of apodoses (Robert Biggs, "More Babylonian Prophecies," *Iraq* 29 [1967]: 117:32. This conclusion is supported by Grayson (A. K. Grayson, *Babylonian Historical-Literary Texts* [Toronto, 1975], 15). However, Biggs has recently suggested that this text still ought to be considered along with the Akkadian prophecies because of certain shared genre characteristics.

The length of the major long prediction which runs to some 24 lines is without parallel in any omen text, and furthermore appears not to be

This late Assyrian copy from Assur is dated to the seventh century B.C.[2]

Manuscript Data
VAT 10179, first published in 1919.

Publication Data
Text:
  E. Ebeling, KAR 421.
Transliteration:
  A. K. Grayson and W. G. Lambert, JCS 18 (1964): 12–14.
Translation:
  ANET, 606–7 (Biggs).

Content
Twelve unnamed kings are treated, with descriptions of either good or bad things that accompanied each reign. The comments connected to each king include cultic, military (both foreign and domestic matters), and social accomplishments and events. William Hallo suggests that the text describes the reigns of several kings in the Second Dynasty of Isin in the twelfth and eleventh centuries B.C.[3]

II. Marduk Prophecy

Approximate Date of Composition
Generally connected to the reign of Nebuchadnezzar I (1127–1105).[4]

Manuscript Data
A. K. Grayson and W. G. Lambert Text D (Assur text 13348), plus additional texts gathered and listed by R. Borger, "Gott Marduk und Gott-König Šulgi als Propheten," BO 28 (1971): 3–24.

Publication Data
Text and Transliteration:
  R. Borger, "Gott Marduk und Gott-König Šulgi als Propheten," BO 28 (1971): 3–24. See also
  A. K. Grayson and Lambert, JCS 18 (1964), for some of the fragments.

---

associated with any omen protasis. Because of its special character, I prefer not to exclude it categorically from considerations within the context of Babylonian prophecies. It is, in any case, so rich in typical prophecy topoi— such as famine when mothers bar their doors to their own daughters, friends and relatives killing one another, the re-establishment of regular offerings that had ceased, etc.—that it aids in restoring broken passages in the unquestioned prophecy texts (R. Biggs, "Babylonian Prophecies and the Astrological Traditions of Mesopotamia," JCS 39 [1985]: 86, n. 5).

Further fragments of Text B have been published by Biggs in "Babylonian Prophecies, Astrology, and a New Source for 'Prophecy Text B,'" in *Language, Literature and History: Philological and Historical Studies Presented to Erica Reiner*, ed. Francesca Rochberg-Halton (New Haven, 1987), 6–14.

[2] W. G. Lambert, *The Background of Jewish Apocalyptic* (London, 1978), 10.

[3] William Hallo, "Akkadian Apocalypses," IEJ 16 (1966): 236–39; cf. also Lambert, *Background of Jewish Apocalyptic*, 10.

[4] E.g., Joyce Baldwin, "Some Literary Affinities of the Book of Daniel," TB 30 (1979): 84.

Translation:
T. Longman, *Fictional Akkadian Royal Autobiography* (Winona Lake, Ind., 1989).
D. Block, *The Gods of the Nations* (Jackson, Miss., 1988), 169–76.
H. Schmökel, *Near Eastern Religious Texts* (Philadelphia, 1978) (segments).

Content

An address to the high gods by Marduk in which he narrates both his own past history as a wanderer, suffering a totally self-imposed exile, and the bad times in Babylonia that accompanied his exile. This is followed by a prediction that a good king will arise who will restore the cult of Marduk to its glory and thereby establish a period of peace and plenty in the land.[5]

III. Šulgi Prophecy

Approximate Date of Composition
Likely also the twelfth century B.C.

Manuscript Data
K 4445: A. K. Grayson and W. G. Lambert Text C (= K 4495 + 4541 + 15508), of which the Berlin copy is designated VAT 14404.

Publication Data
Text and Transliteration:
R. Borger, BO 28 (1971). For several of the pertinent tablets, see also A. K. Grayson and W. G. Lambert, JCS 18 (1964).
Translation:
H. Schmökel, *Near Eastern Religious Texts* (Philadelphia, 1978) (segments).

Content

Presented as revelation from Ishtar and Shamash. After a lengthy introduction of the speaker as one who is privy to divine conversations, there is a description of a crisis and instability in society. The text then speaks of a future king who will bring deliverance by restoring the cult sacrifices and structures. The text is very uncertain due to its damaged condition.

IV. Uruk Prophecy

Approximate Date of Composition
This copy dates to the early Achaemenid period (late sixth century), according to H. Hunger and S. A. Kaufman (JAOS 95), and to the Seleucid period (third to second century B.C.), according to W. G. Lambert.[6]

Manuscript Data
Warka 22307/7. Found in the German excavations at Warka in 1969.

Publication Data
H. Hunger and S. A. Kaufman, "A New Akkadian Prophecy Text," JAOS 95 (1975): 371–75.

---

[5] Taken from S. Kaufman, "Prediction, Prophecy and Apocalypse in Light of New Akkadian Texts," *Proceedings of the Sixth World Congress of Jewish Studies* (1973), 222.
[6] Lambert, *Background of Jewish Apocalyptic*, 10–11.

Content

The obverse side of the text is sufficiently damaged to obscure the number of kings treated and the description of their reigns. On the reverse, however, six unnamed kings are "predicted" with a general classification of their reigns.

H. Hunger and S. A. Kaufman identify the text as describing the events of the reigns of Eriba-Marduk and his successors in the mid-eighth century B.C., until the time of Tiglath-Pileser III, at which point the text skips to Nebuchadnezzar II. The purpose of the text is seen as legitimizing and supporting Nebuchadnezzar's son and successor, Amel-Marduk.[7]

Lambert, based on the succession of rulers described in the text, suggests that it refers to Merodach-Baladan II as the good king, then Neo-Assyrian rulers Sargon II, Sennacherib, Esarhaddon, and Ashurbanipal as the bad kings, concluding with Nabopolassar and Nebuchadnezzar as the good kings, whose reigns are blessed.[8]

V. Dynastic Prophecy

Approximate Date of Composition

Considered by A. K. Grayson to date to the Seleucid period.

Manuscript Data

BM 40623.

Publication Data

A. K. Grayson, *Babylonian Historical-Literary Texts* (Toronto, 1975), 24–37.

Content

The fragmentary text presents a succession of unnamed kings with a description of their deeds and the events that transpired during their reigns. After telling of the downfall of the Assyrian Empire, the first column deals with the rise of the Neo-Babylonian Empire, probably under Nabopolassar, though Nebuchadnezzar II might be meant. The second column deals with Neriglissar, Nabonidus, and Cyrus. The third column takes up Arses and Darius III, also referring to the eunuch Bagoas. Alexander of Macedon is next and is strangely said to have been defeated by Darius III with Babylonian help after inflicting an initial defeat on the Persians. The very badly preserved last column clearly dealt with one more reign, and perhaps two others also, not to mention what might have been included in the gap between the last two columns.[9]

DISCUSSION

I. Concerning the Genre of the Akkadian Literature

Our first task is to survey some of the observations that have been made concerning the genre and literary characteristics of the Akkadian

---

[7]H. Hunger and S. A. Kaufman, "A New Akkadian Prophecy Text," JAOS 95 (1975): 374.

[8]Lambert, *Background of Jewish Apocalyptic*, 11.

[9]Description taken from Ibid., 12.

material. A. K. Grayson and W. G. Lambert identify the Akkadian genre in the following way:

> Descriptions of the reigns of unnamed kings cast in the form of predictions. The reign of each king is described either in terms of a "good" time or a "bad" time. The descriptions are phrases commonly found in the apodoses of omens and are written with an abundance of ideograms typical of omens.[10]

W. W. Hallo concludes from his summary of the characteristics of the literature:

> We can at once agree with the unanimous opinion of modern commentators that we are dealing here with *pretended* predictions, with classical examples of *vaticinium ex eventu*. The allusions are just vague enough to suggest the style of predictions, but at same time they are not nearly vague enough to escape the suspicion that they were inspired by actual historical events that had already transpired in the remote or not-so-remote past.[11]

H. Hunger and S. A. Kaufman point out, on the contrary, that all of the texts are not alike in either format or function.

> The autobiographical "prophecy" texts of Marduk and Šulgi . . . are different both from our text [Uruk prophecy] and from each other. They both are clearly propagandistic in nature and make use of the literary device of pseudonymity—but only the Šulgi text uses the *vaticinium ex eventu* to lend authority to its "predictions." This device is also used in text A . . . though it is not clear whether or not any actual omens are involved.[12]

In another article, Kaufman further observes:

> The only element shared by all of the prophecy texts (that is to say, their primary feature) is a rather specialized use of mantic terminology (especially the terminology of the apodoses of astrological omens) to describe the favorable or unfavorable reigns of unnamed rulers. It is far from clear that the sharing of this feature is indicative of a literary tradition, however. I would tend to view it as nothing more than the expected use of that terminology which was the traditional terminology of Mesopotamian religious historiography. In any case, it is clear that this primary feature of Akkadian "prophecy" is totally lacking in apocalyptic.[13]

Tremper Longman III suggests that the Akkadian prophecies ought to be considered a subgenre of Akkadian fictional autobiography based on shared genre-identifying features existing on levels of style, mood, content,

---

[10]A. K. Grayson and W. G. Lambert, "Akkadian Prophecies," JCS 18 (1964): 7. Biggs ("Babylonian Prophecies, Astrology. . .") takes issue with the good/bad characterization being considered a feature of the prophecy texts. He suggests that often there are contrasts presented in which those who were suffering will prosper and vice versa.

[11]Hallo, "Akkadian Apocalypses," 235.

[12]Hunger and Kaufman, "New Akkadian Prophecy Text," 375.

[13]Kaufman, "Prediction, Prophecy, and Apocalypse," 226.

setting, and structure.[14] I find his conclusions compelling. There yet remains the question, however, whether this subgenre ought to be classified with prophetical or apocalyptic literature. Longman suggests that instead of separating prophecy and apocalyptic into two distinct genres (which has always been a difficult task), we can posit a single genre containing a prophecy-apocalyptic continuum.[15] On such a continuum, the Akkadian texts can be seen to share a number of the traits from the apocalyptic side of the continuum[16] while not evidencing several others.[17] We could therefore appreciate both the prophetical and apocalyptic traits of the literature and place it on the prophetic/apocalyptic continuum leaning toward the apocalyptic side.

II. Concerning the Genre of Daniel 11

By most any definition, Daniel 7–12 is considered to be well within the confines of apocalyptic literature. Using Longman's model of a prophecy/apocalyptic continuum, the features of Daniel would put it further toward the apocalyptic pole than the Akkadian apocalypses.[18]

It also should be noticed that the book of Daniel is autobiographical. Longman has pointed out that autobiography is a logical foundation of both wisdom-style instruction and of predictions. Knowledge about the speaker is intended to lend credibility to either his instruction or his information.[19]

The Akkadian apocalypses are not just autobiographies but are considered fictional autobiographies. Longman admits that the fragmentary nature of the texts makes this difficult to demonstrate conclusively, but he sees an "impression of fictionality" created by the traits of pseudonymity and *vaticinium ex eventu*.[20] This determination does not create a problem with the Akkadian material, because these traits are admitted by all. Concerning Daniel, however, a different situation exists. A fictionality deduced from pseudonymity and *vaticinium ex eventu* will be unconvincing to conservative exegetes who are unwilling to allow that those are traits of the book of Daniel. Therefore, to suggest that Daniel is proven to contain *vaticinium ex eventu* or to be pseudonymous on the basis of a genre trait of fictionality would be circular reasoning at this juncture.

---

[14]Tremper Longman III, *Fictional Akkadian Royal Autobiography* (Ann Arbor, 1983), 373–77. This is not necessarily in disagreement with Biggs's analysis where differences between the texts are clearly present. He would see the Marduk and Šulgi texts in a separate category primarily because of their date and first-person address. Text A is distinguished by a mythological introduction and phrasing related to the astrological omens (similar to Text B) (Biggs, "Babylonian Prophecies, Astrology . . . ," 3–4).

[15]Longman, *Fictional Akkadian Royal Autobiography*, 387ff. Longman takes his lead in this from Kugel, who suggested a similar continuum for the treatment of poetry and prose in *The Idea of Biblical Poetry* (New Haven, 1981).

[16]Longman lists pseudonymity, esoterism, deterministic view of history/*vaticinium ex eventu*, dualism in ethical and temporal senses, social setting, and the use of a wide scope of history (Ibid., 390–91).

[17]He includes here eschatology, mediation, and symbolism (Ibid., 391–92).

[18]Ibid., 406–8.

[19]Ibid., 408–9.

[20]Ibid., 375.

The conclusion of our genre study would be that the Akkadian apocalypses and Daniel are both part of the same larger generic categories. They are both autobiographies toward the apocalyptic side of the prophetic/apocalyptic continuum. This genre identification does not yet address the issue of Daniel's dependence on Akkadian literature. That will be considered after a discussion of similarities and differences with regard to literary features and content.

A. Similarities

Certainly the most striking similarity between the Akkadian apocalypses and Daniel appears in the predictions of a series of unnamed kings covering a long span of history (Dan. 11). Other similarities that are often identified are deduced from genre identification. The only features that S. A. Kaufman is able to find in the Akkadian literature that are comparable to the genre of apocalyptic are pseudonymity (not present in all of the Akkadian texts), the use of *vaticinium ex eventu*, and a propagandistic purpose.[21] Interestingly enough, though these are considered to be characteristics of biblical apocalyptic, all three would be contested by many as characteristics of Daniel 11.[22] Those who would connect such characteristics to Daniel, however, would also not see such characteristics as limited to apocalyptic literature.[23] It would also have to be admitted that these traits are not characteristic of everything apocalyptic and are certainly not a requirement of everything on the prophetic/apocalyptic continuum. So these traits are not genre exclusive. Not every example within the genre contains them, and they are found outside the genre. As a result, the genre similarities are not sufficient to persuade unconvinced conservative interpreters that Daniel is pseudonymous or propagandistic or that it contains *vaticinium ex eventu*. Many remain unconvinced because of the substantial differences that also exist between the Akkadian apocalypses and Daniel 11.

B. Differences

The differences between Daniel and the Akkadian apocalypses fall into the categories of literary content and theological content.

1. Literary content

Here we find that though the book uses the literary technique of discussing various future kings, the kind of information given about the kings is not that similar. In Daniel there is no length of reign given, and the good/bad evaluation is not as clearly set forth.

Perhaps of greater significance is the connection that exists between the Akkadian apocalypses and the astrological omens. On the basis of a comparative study between the Akkadian apocalypses and the omen texts, Robert Biggs concludes:

> The correspondence between the prophecies and the astrological cor-
> pus—especially the topoi and phrases that are unique to the two genres
> and the geographical concerns of both genres—suggest that the literary

---

[21] Kaufman, "Prediction, Prophecy and Apocalypse," 226–27.
[22] E.g., Joyce Baldwin, "Some Literary Affinities," 77–99.
[23] Kaufman, "Prediction, Prophecy and Apocalypse," 227.

associations of the prophecy predictions are with the astrological corpus and not with any other genre of Mesopotamian omens.[24]

It is of special interest that neither the prophetic topoi that Biggs identifies nor the inclination to use specific geographical terminology are evidenced in Daniel 11. This would argue against Daniel's having borrowed from either the Akkadian apocalypses or even from the astrological omens as these Akkadian texts have. It is likewise futile to attempt correlations between Daniel 11 and any other category of Mesopotamian omens. All of this suggests a more superficial correlation between these two literatures.

2. Theological content

The presentation of Daniel as a mediated revelation creates a substantial theological difference. While this is considered a standard characteristic of apocalyptic literature,[25] it is not a regular feature of the Akkadian apocalypses. The Marduk and Šulgi texts have deity and deified king respectively as their speakers. The other three texts make no mention of anything that suggests a mediated revelation.

A second difference is that the sovereignty of YHWH in Daniel 11 provides a vastly different theological context from that found in the Akkadian literature.

> Because Babylonian gods were partisan their intervention was seen as limited to particular areas, whereas in Daniel the supreme and only God is concerned with all history and with all mankind. It follows that the rationale of the book is distinctive. It represents a totally different world view, based on a totally different theology, which gives rise to an understanding of history unknown in Babylon.[26]

Finally, the primary difference appears in the function of the literature. What was the function of the Akkadian apocalypses? Most agree that they could have only been propagandistic in their intent. Yet we often speak of the *vaticinium ex eventu* as intending to establish the speaker's credibility . Do we really have so little regard for the ancient audiences as to think that they would not have seen this immediately as political propaganda? Most of these texts have their climax in the "prophet's" present, not the future. They are justifications for the administration that is in power (with religious elements as necessary, especially in the Marduk prophecy). A. K. Grayson suggests that the exception to this is the Dynastic Prophecy.

> It is only in the Dynastic prophecy that there appears to be real prophecy at the end of a series of vaticinia ex eventu. A real attempt to predict, preceded by pseudo-predictions, is one of the salient features of apocalyptic. It would appear, therefore, that the Dynastic prophecy

---

[24]Biggs, "Babylonian Prophecies and Astrological Traditions," 90. It should be noted that this goes contrary to the previous conclusions of Grayson that there was no connection between Akkadian prophecies and omen literature. Grayson, *Babylonian Historical-Literary Texts*, 15–16.

[25]Cf., e.g., J. Collins, "Daniel," in *Forms of Old Testament Literature* (Grand Rapids, 1984), 6–11.

[26]Joyce Baldwin, "Some Literary Affinities," 93.

reflects an important stage in the development of apocalyptic literature in the ancient Near East.[27]

However, at this point it must be wondered whether even the Dynastic Prophecy provides us with an exception. As Grayson himself readily admits, the evidence is tenuous.[28] It is not at all clear from the text that the Dynastic Prophecy ends in a prediction.

This then constitutes one key difference between the biblical apocalyptic and the Akkadian texts: there is no element of eschatology in the Akkadian literature.

> To my knowledge no one has yet succeeded in discovering any kind of eschatology in Akkadian literature. Indeed the Mesopotamian idea of the ideal future would seem to be (for those in power, at least) nothing more than an indefinite continuation of the status quo.[29]

This means that the idea that the author of the book of Daniel is establishing credibility by using *vaticinium ex eventu* so that he can make a "real" prediction cannot be supported by referring to the Akkadian apocalypses. The Akkadian apocalypses are using *vaticinium ex eventu* for present propagandistic purposes, grandiose predictions of what the present king will accomplish, almost always relating to renewal of the cult centers and practices. This is clearly not the intent of Daniel.

On the other hand, neither can Daniel be considered to be using *vaticinium ex eventu* for the same purpose as that found in the Jewish apocalyptic use of it. In Jewish apocalyptic, *vaticinium ex eventu* leads into eschatological predictions that are characterized by cosmic upheaval, judgment scenes, epiphanies, and the like.[30] Rather, in Daniel the section that is supposedly *vaticinium ex eventu*, leads into a very specific prediction concerning a historical individual. This is nothing like the "campaign promise" style of the Akkadian apocalypses, nor is it in the least similar to the sweeping eschatological generalities of Jewish apocalyptic.

This leaves no generic parameters to support the interpretation that Daniel 11 contains *vaticinium ex eventu*. Though Daniel falls into the same general generic category as the Akkadian apocalypses, *vaticinium ex eventu* is not characteristic of every piece in that genre. Furthermore, the supposed "real" prediction of Daniel 11 (vv. 40–45) has no parallel in either Akkadian or Jewish apocalypses.

With regard to the question of the influence of the Akkadian apocalypses on Daniel, I would readily acknowledge that Daniel is in all likelihood indebted to Akkadian literature for the literary feature of presenting history using successive unnamed kings, just as he used a four empire scheme well known from the ancient Near East earlier in the book. But here, as there, the influence seems to stop at a very superficial level.

---

[27] Grayson, *Babylonian Historical-Literary Texts*, 21–22.

[28] Ibid., 17, n. 22.

[29] Kaufman, "Prediction, Prophecy and Apocalypse," 226. While some may feel that the concept of a divine plan in Akkadian literature is defensible (cf. H. W. F. Saggs, *The Encounter with the Divine in Mesopotamia and Israel* [London, 1978], 81–87), here I would delineate eschatology as a divine plan with consummation.

[30] Cf. Collins, "Daniel," 12–13.

EXCURSUS: ECCLESIASTES

In the chapter on wisdom literature it was noted that Ecclesiastes generally fit into the dialogue/monologue category and into the subcategory of pessimism literature. It could further be noticed that there is some similarity between particular statements in Ecclesiastes and those found in the wisdom comments scattered through the Gilgamesh Epic.[31]

A third level of comparison could be identified in the structure and form that is shared between Ecclesiastes and the Akkadian Royal Autobiography analyzed by Tremper Longman III.[32] In comparing Ecclesiastes with the Cuthean legend of Naram-Sin, Longman finds that once we move beyond the prologue and epilogue of the former (1:1–11; 12:9–14), the work itself may be seen to include a first-person introduction (1:12–18), a first-person narrative (2:1–6:9), and a first-person instruction (6:10–12:8). This is identical to the structure of the Cuthean legend of Naram-Sin, thus offering advice based on experience.

Just as the monologue and pessimism of Ecclesiastes served to identify it with a particular branch of wisdom literature, so Longman suggests that the style of an author addressing himself identifies Ecclesiastes with fictional royal autobiography. Furthermore, Longman suggests that the genre identification is sound enough to determine that royal fiction is also a characteristic of Ecclesiastes.[33] By this he means that the writer is not really Solomon. The material is presented as the wisdom of Solomon and stylistically framed in the first person.

A combination of all of these features suggests that the author of Ecclesiastes was truly cosmopolitan in the breadth of his literary exposure. Deft and sophisticated uses of several ancient Near Eastern genres make him a fine example of Israel's literary elite.

---

[31]Compare 10:iii:1–10 (ANET, 90) of the Old Babylonian version with Ecclesiastes 9:7–9; and tablet 3, lines 141–43: "Only the gods live forever under the sun. / As for mankind, his days are numbered. / Whatever he does is just wind. Cf. Longman, *Fictional Akkadian Royal Autobiography,* 245–46.

[32]Ibid., 246–49.

[33]Ibid., 248.

FOR FURTHER READING

Baldwin, Joyce. "Some Literary Affinities of the Book of Daniel." TB 30 (1979): 77–99.
Biggs, Robert. "More Babylonian Prophecies." *Iraq* 29 (1967): 117–32.
_____. "The Babylonian Prophecies and the Astrological Traditions of Mesopotamia." JCS 39 (1985): 86–90.
_____. "Babylonian Prophecies, Astrology, and a New Source for 'Prophecy Text B.'" In *Language, Literature and History: Philological and Historical Studies Presented to Erica Reiner.* Ed. Francesca Rochberg-Halton. New Haven, 1987, 1–14.
Grayson, A. K. *Babylonian Historical-Literary Texts.* Toronto, 1975.
Grayson, A. K., and W. G. Lambert. "Akkadian Prophecies." JCS 18 (1964): 7–30.
Hallo, William. "Akkadian Apocalypses." IEJ 16 (1966): 231–42.
_____. "Apocalyptic Origins Updated." Forthcoming: listed in Longman dissertation.
Hunger, H., and S. A. Kaufman. "A New Akkadian Prophecy Text." JAOS 95 (1975): 371–75.
Kaufman, Stephen. "Prediction, Prophecy and Apocalypse in the Light of New Akkadian Texts." *Proceedings of the Sixth World Congress of Jewish Studies.* Vol. 1. Jerusalem, 1977.
Lambert, W. G. *The Background of Jewish Apocalyptic.* London, 1978.
Longman, Tremper, III. *Fictional Akkadian Royal Autobiography: A Generic and Comparative Study* (Ann Arbor, 1983). To be published in 1989 by Eisenbrauns.
Thomas, J. Douglas. "Jewish Apocalyptic and the Comparative Method." In *Scripture in Context.* Ed. Carl Evans, William W. Hallo, and John B. White. Pittsburgh, 1980, 245–62.
Yamauchi, Edwin. "Hermeneutical Issues in the Book of Daniel." JETS 23 (1980): 13–21.

Chapter 10

SUMMARY AND CONCLUSIONS

Following is a summary of the major similarities and differences that were identified throughout the book, as well as an overall look at the issue of the dependence of the Israelite literature on that of the ancient Near East.

I. Summary of Similarities and Differences in Literature

A. Chapter Summary of Similarities

1. Cosmology

a. Form.

There may be some similarity overall between the shape of Genesis 1–11 and a work like the Eridu Genesis, but only in broad outline. There is little or no genre overlap in this category, so formal similarity would not be expected.

b. Content.

Except in occasional minor details, there is little similarity within the cosmological materials.

2. Personal archives and epics

a. Form.

The patriarchal narratives are of a genre that so far is unknown in the literature of the ancient Near East.

b. Content.

Similarities to some of the content of the patriarchal narratives are found in texts such as those from Nuzi, but this type of comparison is sociological comparison, not literary comparison.

3. Legal texts

a. Form.

The casuistic form that is used widely in Exodus, Leviticus, and Deuteronomy is also the primary form used in the legal collections of the ancient Near East.

b. Content.

The matters of legal formulation overlap considerably, but such would be the case in any two societies. More importantly, the formulations and penalties often show great similarity.

4. Covenants and treaties

a. Form.

Covenants of the Old Testament share the closest formal similarities with the Hittite treaties of the second millennium B.C. Comparison reveals that, typically, similar paragraphs are often in the same order. Furthermore, the apodictic form used in the Decalogue and elsewhere in the Old Testament is also paralleled in the stipulations sections of the Hittite treaties.

b. Content.

The content of the treaties is similar to the covenant in broad outline, but since the covenants of Israel are religious documents while the treaties of the ancient Near East are political documents, the similarity is not carried into the detail.

5. Historical literature

a. Form.

There is little parallel between the historiographic forms of the Old Testament and those of the ancient Near East. The Old Testament historical books are theological in nature and use the raw materials of history (e.g., royal inscriptions or annals) as sources. In the ancient Near Eastern materials, the raw materials are largely extant. The other historiographical literature, such as the Hittite Apologies, are still not similar enough in genre for close comparison.

b. Content.

Israel's concept of history is more similar to the general ancient Near Eastern perspective than to our own modern Western view, especially with regard to the role of Deity in history.

6. Hymns, prayers, and incantations

a. Form.

There are certainly some formal similarities between Israelite and Mesopotamian psalmic literature, but there are no parallels that extend all the way through any of the genres; rather they occur sporadically.

b. Content.

There is general similarity in the praises and laments of Israel and Mesopotamia. People in Israel and Mesopotamia have many common complaints, and they offer praise to deity for common thanksgivings.

7. Wisdom literature

a. Form.

The dialogue/monologue forms, instructional literature, pessimism literature, and love poetry are all genres common to both Israel and the ancient Near East.

b. Content.

The wisdom of the Old Testament is not unlike the wisdom of the ancient Near East on "secular" matters. Books like Job, Proverbs, and Ecclesiastes share a general content, though not necessarily a similar perspective, that is found throughout the ancient Near East.

8. Prophetic literature

a. Form.

The prophetic literature of the Old Testament has no parallels in any genres or literatures of the ancient Near East.

b. Content.

Certainly the prophetic institution was a common sociological phenomenon in the ancient Near East, and the issues that drew the prophets' attention—Israel's prophets included—are generally similar; military matters and cultic practice are among the most common.

9. Apocalyptic literature

a. Form.

The presentation of history using successive unnamed kings is a motif found in Daniel 11 and in the so-called Akkadian Apocalypses. With regard to genre identification, the Akkadian materials were tentatively identified as a subset of the Akkadian Royal Fictional Autobiography genre. The closest comparison to this genre is not the apocalyptic literature of the Old Testament but the book of Ecclesiastes.

b. Content.

No similarities are found here with the exception of those connected to the general motif mentioned above and the four-empire scheme known in the ancient Near East.

B. Chapter Summary of Differences

In the summary below I have drawn from the discussion of each chapter to highlight the sharpest contrasts between Israel and the ancient Near East. By the very nature of this summary, many of these statements are overgeneralized and, at times, overpolarized. Almost every statement here needs qualification, and for this the reader is referred to each respective chapter. This listing is solely for summary purposes and is not intended to stand on its own.

1. Cosmology

a. Theogony versus cosmogony.

In the ancient Near Eastern cosmologies, the major components of the cosmos originated through the deities connected with those components. As a result, the only cosmogony evident in the ancient Near East is a theogonic one. These concepts are not found in the Israelite perspective.

b. Organization versus creation.

Especially in Mesopotamia, much of the creative work done by deity is organizational in nature. Actual creation by the gods is rare in the works available to us.

c. Creation through conflict.

The Canaanite and Mesopotamian cosmologies depict creation arising out of conflict in the divine realms. Though some scholars contend that the language of the cosmological poetic literature of Israel may reflect this element, it is certainly not a part of the normative Genesis accounts.

d. Monogenesis.

The Israelite concept is that originally only one human pair was created, and all of humankind is descended from them. In contrast, the creation of humankind is everywhere else in the Near East a matter of mass production.

e. Dignity of humankind.

In the book of Genesis, dignity is conferred on humankind because only humans are in the image of God. All of the cosmos is created for people and with people in mind. In the ancient Near Eastern perspective, humankind is an afterthought and even a bother. There is no dignity to be found in the created status of humanity. Humankind is created to be slaves rather than to rule. Dignity in Mesopotamia, for example, is therefore found in the function of humankind—the gods need them to provide housing (temples) and food (sacrifices).

2. Personal archives and epics

The epics of the ancient Near East, though taking different forms, show nothing similar to the patriarchal narratives. Some epics use mythological motifs (e.g., Adapa) or include extensive conversation in divine realms (e.g., Keret, Aqhat), while others contain little if any involvement of the divine (e.g., Sinuhe, Wenamun). Whatever genre designations are assigned to these ancient Near Eastern works, they do not share a sufficient number of genre indicators with the patriarchal narratives.

3. Legal texts

a. Revelatory nature.

The Torah (Law) in the Pentateuch is clearly presented as a revelation from the God of Israel. This element of revelation is absent from any of the ancient Near Eastern collections.

b. Cultic law component of legal texts.

The legal texts of Israel not only contain cultic law but are cultic in their orientation, even when civil or criminal law is discussed. The ancient Near Eastern collections do not include cultic law; rather, their focus is on civil law. As a generalization, in the ancient Near East violation of law is an offense against society. In Israel a violation of law is an offense against deity.

c. Use of apodictic.

The rare use of apodictic formulation of law in the ancient Near East makes the Decalogue unique.

d. Motive clauses.

Biblical law features a much higher proportion of motivated laws that differ in form, function, and content from motive clauses used in Near Eastern law.

e. Justice versus morality (order/chaos versus right/wrong).

The biblical material presents us with a detailed legal development of some of the forms that morality or holiness would take in society. The ancient Near Eastern material presents us with a detailed legal development of some of the forms of justice in society. The ancient Near East emphasized achieving order within society, while Israel emphasized right behavior in the eyes of God.

4. Historical literature

a. Propagandistic versus didactic.

Much of the historiographical literature of the ancient Near East has a propagandistic function. Biblical historiography is theological in orientation and primarily didactic in nature.

b. Single corpus.

No literature in the ancient Near East presents a single corpus of historiographical literature reflecting a large scope of history with a unified purpose.

c. Divine intervention.

While divine intervention is depicted in the historical literature of all of these cultures, only in Israel is deity's intervention focused toward an established and consistent goal. The intervention of YHWH in Israel's history goes far beyond either preserving or changing the status quo.

d. Election of Israel.

The covenant and the election of Israel as God's chosen people are the two elements that give a framework to all of Israelite historiography. There is nothing remotely similar in ancient Near Eastern literature.

e. Omens.

The use of and dependence on omens play a major role in the view of history in the ancient Near East but not in Israel. While a "recurrence" model may have legitimacy in either system, the basis of recurrence in the Israelite view is totally detached from omens.

5. Hymns, prayers, and incantations

a. Declarative praise.

The declarative praise in the Israelite psalms is generally offered by the individual recalling a specific, past incident of God's intervention or deliverance. This form does not exist anywhere else in the extant literature of the ancient Near East.

b. Types of descriptive praise.

Descriptive praise is common in the hymnic literature of the ancient Near East, but it takes different forms in different cultures. Mesopotamian works tend to use attribute enumeration or simply the listing of epithets of deity. In Egypt descriptive praise typically depicts praise in process and focuses on physical attributes of deity. In contrast to both of these, the Old Testament emphasizes the imperative call to praise.

c. Nature of petition.

In the laments of Mesopotamia, the psalmist is most frequently seeking to appease the offended deity. In Israelite laments, the psalmist typically is seeking vindication.

d. Incantations.

The lament psalms of Mesopotamia were most frequently used in conjunction with magical rituals and incantations. There is no hint of this in the biblical material. The aspect of magical efficacy or the accompaniment of sacrifices is not evident in the Israelite psalms.

e. Guilt or innocence.

This element is connected to the nature of the petition. The Israelite is more inclined to consider himself innocent in most of the psalms of lament and therefore seeks vindication. In the Mesopotamian laments, the worshiper cannot necessarily determine whether the deity's anger is justified or not. He accepts the fact that the deity is angry and seeks to appease him. He therefore is quite willing to acknowledge guilt.

f. Nature of offense.

In the ancient Near East offenses tend to be of a ritual nature—some cultic act has not been performed. Though ethical offenses are not unknown in Mesopotamian literature, in Israel ethical considerations are the primary focus of offenses.

g. Divine obligation.

The Israelite reminds God of the ways in which he has obligated himself (generally by covenant or attribute). The Mesopotamian seeks to bring deity under obligation by performance of ritual and recitation of suitable incantations.

6. Wisdom literature

a. Antithetical mode of expression.

In the instructional literature found in the Israelite book of Proverbs, antithetic formulation is common, yet it is practically unknown in the extant literature of the ancient Near East.

b. Theodicy controversy.

While the controversy concerning the righteous sufferer is a major theme of ancient Near Eastern wisdom literature, the resolutions to the issue take different forms. The book of Job rejects the "easy" answers found in the Mesopotamian literature, suggesting rather that the foundational premise of humankind's worldview is faulty.

7. Prophetic literature

a. Classical prophecy.

While the prophetic institution is not an uncommon sociological phenomenon in the ancient Near East, there is nothing to parallel the Israelite development of what we call classical prophecy. Differences in the audience and themes that set the literature of the classical prophets apart can possibly be related to the covenant orientation of the prophetic literature.

b. Eschatological focus.

Because of the differences noted in our analysis of the historical literature (see Divine Intervention), it is no surprise that there is no observable eschatology in Mesopotamia. This focus in Israelite prophecy is again covenant related and unparalleled.

8. Apocalyptic literature

a. Function.

The so-called Akkadian Apocalypses are clearly propagandistic in their function. They focus on the "prophet's" present, not his future. In contrast, the book of Daniel has a more theological or eschatological function, though it is not nearly so eschatological as Jewish apocalypses of the Greek and Roman periods.

II. Summary of Case for Alleged Borrowing

We have found very little in any of the literary categories to substantiate borrowing from specific literary pieces by the Israelites. Certainly there are cases where common roots of society and culture are evident. Likewise, it is not unusual to see common motifs employed. Furthermore, it is evident that a number of the genres of the ancient Near East were utilized by Israelite authors and composers. Nevertheless, these points offer no ground to suspect that Israel borrowed from a specific piece of literature to compose another piece of literature.

Probably the strongest case for the actual borrowing from a specific piece of literature could be made for Proverbs' use of Amenemope. Even here, however, the evidence cannot support direct borrowing, though it may suggest familiarity with Amenemope on the part of the composer of Proverbs.

Based on these findings we can appreciate the extent of Israel's participation in the literary heritage of the ancient Near East, but we are not compelled to view Israelite composers simply as theological editors of well-known pieces of pagan literature. Israel had significant contributions to make to the literary creativeness of the ancient world. In its role, Israel often drew from the contemporary literary milieu and motifs to shape its unique theological perspective. Partaking from the common heritage is a far different matter than adapting specific pieces of literature. The former is evident and to be expected. So far, however, the latter is undemonstrated.

III. Summary of Fundamental Religious Distinctions

Finally, we need to assess how this study has helped us to better understand the religion of Israel. Throughout this study two major areas that distinguished Israel from her contemporary cultures consistently emerge.

A. Concept of Deity

In each of the areas discussed above, and in virtually every topic discussed in this book, the primary distinction between Israel and the surrounding world is the concept of deity. The significance of this difference cannot be overstated. The difference between a polytheistic system and a monotheistic system reflects an entire philosophy of expectations of the divine realm and its relation to the total operation of the universe. Six key areas delineate the difference between Israel and Mesopotamian and Egyptian interpretations of deity.

1. Deity in Mesopotamia

a. Ultimate power.

Yehezkel Kaufmann has identified as the "fundamental idea" of pagan religion the fact that there is no entity in the universe that possesses ultimate power. His examination of the various embodiments of pagan religion leads him to the following significant conclusion:

> Yet all these embodiments involve one idea which is the distinguishing mark of pagan thought: the idea that there exists a realm of being prior to the gods and above them, upon which the gods depend, and whose decrees they must obey. Deity belongs to, and is derived from, a primordial realm. This realm is conceived of variously—as darkness, water, spirit, earth, sky, and so forth—but always as the womb in which the seeds of all being are contained. Alternatively, this idea appears as a belief in a primordial realm beside the gods, as independent and primary as the gods themselves. Not being subject to the gods, it necessarily limits them. The first conception, however, is the fundamental one. This is to

say that in the pagan view, the gods are not the source of all that is, nor do they transcend the universe. They are, rather, part of a realm precedent to and independent of them. They are rooted in this realm, are bound by its nature, are subservient to its laws. To be sure, paganism has personal gods who create and govern the world of men. But a divine will, sovereign and absolute, which governs all and is the cause of all being— such a conception is unknown. There are heads of pantheons, there are creators and maintainers of the cosmos; but transcending them is the primordial realm, with its pre-existent, autonomous forces. This is the radical dichotomy of paganism; from it spring both mythology and magic.[1]

The limited nature of deity in Mesopotamian religious belief may be viewed from two perspectives. On the one hand, as stressed by Kaufmann, the divine realm as a corporate entity had some limitations, though the gods were conceived of as the highest active power operating in the universe.[2] On the other hand, any given deity was limited within his sphere of activity and was subject to the decrees of the assembly of gods.

> The interdependence, or interrelationship, of the gods has been aptly characterized as an "integration of wills"; this integration resulted in the conception of "the cosmos as a state." . . . The autonomy of the god within his or her sphere meant that viewed as a polity the gods, whether acting individually or collectively, could never exert absolute universal sovereignty. . . . Being restricted, or unable to realize themselves fully as individual personalities, the gods could not give their undivided attention to the concerns of mankind, since the cosmic equilibrium required first and foremost that they keep an eye upon each other.[3]

This issue of ultimacy, then, is a key distinction between the polytheistic religion of Mesopotamia and the monotheism of Israel. J. J. Finkelstein sums up the essence of polytheism as a theological system as follows: "It implies the existence of a plurality of superhuman wills. This very condition precludes the absolute omnipotence of any one of these wills."[4] In contrast YHWH is viewed as the ultimate power in the universe, with no limitations and no competition.

b. Manifestation of deity.

H. W. F. Saggs has suggested that the sense of Israelite thought, and therefore the best way to draw distinctions between Israelite and Mesopotamian religion, is found by examining the "negative"—that is, "Not by what God is but by what he is not": "He is not immanent in the heavenly bodies or the wind, and . . . God is not representable in human form or animal form, and . . . the divine has not a multiplicity of forms."[5]

These are all elements that distinguish YHWH from the gods of the

---

[1] Y. Kaufmann, *The Religion of Israel* (New York, 1972), 21–22.

[2] See T. Jacobsen, *Treasures of Darkness* (New Haven, 1976), 86.

[3] J. J. Finkelstein, *The Ox That Gored, Transactions of the American Philosophical Society* 71:2 (Philadelphia, 1981), 10.

[4] J. J. Finkelstein, "Bible and Babel", *Commentary* 26 (1958): 438.

[5] H. W. F. Saggs, *The Encounter with the Divine in Mesopotamia and Israel* (London, 1978), 92.

nations at large. As T. Jacobsen has pointed out in his discussion of the development of Mesopotamian religion, the earliest perception of the gods in Mesopotamia was in the form and by the names of the natural phenomena that they represented.[6] While this falls short of pantheism, it nevertheless requires a much closer relationship of the gods with nature than the most phenomenistic of biblical passages allows or suggests for YHWH.

As time progresses, a change can be perceived as the gods become more and more made in the image of man. This anthropomorphizing tendency becomes apparent in the Early Dynastic period (2900–2300 B.C.).[7] In this stage, "the Sumerian gods, as illustrated by the Sumerian myths, were entirely anthropomorphic; even the most powerful and most knowing among them were conceived as human in form, thought, and deed."[8] While this scenario for the development of anthropomorphization is speculative and may be replaced as more information becomes available, the distinction remains that YHWH was "wholly other," despite the use of anthropomorphisms, while the Mesopotamians succeeded in making the gods in their own image to a much greater extent. Though the gods of the Mesopotamians were more powerful than their human foils, they existed in the same realm and shared, in many respects, the same nature.

c. Disposition of deity.

What Aristotle later observed about Greek religion was just as true of Mesopotamian religion: "Men imagine not only the forms of the gods but their ways of life to be like their own."[9] Like human conduct, then, the conduct of the gods lacked consistency and was for the most part unpredictable. There was no absolute morality characteristic of divine conduct and no code to which the gods were bound. The gods were not obliged to be moral, ethical, or even fair, and integrity could never be assumed. The divine decrees that theoretically constituted the guidelines of divine behavior and the sum total of the decisions of the assembly were not "revealed" (in the theological sense) and could frequently be circumvented. Even the various domains of any particular deity demonstrated no essential unity or consistency. So, for instance, the following list is given for Inanna:

> To pester, insult, deride, desecrate—and to venerate—is your domain, Inanna.
> Downheartedness, calamity, heartache—and joy and good cheer—is your domain, Inanna.
> Trembling, affright, terror—dazzling and glory—is your domain, Inanna.[10]

We find then that two of the most cherished and emphasized of YHWH's attributes, consistency and absolute morality, are not part of the disposition of the Mesopotamian gods.

---

[6] See Jacobsen, *Treasures*, 5–6; and "Formative Tendencies in Sumerian Religion," reprinted in *Toward the Image of Tammuz* (Cambridge, 1970), 2–5.
[7] Jacobsen, "Formative Tendencies in Sumerian Religion," 10–11.
[8] S. N. Kramer, *The Sumerians* (Chicago, 1963), 117.
[9] Aristotle, *Politics*, 1252b.
[10] Jacobsen, *Treasures*, 141.

d. Autonomy of the gods vis-à-vis man.

As mentioned above, since humans were created to do work for the gods, the gods were seen to depend on people to provide for them. This primarily involved two basic elements: the sacrifices provided food for the gods, and the temples provided shelter and housing for the gods. The fact that the gods were seen to need what humans could provide created a situation in which they had a bargaining chip when dealing with the gods. There was mutual benefit in a relationship that worked smoothly. The result of this can perhaps be seen most clearly in the wisdom literature in a work referred to as the "Dialogue of Pessimism."

> "Slave, listen to me."
> "Here I am, sir, here I am."
> "Quickly fetch me water for my hands, and give it to me so that I can sacrifice to my god."
> "Sacrifice, sir, sacrifice. The man who sacrifices to his god is satisfied with the bargain: He is making loan upon loan."
> "No, slave, I will by no means sacrifice to my god."
> "Do not sacrifice, sir, do not sacrifice. You can teach your god to run after you like a dog, Whether he asks of you rites, or 'Do not consult your god,' or anything else."[11]

While this certainly represents the more cynical perspective on religion, it is nevertheless one of the natural results of the needs of the gods being filled by humans. The desperate state of the gods can also be seen in the flood stories in the gods' response to the sacrifice of the hero after he leaves the boat. The picture of the famished gods gathering like flies[12] around the sacrifice is certainly an indication of the way divine dignity at times was compromised by need. In a third example, the ability of humankind to pressure the gods to act benevolently can be seen in Atraḫasis when Enki advises Atraḫasis that the way to bring an end to the plague is for all of the people of the city to devote themselves solely to Namtara, the god responsible for the plague. The deity is so flattered that the plague is brought to an end (I:372–413).

In contrast, the prophets have to continually remind Israel that YHWH is not a God who depends on them for anything. This is also made clear in passages such as Psalm 50:7–15, in which YHWH avers, "If I were hungry, I would not tell you; / For the world is Mine, and all that it contains" (v. 12 NASB). The "manipulation factor" succeeded with the gods of the ancient Near East; it failed with YHWH. He could not be blackmailed or manipulated so that he became man's lackey. In Mesopotamian perceptions of deity, manipulation was much more of a possibility. That does not mean that it was safe, for in the end, the gods usually had the last laugh. But the very possibility of manipulation in itself is something that distinguishes a Mesopotamian view of deity from the uncorrupted Israelite view.

---

[11] BWL, 147, 149, lines 53–61; ANET, 438

[12] For an attempt to see similarity between the flies motif here and the rainbow motif in Genesis, see Anne D. Kilmer, "The Symbolism of the Flies in the Mesopotamian Flood Myth and Some Further Implications" in *Language, Literature and History*, ed. Francesca Rochberg-Halton (New Haven, 1987), 175–80.

e. Requirements of the gods.

In Mesopotamia there was no revelation given by the gods regarding what they expected of human beings. Rather, people had to attempt to stay in harmony with the status quo of society and civilization, with their good and bad aspects, for that was what the gods had ordained. Justice was something the gods had instituted and that contributed to the smooth operation of society. Injustice, therefore, could fall into the realm of offense but not because injustice was immoral; rather it was an offense insofar as it was a threat to society. The major responsibility of the god Utu-Shamash, the god of justice, was to protect the vulnerable classes against injustice. Yet even Shamash is appeased, not by just conduct, but by ritual.[13] There is no question that the gods preferred moral or ethical conduct on the part of people, but that conduct was not part of the religious requirement made on them by the gods. The gods themselves were not characterized by such conduct.

It was not revelation that provided knowledge of what the gods demanded in general; tradition was the source. When special instructions were required, revelation was looked for through divination. Both of these areas, revelation and divination, are addressed by Jacobsen:

> In part such knowledge [what the gods wanted] was, of course, given with tradition. The gods were certain to want their temples looked after, their cult performed correctly, their festivals celebrated at the proper times, and attention and reverence from their people generally. But these—one might call them the "standing" orders—was not all. Situations were bound to develop in which the divine will might not be so clear. Did the god want a new high priest or high priestess and, if so, whom? Did the god wish that his old temple be rebuilt now or later? Or not at all? Did he think one should go to war against an encroaching neighbor, or was he inclined to use diplomatic means? And, of course, the god might harbor a wish that one could not guess, but which nevertheless had to be divined and carried out. For such cases—one might call them the "specific" orders—the ruler had to rely on messages from the gods in dreams or visions, on signs and portents, or on one of the traditional ways in which one would approach the gods and obtain—if one was lucky—an answer.[14]

Lacking information concerning the kind of conduct required by the gods, the people found themselves depending on their circumstances in life to determine their status with deity. If things were going well for them, they would assume that at least they were not doing anything to attract the gods' disfavor. They could only discern offense on their part when life began to go wrong. Then would begin the long, frustrating process of attempting to discover what offense had been committed and against which god. In this regard the "Prayer to Every God" found in Ashurbanipal's library is very instructive:

> May the fury of my lord's heart be quieted toward me.
> May the god who is not known be quieted toward me;
> May the goddess who is not known be quieted toward me.

---

[13]See BWL, 135:130–31; also Jacobsen, *Treasures*, 134.
[14]Jacobsen, *Treasures*, 84.

May the god whom I know or do not know be quieted toward me;
May the goddess whom I know or do not know be quieted toward me.
May the heart of my god be quieted toward me.
May the heart of my goddess be quieted toward me.

In ignorance I have eaten that forbidden of my god;
In ignorance I have set foot on that forbidden by my goddess.
O Lord, my transgressions are many; great are my sins.

The transgression which I have committed, indeed I do not know;
The sin which I have done, indeed I do not know.
The forbidden thing which I have eaten, indeed I do not know;
The prohibited (place) on which I have set foot, indeed I do not know.
The lord in the anger of his heart looked at me;
The god in the rage of his heart confronted me;
When the goddess was angry with me, she made me become ill.
The god whom I know or do not know has oppressed me;
The goddess whom I know or do not know has placed suffering upon
    me.
Although I am constantly looking for help, no one takes me by the hand;
When I weep, they do not come to my side.
I utter laments, but no one hears me;
I am troubled; I am overwhelmed; I cannot see.

Man is dumb; he knows nothing;
Mankind, everyone that exists—what does he know?
Whether he is committing sin or doing good, he does not even know.
O my lord, do not cast thy servant down;
He is plunged into the waters of a swamp; take him by the hand.
The sin which I have done, turn into goodness;
The transgression which I have committed, let the wind carry away;
My many misdeeds strip off like a garment.[15]

Here the worshiper assumes that he has committed grave offenses because serious things have gone wrong for him. He has no idea what he has done wrong or whom he has offended. He can only throw himself on the mercy of the unknown deity who is the cause of his trouble.

Another difficulty that existed in polytheistic systems was that not only was each particular god inconsistent in his demands (i.e., what was pleasing to him one day might not be acceptable at another time), but even if the individual managed to act in accordance with the demands of one deity, he might find himself in disfavor with another deity. Logic was not sufficient to discern what would be pleasing to deity. One frustrated worshiper, after considering a whole list of cultic acts, has the following comment:

I wish I knew that these things were pleasing to one's god! What is proper to oneself is an offence to one's god, What in one's own heart seems despicable is proper to one's god. Who knows the will of the gods in heaven? Who understands the plans of the underworld gods? Where have mortals learnt the way of a god?[16]

If an offense was committed against deity, the deity deserted the offending individual, leaving him vulnerable to the attack of demonic forces.

---

[15]ANET, 391–92:1–7, 19–21, 26–38, 51–58.
[16]W. G. Lambert, "Ludlul Bel Nemeqi," BWL, 41:33–38; ANET, 597.

The demonic forces could be combatted with incantations, but if an offense was the cause of the problem, the incantation needed to name the offense.

> On this basis there grew up the Incantation Series known as Šurpu, which contains long lists of possible offences, some ritual (such as eating tabooed food), some ethical (such as lying or cheating), and others social (such as causing estrangement within a family group).[17]

By reading through the list, there was the hope that the offense, though unknown to the individual, might be mentioned, thus lending efficacy to the incantation.

The great boon granted to Israel by YHWH was the privilege of having revelation, the Torah from Sinai, as well as the admonitions of the prophets, concerning precisely what their God expected of them. These demands included, not only cultic acts, but also ethical and moral responses. This leads us to the last section.

f. Response to the gods.

The primary distinction we will draw here between Israelite and Mesopotamian religions may be generalized as the distinction between piety and ritual. This is not to say that either religious practice lacked either of those elements; rather it is a matter of emphasis and priority. We may start with the observation of A. L. Oppenheim:

> Religious life in Mesopotamia remains concentrated in sanctuary-centered cults. A system of "inside" religious practices evolves in contrast to those enacted for the outside world. Adorations, ceremonial offerings of food, decorating images, and whatever purification rites and specific cult activities are required by tradition for an individual deity take place within the sanctuary, whereas occasional appearances and exhibitions of statues, even travel between sanctuaries (to express theological or, rather, political relationships between gods), display the pomp and splendor so dear to the community of citizens. No personal piety or emotional involvement is required, not even of the king or of the deity's high priest. The common man's relationship to his gods and goddesses is difficult to discern, although the extremely pious onomasticon would suggest not only personal piety but also a wide range in the intensity and nature of the god-man relationship of Mesopotamian man.[18]

We contend that personal piety and morality constitute a basic element in the religious practice of Israel as it was supposed to be conducted. Any reading of the prophets will show that Israelites had difficulties grasping this. Moral conduct was demanded by YHWH and was necessary to please him. Ritual not backed up by proper attitudes and conduct was useless and unacceptable.

This emphasis underscores the stark contrast to Mesopotamian religion where "the gods, for their part, appreciated and even demanded moral and ethical conduct on the part of mankind, but they could offer no guarantees in

---

[17]Saggs, *Encounter*, 117. The Šurpu series is published by Erica Reiner, *Šurpu, A Collection of Sumerian and Akkadian Incantations* (AfO *Beiheft* 11), Graz, 1958.

[18]A. L. Oppenheim, *Letters From Mesopotamia* (Chicago, 1967), 29.

return."[19] Ritual in and of itself was sufficient and efficacious, as evidenced by the following section from the Babylonian "Counsels of Wisdom."

> Every day worship your god.
> Sacrifice and benediction are the proper accompaniment of incense.
> Present your free-will offering to your god,
> For this is proper toward the gods.
> Prayer, supplication, and prostration
> Offer him daily, and you will get your reward.
> Then you will have full communion with your god.
> In your wisdom study the tablet.
> Reverence begets favor,
> Sacrifice prolongs life,
> And prayer atones for guilt.[20]

The obligation that the Mesopotamian worshiper had toward the gods, then, had little effect on how he lived his life.

> One obtains the impression—confirmed by other indications—that the influence of religion on the individual, as well as on the community as a whole, was unimportant in Mesopotamia. No text tells us that ritual requirements in any stringent way affected the individual's physiological appetites, his psychological preferences, or his attitude toward his possessions or his family. His body, his time, and his valuables were in no serious way affected by religious demands, and thus no conflict of loyalties arose to disturb or shake him. Death was accepted in a truly matter-of-fact way, and the participation of the individual in the cult of the city deity was restricted in the extreme; he was simply an onlooker in certain public ceremonies of rejoicing or communal mourning. He lived in a quite tepid religious climate within a framework of socio-economic rather than cultic co-ordinates. His expectations and apprehensions as well as his moral code revolved within the orbit of a small urban or rural society.[21]

The duty having a greater effect on daily life was the duty that each individual owed his society. This is not at all unrelated to religious practice, for the gods had set up society and were concerned that the status quo be maintained.

> Everything in the universe, material or immaterial, human or divine, was laid down by decree. Man's duty was to conform to these regulations. The contrast was not, as among the Hebrews, between morally right and wrong, but between order and disorder. Civilization was the ideal: the well ordered society.[22]

Response of the Mesopotamian worshiper was expected in two basic areas. First, he was expected to play whatever role was open to him in the performance of cultic ritual. This was his part in providing for the care and

---

[19] Finkelstein, "Bible and Babel," 439.

[20] BWL, 105:135–45; see ANET, 427.

[21] Oppenheim, *Ancient Mesopotamia* (Chicago, 1977), 176.

[22] Lambert, OTS 17 (1972): 67; Saggs (*Encounter*, 76) finds disagreement with this statement, not for how it reflects Mesopotamian thinking, but on the basis of his conclusion that order versus disorder was also an important element of Israelite metaphysics.

feeding of the gods. It required no particular attitude or lifestyle on his part, and any concept of "faith" in deity is the exception rather than the rule.[23] Second, he was expected to contribute to the smooth operation of a well-ordered society by maintaining its status quo and conforming to accepted social standards.

The response expected of the Israelite worshiper was, above all, obedience to the revealed law of YHWH. This included social and cultic responsibility but was in the end an issue of morality.

In each of the six areas that we have examined, we have contrasted what the literature suggests to us were the major concerns and concepts of Mesopotamian religion with what the Bible tells us Israelite religion was supposed to be like. As frequently noted, however, the Israelites did not always conform their practice to what was dictated by their religious theory. We suggest that this is because their religious theory was not their own invention but something imposed on them by God. Their tendency, however, was to neglect the commands, admonitions, and assertions of YHWH in preference for the religious ideals of their neighboring cultures (influenced by Mesopotamian and Egyptian theology). For this reason, we often see the Israelites being rebuked for their pagan practices or concepts. So, for instance, Isaiah frequently stresses the ultimacy of YHWH (e.g., 43:13; 45:6, 21; 46:9). The proper response to deity and clear statements of his requirements may be found in passages such as Isaiah 1:11–20; Deuteronomy 10:12; Amos 5:21–24; and Micah 6:8. We have already mentioned Psalm 50:12 with regard to the autonomy of YHWH, and many passages address his attributes of justice, holiness, righteousness, etc.

While it seems fair to say that most polytheists had little or no comprehension of the presuppositions and implications of Israel's monotheistic system (sometimes, judging from the prophets, the implications even escaped Israelites), there has also been the suggestion that the Israelites likewise completely misunderstood what idol worship was all about and as a result reduced it to mere fetishism.[24] There can be no doubt that such distortion took place on the popular level, as is often the case in any religion. It is difficult to judge, however, whether the more educated in Israel suffered from the same delusions. Whatever the case, this would not have affected some of the other areas of syncretism, such as the issues of ultimacy and response to deity, where Israelites show understanding and acceptance of pagan ideas.

As has frequently been noted in the history of scholarship, it is this distinction between monotheistic and polytheistic systems that is responsible for many of the differences in the respective worldviews of Israel and her neighbors. In most areas where differences are posited or observable between cultures, it is this theological element that provides an explanation. In areas where this theological difference has no effect, we have found Israel remarkably similar to her neighbors.

---

[23]Cf. G. Buccellati, "Adapa, Genesis, and the Notion of Faith," UF 5 (1973): 61–66.

[24]Y. Kaufmann, *Religion of Israel*, 7–20; John MacKenzie, "The Hebrew Attitude Towards Mythological Polytheism," CBQ 14 (1952): 323ff. To bring balance to this see also T. Jacobsen, "The Graven Image" in *Ancient Israelite Religion*, ed. P. D. Miller, P. D. Hanson, and S. D. McBride (Philadelphia, 1987), 15–32.

2. Deity in Egypt

Though the conception of deity in Egypt differs in many important respects from the conception of the Mesopotamians, the issue may be discussed in the same categories.

a. Ultimate power.

As in the Mesopotamian system, neither any particular deity nor the realm of deity as a whole represented ultimate power in the universe. So E. Hornung can conclude after his study of the characteristics of the gods: "We must accustom ourselves to the fact that by their nature Egyptian gods are neither transcendent nor eternal, unconditional, absolute."[25] He points out that the gods along with man inhabit the ordered world of creation, while the transcendent realms are "reserved for the 'enemies,' the powers of chaos."[26] One of the most startling evidences for the limitations of the Egyptian gods is that not only are they born; they also die.[27] Having said this, however, it must be remembered that in Egyptian thinking, death does not mean the end of existence but is rather like a rejuvenation process by which one enters another sphere.

It is further evident that the Egyptian gods were generally restricted to particular localities or functions, much more so than the Mesopotamian deities. The power of any particular deity within his own realm was great indeed, but it was not unlimited. This creates a system that has the appearance of henotheism. That is, even though a multitude of gods was considered to exist, most individuals approached a single deity or one deity at a time. The individual worshiper would interact with the deity of his particular city. Each deity was not a source of power or even a lord of power but rather should be seen as an exponent of power[28] or as a power broker. Power (mana) existed before the gods. As in Mesopotamia, it was represented as an impersonal magical force. This force had brought about creation and maintained it. Each god had access to this force through its incorporation into his essence, but that essence was diluted through the diversification process. E. Hornung describes diversity as the "intellectual foundation of Egyptian polytheism."[29] This likewise constitutes a limitation to any deity's power.

b. Manifestation of deity.

Above all in the Egyptian system, unlike any other system in the ancient Near East, the king was the primary manifestation of the deity. The Egyptians also made wide use of images, but these were in no way thought to be the gods themselves. Rather the ba of the deity (his essence) was thought to indwell the image. The analysis of the relationship of the god to his image and the significance of depicting the gods in human form with animal heads goes well beyond the scope of this work. Though the concepts

---

[25] E. Hornung, Conceptions of God in Ancient Egypt (Ithaca, N.Y., 1982), 195.
[26] Ibid.
[27] E.g., Osiris; S. Morenz, Egyptian Religion (Ithaca, N.Y., 1973), 24; Hornung, Conceptions, 143.
[28] Morenz, Egyptian Religion, 18.
[29] Hornung, Conceptions, 176.

are different from those found in Mesopotamia, they are much more like the manifestations of deity as understood in Mesopotamia than like those found in Israel. This uniqueness of Israel is again embodied in the prohibition of images of YHWH.

c. Disposition of deity.

The conduct of individual gods is not as evident in the mythology of Egypt as it is in Sumerian and Babylonian myths. There is an element in Egyptian thinking, however, that differentiates it from Mesopotamian thought. That is the pervasive significance of *ma'at*. *Ma'at* is an abstract concept and is not easily defined. S. Morenz characterizes it as right order in nature and society. It is the foundation of Egyptian conduct and ethics. It is established by an act of creation and is the inherent structure by which the system operates.[30] It is the basis of the conduct of the gods as well as of humans. While it is not the same as an absolute morality, in effect it has a similar result: it provides a standard for acceptable behavior. Thus the Egyptian gods do not exhibit the same perversity in their conduct so evident in the Mesopotamian and Canaanite deities. Nevertheless, they are not totally free of inappropriate behavior, as the feuding between Horus and Seth demonstrates.[31] There are also hostile gods against whom people need protection, so the gods should not be considered "good" in every sense.

d. Autonomy of the gods vis-à-vis man.

Again we find ideas that fall between those of Mesopotamia and those of Israel. The view that the cultic act has an automatic efficacy and places deity under obligation (so prevalent in the Mesopotamian system) is not so obvious in Egyptian theology. In theory, the king alone was entitled to communicate with the gods and carry out the daily ritual.[32] Though the king was deity incarnate, he sought to oblige the gods to bless Egypt by his cultic presentation. The people also practiced a system of manipulation by sacrifice within the popular cults in their own small chapels like those at Deir el-Medina.

e. Requirements of the gods.

Just as the conduct of the gods was based on *ma'at*, so *ma'at* delineated the requirements that the gods placed on human beings. *Ma'at* is seen to be man's task in life, his goal in life, and his reward in the afterlife.[33] It does not come about by revelation but can be learned. It is equated with insight and experience and is the result of divine guidance from within. It is a sense of what is proper, right, wise, true, and just. It is associated with wisdom. Behavior in accordance with *ma'at* is required and expected of man by the gods, but it is not necessarily sin to fail to do *ma'at*; sometimes it is merely ignorance or inexperience. An evil lifestyle is sometimes claimed to constitute disobedience to divine commands, but in general ethical teachings

---

[30]Morenz, *Egyptian Religion*, 113–18.
[31]ANET, 14–17.
[32]Morenz, *Egyptian Religion*, 40.
[33]Ibid., 113.

are not associated with divine commands.[34] It is interesting to note that the Egyptian expected to be judged in comparison to *ma'at* after death, but he also expected that the judgment could be side-stepped by the use of the proper magical spells. Nevertheless, the practical result of *ma'at* created a system that was much closer to the Israelite system than it was to the Mesopotamian.

f. Response to the gods.

As already mentioned, religious response in the Egyptian system was primarily through the cult. It should also be noticed that piety seems much more evident in Egyptian religious practice than it does in Mesopotamian. For instance, in the "Instruction for Merikare" is a line that sounds like it came from the Old Testament: "More acceptable is the character of one upright of heart than the ox of the evildoer."[35] The ancient Near Eastern gods were perceived to be farther removed; however, Israel and her God were on more intimate terms. It should be remembered, though, that even these observations are general and liable to be greatly affected by the extant literature of each of the civilizations, as well as by the presuppositions of modern interpreters of that literature.

In summary, we would have to conclude that on the practical level, the actual interaction of an individual with deity, the Egyptians had much more similarity with the Israelites than the Mesopotamians (or Canaanites) did. In actual theology though, there were still vast differences. In Egyptian practice the absence of ultimate power in the realm of deity did not elicit the same response as it did in Mesopotamia. Nevertheless, that absence still comprises a major theological distinction from the monotheism of the Israelites. It is not so much the Egyptian way of thinking that is identified as a threat to Israel by the prophets. The Mesopotamian/Canaanite distortions were considered much more dangerous.

B. Covenant

The second element that clearly and everywhere distinguishes Israel from her neighbors is the covenant. Revelation from deity was something that was claimed in every culture; though, as mentioned in the previous section, Israel enjoyed more of it and in different areas (e.g., law). But the covenant concept goes far beyond simple revelation. Here we have election, revelation, intervention, and eschatology all combined together into a theological concept that, not only defined the relationship between YHWH and Israel, but was responsible for Israel's identity and self-image. There may be other peoples who would have said that their god singled them out for special blessing, saying, "I will be your God and you will be my people," but in no other culture does that mean so much and serve as a foundational theological premise for so long.[36]

---

[34]Ibid., 62.

[35]ANET, 417, line 129.

[36]For treatment of some of the differences in concept of deity that are observable in national theology, see D. I. Block, *The Gods of the Nations* (Jackson, Miss., 1988), 162–68.

FOR FURTHER READING

Finkelstein, J. J. "Bible and Babel." *Commentary* 26 (1958): 431–44.

_____. *The Ox That Gored. Transactions of the American Philosophical Society.* 71:2. Philadelphia, 1981, 8–13.

Frankfort, Henri, et al. *Before Philosophy.* Harmondsworth, 1949.

_____. *Ancient Egyptian Religion.* New York, 1948.

Hornung, Erik. *Conceptions of God in Ancient Egypt.* Ithaca, N.Y., 1982.

Jacobsen, Thorkild. "Ancient Mesopotamian Religion: The Central Concerns." In *Toward the Image of Tammuz.* Ed. W. L. Moran. Cambridge, 1970, 39–47.

_____. "Formative Tendencies in Sumerian Religion." In *Toward the Image of Tammuz,* 1–15.

Kaufmann, Yehezkel. *The Religion of Israel.* New York, 1960, 21–59.

Lambert, W. G. "Morals in Ancient Mesopotamia." JEOL 15 (1958): 184–96.